IF THIS BOOK IS YOURS WRITE IN IT EXPRESS YOURSELF

YOU

THE PSYCHOLOGY OF SURVIVING AND ENHANCING YOUR

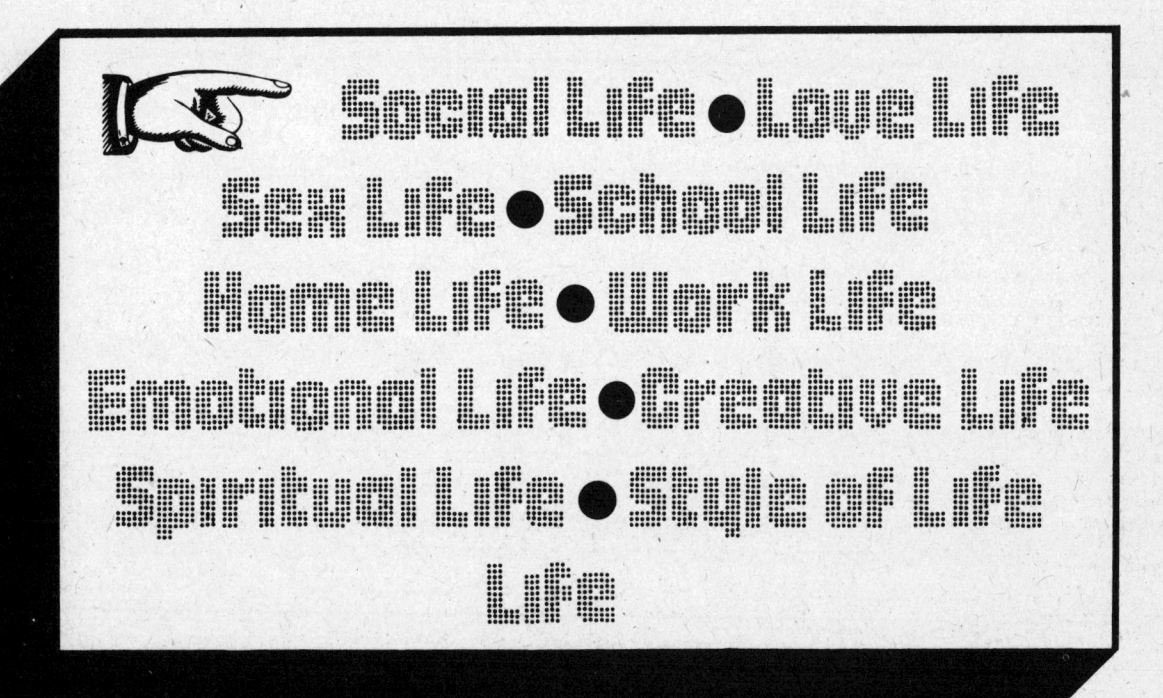

☞ Social Life • Love Life • Sex Life • School Life • Home Life • Work Life • Emotional Life • Creative Life • Spiritual Life • Style of Life Life

by SOL GORDON with Roger Conant

A Strawberry Hill Book
Published with Quadrangle/The New York Times Book Company

The Momma cartoons on pages 96 and 99 are used with permission of the author, Mell Lazarus, and Publisher's-Hall Syndicate; copyright Field Enterprises. The Family Circus cartoon by Bill Keane on page 70 is reprinted courtesy of The Register and Tribune Syndicate. The Lynd Ward woodcut on page 127 is from *Storyteller Without Words,* © 1974 by Harry N. Abrams, Inc., New York, and is used by permission of the artist and publisher. Excerpts from *Notes to Myself,* by Hugh Prather, © 1970, Real People Press, used by permission of the author and publisher.

A Strawberry Hill Book
Published with Quadrangle/The New York Times Book Co.

YOU
© 1975 by Sol Gordon
All rights reserved, including the right of reproduction in whole or in part in any form. For information, address: Quadrangle/The New York Times Book Co., 10 East 53 Street, New York, New York 10022. Manufactured in the United States of America. Published simultaneously in Canada by Fitzhenry & Whiteside, Ltd.; Toronto.

Composition by David E. Seham Associates, Inc.

Design by Hermann Strohbach

Edited by Richard Roberts

Library of Congress Cataloging in Publication Data

Gordon, Sol, 1923–
  You! : The psychology of enhancing your social life, love life, sex life, school life, work life, home life, emotional life, creative life, spiritual life, style of life, life.

  SUMMARY: Helps the teenager to examine himself as a person and to cope with school, sex, work, parents, religion—and life in general.
  1. Success. [1. Identity. 2. Interpersonal relations. 3. Adolescence. 4. Conduct of life] I. Conant, Roger, 1909– joint author. II. Title.

BF637.S8G65   158.1   74-26015
ISBN 0-8129-0548-2

CREDITS:

Photo, pg. **1**, by Bert Peate; Woodcut, pg. **16**, by Albrecht Dürer; Photo, pg. **23**, by Sol Gordon; Photo, pg. **35**, by Richard Kasak; Photo, pg. **40**, by Lester Blumberg; Photo, pg. **49**, by Richard Kasak; Photo, pg. **50**, by David Teich; Photo, pg. **52**, by Richard Kasak, Photo, pg. **56**, by Sol Gordon; Photo, pg. **71**, by Doug Cunningham; Drawings, pgs. **73**, **77**, **105**, by Jack Nelson; Photo, pg. **83**, by Bert Peate; Self-Xerox portrait, pg. **89**, of David Teich; Photo, pg. **94**, by Richard Kasak; Photo, pg. **99**, by Sol Gordon; Photo, pg. **112**, by Lester Blumberg; Drawing, pg. **114**, by Lisa Mannheim; Photo, pg. **125**, by Sol Gordon; Photo, pg. **126**, by Richard Kasak; Portrait of the author, pg. **138**, by Rita Dominguez; Photo, pg. **144**, by Richard Kasak.

My part of the book is in the memory of my parents—and for my wife Judith, son Josh, sister Ethel and brother Henry— and our extended families.

I also want to acknowledge
Roger Conant
who dedicates his part to his wife, Marlene, and their new son, James Roger.

We are both grateful to
Richard Roberts, Richard Kasak and Hermann Strohbach, as people who know how to inspire.

Some of the ideas in this book have appeared in another form in my text "Psychology For You," published by Oxford/Sadlier. I am delighted also to have been able to include the works of many of my friends.

But mostly this book is for

February 1975
Sol Gordon

> If you are true to yourself,
> you are positively weird.
> (You are definitely not average.)

CONTENTS

Comic Books

Gut News for Modern Eaters	18
Juice Use — Special Hangover Edition	50
Ten Heavy Facts About Sex; Protect Yourself From Becoming an Unwanted Parent; V.D. Claptrap	82
What do you do when you're all Drug Doubt?	114

What Do You Do After You Find Yourself?   xi

WHAT IS NORMAL?   1

Includes "what is not abnormal," "a scale for measuring your adjustment/maladjustment," "six signs of very poor adjustment," "fantasy, reality and normality," "is society abnormal?" and "questions to ask yourself."

DISCOVERING WHO WE ARE   7

This section is kind of a "how not to do it guide to what you really want to do." Includes "the 10 most unnecessary fears."

FOR PEOPLE WHO:

. . . Suffer From Being a Minority	13
. . . Don't Think They Are Attractive	14
. . . Are Especially Bright or Sensitive	15
. . . Have Been Insulted	16
. . . Demand Everything — or Nothing	17
. . . Smoke, Smoke Smoke . . . Smoke That Cigarette	18
. . . Would Like to Know How the Comic Books Were Born and Some People's Reactions to Them	19
. . . Want to Play a Sneaky Trick	22
. . . Are Allergic to Ideas	22
. . . Think They Can't Write a Poem	23

A HODGEPODGE OF POETRY AND OTHER STRANGE STUFF	24

If you tune yourself in, one good poem can tell you more than a hundred textbooks. Are you aware that many of your friends write poetry (mostly in secret)? The only trouble is, most of them have the odd idea that for a poem to be good it has to rhyme.

ELEVEN LAST-MINUTE SURVIVAL IDEAS	38

NEW EXPERIENCES	41

Variety isn't just the spice of life, it's more like the salt of life: it's hard to live without it.

WHEN YOU ARE BORED, YOU ARE BORING TO BE WITH	47

Includes a list of the most boring things you can do and ways to shake yourself loose from boredom and depression.

STAYING SANE — DESPITE SCHOOL	53

How do you protect your mind and your dignity and still get what you need, whether from high school or, possibly, college?

WORK	60

What are you working *for*? Includes "what you should know about jobs."

SEX	63

Includes "will the real sexual revolution stand up?"; "is bed-ed dead?"; "sex, ready or not!"; virgin rights; hetero, homo, auto and bi sexuality; arousal; sex thoughts; sex problems, and whom to see for help; and "toward a psychology of being sexually very healthy."

THE WOMEN'S LIBERATION MOVEMENT HAS A LOT TO SAY TO ALL OF US	81

It's boring to be unliberated.

BEING REASONABLE WITH YOURSELF — 89

What can you say to yourself if you get upset easily or if you are insecure?

COPING WITH YOUR PARENTS — 95

You're more mature than your folks give you credit for, but . . .

FOR TEENAGERS WHOSE PARENTS ARE ABOUT TO BE OR HAVE RECENTLY BECOME DIVORCED OR SEPARATED — 100

It hurts . . . but don't let it ruin you.

THIS PAGE IS FOR PARENTS — 102

IF YOU EVER BECOME A PARENT, DO IT RIGHT YOUR TIME AROUND — 103

Do you know what your kid's most important emotional needs would be?

LOVE IS . . . — 109

Mature or immature? Also: "On being intimate with a chestnut" (a nutty idea, no?).

WHOM NOT TO MARRY (If You Do Marry) — 113

Don't be like almost everyone else . . .

MENTAL ILLNESS — 114

If you think you might be going crazy; if you think somebody else is crazy; most important facts about mental illness; if you're concerned about suicide . . .

DEATH — 117

We aren't into death, and we have just a few things to say about it.

IS RELIGION DEAD?   118

If you don't have a religion, really — discover your own.

TWO BOOK REVIEWS:

Pro: *The Catcher in the Rye*   120
Interlude: Be the first kid on your block to read these 10 recently forgotten novels   122
Con: *Jonathan Livingston Seagull*   123
Special: 142 modern writers we think you'll like   123/124

LIFE IS AN OPPORTUNITY CLASSIFIEDS   127

If you're looking for something to get into, here's a slew of possibilities.

ABOUT THE AUTHORS (by the authors)   137

ABOUT YOU (by yourself)   143

WHAT DO YOU DO AFTER YOU FIND YOURSELF

An old sage* once said:

>when all is
>sad and done
>the way
>to have fun
>is with
>someone

You know, I think after "everything" has been tried—meditation, basketball, yoga, marathons, macrobiotic diets, tripping, finding oneself, occult, I Ching, Jesus, psychotherapy, Kung Fu, masturbation, alcohol, TV, streaking, politics, volunteering, sex, Nader (and even if what we try works for us)—we are left with ourselves.

The guy/gal on the make still needs to make it with someone s/he cares about.

The meditator still needs someone to talk to about it.

The black garter/belt still needs someone to admire him/her.

The finder of oneself still needs someone to share "it" with.

Kung Fu still needs a disciple.

Even TV addicts need someone, but no one wants to be with them because they are so boring to be with.

None of us can find ourselves by ourselves

That's our message.
No one thing or combination of things is salvation.
Find yourself
    things to do and believe in.
Yes
but

*Me

Life is not *a* meaning,
It's an opportunity.
When "all" is being said and done and tried, *it* will be *tested* by our ability to love and care for at least one other person.

SPECIAL ALERT

 Everything funny in this book is seriously intended.

Some people may be taken aback by the *form* of this book, more than by what it has to say. It deliberately contains some surprises, some repetitions and some apparent incongruities.

But that's what life is like—isn't it?

This book is designed so that it can be begun at any point. It *does not* get into heavy trips about the culture or counter-culture, music or counter-music, sports or the way people dress or current fads and follies. There is plenty already written about that. None of the sections are overloaded with references. (Near the back of the book, however, is a Life Is An Opportunity Classifieds.)

We want to get into you, your trips and your vibrations. We are dedicated to the idea that life is what happens to you while you're busy making other plans.

★ ★ ★ BULLETIN ★ ★ ★

If you are allergic to ideas, turn immediately to page 77.

EXTRA EXTRA

You'll need a pencil on hand while you go through this book. After you fill in the blanks, answer the questions, write the poems and do the other things you can do with the free spaces, give this book to someone you really care about. You can always get another copy for yourself.

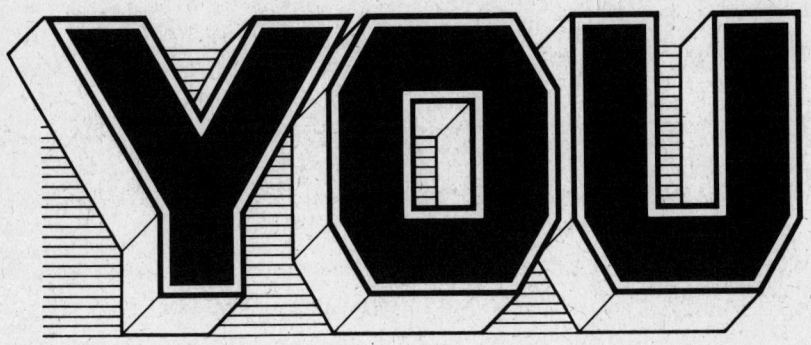

WHAT IS NORMAL?

Normal is a word. But not a normal word. It is a *loaded* word. And like other loaded words, it is sometimes used as a weapon to keep you in line.

For example, people often use "normal" as a label to describe people and situations they consider to be "safe" or non-threatening. Likewise, people often call "abnormal" the people and things they don't like, don't agree with or that are just "different."

Some people feel that you are normal when you are able to adjust to and accept the status quo and other written and unwritten "rules" handed down by the Establishment (as those in positions of power are sometimes called). That is, normal behavior is frequently thought to be behavior which *conforms* to society's jumble of taboos, fears, customs, rules and laws. If what you are doing does not conform to what parents, friends and teachers expect, they say you are not dealing with "real" things and that this isn't normal. They may be right, but,

 when you get down to it
only you
can decide
what is true
for you

reality
can change as
you grow

If *normal* means conformity to rules and regulations (which change from culture to culture and from time to time), then dissenters, reformers and creative people will be branded as *abnormal*.

Similarly, we must be wary of accepting the majority's view as the norm. For example, prejudice against minority groups, such as blacks, Mexican-Americans, Puerto Ricans, Indians and Jews is common in America. But is it normal to be prejudiced against some people just because many, or most, members of your own group are prejudiced against these "outsiders?" Is it normal to follow the latest fashions or fads because "stars" are doing it or because the mass media tell us what is "in" and "out"?

Rather than worry about what is normal, we might think about *what is not abnormal*.

For one thing, it is not abnormal to refuse to accept and adjust to all existing conditions. Martin Luther King, for example, refused to go along with segregationist laws and customs. By intelligent, well-planned protest and opposition, he was able to trigger off important changes (including the 1964 Civil Rights Act). Likewise, it is not abnormal for us to crusade against common evils like pollution, slums, corruption in business and government or the exploitation of one person by another.

Conformity for its own sake is not a measure of normality.

Super-conformists or super non-conformists, at best, tend to lead boring lives.

Non-conformity as an act of conscience can be a courageous and enriching force in a person's life, as demonstrated by the thousands of young men who refused to be drafted for the war in Vietnam. In a sense these resisters can be accused of premature morality.

A SCALE FOR MEASURING ADJUSTMENT AND MALADJUSTMENT

Perhaps, when discussing purely personal behavior, it would be better to abandon the notion of normality altogether. Rather than casually brand someone as "normal" or "abnormal" we might think in terms of an "adjustment—maladjustment" scale, as follows.

You have:

- **Excellent adjustment** if you enjoy life, have friends, work close to your maximum abilities, have a sound relationship with your family, make satisfying use of your leisure time, and if you can generally cope with your problems.

- **Good adjustment** if your behavior is excellent in most areas of everyday life and personality development, but is less than excellent in a few areas.

- **Adequate adjustment** if you get along reasonably well and have no problems so serious that they overwhelm you. You have ups and downs, but you also have friends and enjoyable interests.

- **Poor adjustment** if you have at least one serious problem (see the following list of six) but still do well in at least one area, such as schoolwork or relationships with friends.

- **Very poor adjustment** if you have one or more problems so severe as to be disabling, or with symptoms that threaten future personality development. Poorly adjusted young people often appear to be on the road to mental illness or delinquency, or give the impression of being grossly inadequate.

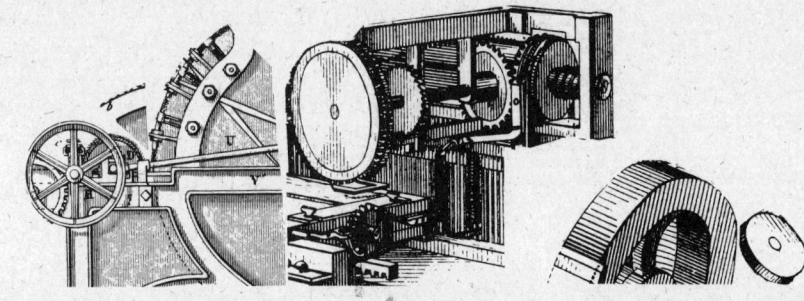

SIX
SIGNS OF VERY POOR ADJUSTMENT

You have made a poor or very poor adjustment to life if you show at least one of the following signs:

1. An inability to learn at a level close to what your intelligence would call for. (And if this gap is not caused by brain damage or other health problems; or by language barriers resulting from recent immigration; or by a move from an area with a backward educational system; or by temporary conditions, such as grief over the breaking up of an important relationship).
2. An inability to build and maintain satisfactory relationships with other people, especially people in the same age group. (This sign is important only if it lasts for a long time.)
3. Continued inappropriate or immature behavior in everyday circumstances. Such behavior might include silliness, bizarre mannerisms, or frequent aggressive outbursts, as well as apathy as a common response to frustration.
4. A persistent mood of unhappiness or depression. This does not refer to a temporary reaction of shock triggered by the death of a loved one, for instance. And it does not apply to occasional anxiety, tension and unhappiness, which are all part of *normal* growth and development.
5. Fears or physical symptoms (such as stuttering, tics, pains, and phobias) that develop in response to personal and school problems.
6. Compulsive behavior. Almost everyone has a bad habit or two, but sometimes behaviors get far enough beyond your control (such as overeating or superorderliness) that they become the focus of a lot of anxiety.

Remember: The poorly adjusted person doesn't necessarily show all these symptoms. Also, even the most maladjusted person may sometimes have areas of adequacy, or even demonstrate exceptional talents and accomplishments. Jimi Hendrix and Janis Joplin, for instance, were tremendous musicians but evidently couldn't cope with the rest of life.

FANTASY, REALITY & NORMALITY

All of us have a *fantasy life*.

This is made up of dreams, imaginings, wishes, impulses and the like, which often originate in the unconscious. At the deeper levels of the mind, these elements represent the raw, primitive, amoral forces in the personality. Thus, from time to time, we become aware of impulses or desires which may seem murderous, suicidal, sensuous, sadistic, romantic, weird, sexual, heroic or incestuous.

If we feel guilty or frightened by these ideas, they are likely to occur again and again. *Guilt provides the energy for the compulsive (involuntary) repetition of images which are unacceptable or even repulsive to us.* This is a very important idea, and we repeat it elsewhere in this book.

The point to keep in mind is that fantasizing and daydreaming are entirely normal. They are a healthy and, indeed, a necessary part of life. For example, we may enjoy fantasies of a sexual nature, and we may choose to repeat them again and again, even though we know that we cannot carry them out. In one sense, fantasy is part of the reality of preparing for life as an adult. In fact, in all of us, *fantasy is part of the reality of life*.

Thus, you should reject the fear that any kinds of thoughts can in themselves be abnormal or can drive you crazy.

However, it is clear that fantasy can also become an escape, a cop-out, a way of avoiding life. Guilt-ridden, uncontrolled fantasizing is a symptom of internal conflicts, such as feelings of inferiority.

IS SOCIETY ABNORMAL?

As R. D. Laing has pointed out, in the last 50 years, "normal" people have killed more than 100 million of their fellow normal people.

No one can make you feel inferior without your consent

---

4 QUESTIONS:

The next time you think of anyone, including yourself, in terms of normal and abnormal, consider the following questions:

1. Is the use of the concept of normality the real issue — or is it really a means of avoiding the issue?
2. Is it being used as an attack against a non-conformist who may be a creative, healthy person with ideas that you don't like?
3. Is it being used on the basis of an unexamined assumption that anything the majority does, thinks, or likes is thereby good—and "normal"?
4. Is it being used as a way of debasing or hating yourself?

☞ HAVE YOU EVER HEARD OF ANYONE WHO ENJOYS LIFE WHO DOESN'T ALSO ENJOY DAYDREAMING?

DISCOVERING WHO WE ARE

Do you find yourself looking for yourself? What does that mean? I am not sure *I* know, but a lot of young people come to me and say they can't find themselves or that life, for them, has no meaning. They want to get it together, so they go on trips. Sometimes after these trips they come to me and confess, "I've never been so lonely and unhappy in my life." This is what I say: Life is not a meaning. It is an opportunity. Life is made up of a series of meaningful experiences which often last only a short time.

One of the most important survival tips for lonely people to know is this: Don't trust anyone who says that s/he is not trying to influence you. Be especially critical of people who claim they are fair, objective, perfectly honest and who start sentences with, "To tell the truth." Never, never trust anyone who says, "You can trust me."

Are you puzzled? Why should you be? I don't expect you to trust me. And besides, I only give advice that people find hard to follow. I have too much respect for the complexity of personality to expect that people can follow advice. Try these for size:

> If you are worried about gaining weight: Don't eat so much.
> If you are horny: Think of something else.
> If you feel life is passing you by: Try to make the most of it.

I think that if people can, in fact, follow your advice, you are insulting them by offering it. The only advice worth giving is advice people cannot easily follow:

Not "advice" like
    Be Good
    Pay Attention
       which is never worthwhile, but

Let me make another point first. Behavior based on trust is often a way of avoiding responsibility. If you want to do something, do it as a risk, an unselfish act, an opportunity—but not because someone asks you to trust him/her. Take responsibility for what you do!

7

Say (to yourself): "I am telling you (a friend) my innermost secrets because I have a need to tell someone, and because I want to risk the possibility that you may betray me. If you do betray me I will be hurt and disappointed. If you prove to be a good friend I will be joyful." But don't say (or cry), "I told you my secrets because I trusted you." Or (the ultimate immaturity), "Now I can't trust anybody." Translation: *I will act as though everybody hates me.*

I tell people what I'm telling you now: Don't do anything on trust alone. You may continue to operate on trust, but if it doesn't work out you will remember what I said and after more mistakes later you may be able to change your behavior. The price? Change may make you tense, uncomfortable and nervous. It's hard to shift gears. The reason people overeat is that eating relieves tension. If you reduce your intake you become very anxious. Having to tolerate the tension is the price you pay for weight reduction.

Sometimes, no matter how much you try, and despite your best intentions, you can't change the behavior you find unacceptable. This is because your personality needs that behavior; it is a defense against some worry or fear that is worse.

> A young man thinks he wants to stop stuttering but discovers that he doesn't really want to because he needs it so that people can feel sorry for him. No amount of speech therapy will help him until he can gain some confidence in himself.
>
> A mother overprotects her child because she has never felt secure as a mother and if anything happened to the child it would be "her fault." Telling her that she is being overprotective will fall on deaf ears until she works out the problem of her own insecurity.

The two examples given above illustrate conflicts that can require professional help from a trained social worker, psychologist, counselor or psychiatrist.

So what I am saying is that if you can't work out your problems by yourself or with the help of parents or friends, seek out professional guidance. But (warning) do not respond to your impulse to trust or not to trust the helper. Tell him/her what is on your mind but:

DO — risk the helper's not helping
                not understanding
                not having the time or interest

 miss out on an opportunity

the helper will like you
       will help you
       will influence your life

If you must always be in control, you will never feel secure.

Now I will give advice to people who can profit from advice that is awfully hard to follow.

If you are in a situation that is bad, try to improve or change it. If you can't, it may be because you are too young or too chicken or because the odds against you (as with some schools and families) are too heavy. In that case discover strategies of toleration and compromise but:

because of someone else's problem.

Pass the course you hate. Why punish yourself twice by having to take it over again?

- Don't continue a relationship only because you don't want to hurt the other person's feelings. This is punishing yourself and the other person while giving you a false sense of being a nice person.

- Sometimes it is possible to change things and feel good about it. One group of students persisted in their demands for a birth-control clinic on campus (and won). Another group "forced" the introduction of sex education, another is still struggling for a more flexible curriculum.

The point is that feeling rotten about yourself — whether expressed in terms of "the world is evil," "school is irrelevant," or "there is nothing to do"—is a cop-out. It is helpful to no one, even if the motivation for your view of the world seems to be sympathy for the poor or opposition to dictatorships. Sometimes you can't do much about the outside world except wait (painfully) until you are able to achieve a position of power and influence.

People who are messed up spend most of their time and energy hurting themselves and/or others. Their behavior tends to be involuntary, repetitive and exploitative.

A kid into heavy drinking lies to friends and parents about how he is going to change. He maintains his habit by stealing and borrowing money, which he will never return. He hates himself because he is most hateful to people who care about him.

A girl spends most of her time thinking about all the people who hate her. All the people who are supposed to hate her don't even know she exists.

A boy finds school irrelevant, the world meaningless. He spends most of his time sleeping, not doing his school work, and quarreling with his brother and mother. He is so busy not doing things and fighting that he has no time for friends and pleasure. His current anger is that his parents do not want to reward him for his hostility by giving him a motorcycle (and some bread besides) so he can travel around the country "finding himself."

A pretty girl is fed up with all the superficiality in life. She wants to be liked for her own sake. She dresses unattractively, doesn't wash much, and is more or less accepted as one of the boys—but she cannot understand why no boy wants to take her out (though quite a few wouldn't mind sleeping with her).

The meantime determines very largely what will happen in your future. Waiting until you get the courses you like ("and then I'll study") often means you won't reach that point. Trying to improve a marriage by having children usually ends up making matters much worse. (Who was it who said, "The road to hell is paved with good intentions"?)

It is not difficult to know when you are doing the wrong thing. (You really have to be in a bad way not to know—like a criminal who feels there is nothing wrong with what he does except if he gets caught.)

The chances are that if you are not doing what is right for you, symptoms, such as these, will appear:

◆◆◆◆◆◆◆◆◆◆◆◆◆◆◆◆◆◆◆◆◆◆◆

Overdependency, overeating, oversleeping, overtalking
Fear of high, low, tight or empty places
Anxiety
Underachievement
Loneliness
Accident-proneness
Tension headaches
Sexual hangups

And then there is boasting (what a bore),
not having anything to do
(what a drag),
or not ever enjoying being alone (what a pity).

◆◆◆◆◆◆◆◆◆◆◆◆◆◆◆◆◆◆◆◆◆◆◆

We all get depressed at times. Sometimes feeling down in the dumps lasts a long time. Professional help may be needed to get out of it, but more often than not an opportune phone call will put you in good spirits. Let me, however, suggest a strategy that can occasionally be used to speed up getting back into the swing of things. You are depressed, upset, moody, irritable, bitchy, or whatever. Look up a new word in a dictionary, glance at an encyclopedia, almanac, or one of the news weeklies. Learning something new is very stimulating. The next step is calling someone and having a long conversation, or going out for a walk or run (or standing on your head). Before you know it, the down cycle is broken. The more you do, the better you feel. This is especially true of people who spend a lot of time thinking about what they'd like to do or all the things they feel guilty about (or people who are chronic worriers). Remember, too, that even if you have a lot of self-awareness it is of little practical value unless you can act on it.

THE 10 MOST UNNECESSARY FEARS

(in order of unreasonable fearsomeness):

1 FEAR OF THE OPPOSITE SEX
2 FEAR OF THE SAME SEX
3 FEAR THAT YOU MIGHT BE A HOMOSEXUAL
4 FEAR THAT NO ONE WILL WANT TO HAVE SEX WITH YOU
5 FEAR OF INTIMACY
6 FEAR THAT YOU WON'T MEASURE UP TO SOMEONE ELSE'S STANDARDS
7 FEAR OF RISKING NEW EXPERIENCES
8 FEAR THAT IF YOU ARE NICE TO PEOPLE, THEY WILL TAKE ADVANTAGE OF YOU
9 FEAR THAT LIFE WILL PASS YOU BY
10 FEAR THAT ALL THERE IS TO LIFE IS WHAT YOU'VE EXPERIENCED ALREADY

 # WARNING

Try not to be desperate about anything you do. Cool it, be patient. If necessary, pretend you have savoir faire (if you don't know what it means, look it up). Live in the present. Stop trying to please the people you don't care about.

If, after reading this book, you still have one or more of the above 10 fears, you have not read it carefully or taken it seriously enough. So read it again. Discuss it with a friend. And if you still have at least one of those fears, get help (see page 131).

If you don't know what to say, listen to what other people are saying. You might have something to say (after all).

You don't have to be a big psychologist to appreciate that the process of not learning is exhausting. Students who don't learn much at school are tired at the end of the day. If you want energy during after-school activities, learn for your own protection.

If you want to know whether you were oversleeping (let's say for 12 hours or more) because you physically needed it or because you were psychologically afraid to face the next day, you can *always* judge it by whether, after oversleeping, you were refreshed or woke up tired.

If you have a persistent, uncomfortable dream or nightmare, your unconscious is giving you a message that you have an unresolved conflict. If you resolve the conflict you will no longer have the repetitive dream.

Real guilt can be distinguished from fake guilt by how you handle it. Genuine guilt organizes you. It helps you avoid making the same mistake again and has a tendency to make you feel better about yourself. Fake guilt encourages a tendency for self-pity or a wish for punishment so you can feel free to do *it* again. Rational guilt (something you should feel after doing something wrong) is healthy. Irrational guilt (something you feel despite the fact that you did nothing wrong—the worst kind being when you feel guilty about thoughts and fantasies) always makes you feel rotten about yourself and the energy of the rottenness keeps the guilt alive and unwell.

What counts is not what a person says so much as what he does. Sometimes behavior such as forgetting or passivity communicates more hostility than a big verbal argument. "I love you" is worth only as much as how it is expressed in day-to-day behavior.

There is no way of avoiding tension, upsets and frustrations, but when these become the dominant forces in life, then life becomes one big hassle, whether it is expressed in terms of "life has no meaning" or "everybody hates me." People who are striving to find meaning in a mature way are people whose lives are made up of meaningful choices. They always have more to do than there is time for. They have alternatives. They take risks. They can enjoy being alone at times. They know that when it is more important to them to meet the needs of the other person than to satisfy their own, they are in love.

If you don't feel that your life has just been described, work to make it psychologically healthy.

It's hard work. Life is hard work. If you have a genuine problem, the shift from the conflict to a state of health is rarely easy or automatic. The shift (the work of resolving the conflict) usually requires boring, mechanical and tension-producing efforts.

If your hangup is studying and it is important *for you* to do your work—you will seldom reach a point when you really feel like doing it. You must do it despite your feeling of not wanting to. Set yourself realistic goals. "I'll study for 30 minutes, then I'll watch TV for 30 minutes, then I'll study for 40 minutes and then I'll eat a snack," etc. "I'm going to study for four hours straight" usually ends up in not studying at all.

If your hangup is being afraid of girls/boys there is no way you are going to feel comfortable with them without having a lot of experience of being comfortable with yourself first, being comfortable with members of your own sex second and then slowly working through your conflicts with the opposite sex. Upon reaching the third stage you can't help but *feel* uncomfortable and awkward on your first dates. And unless you *are* willing to risk rejection, you won't even reach the stage of your first date. What is not often understood is that *risking rejection is also risking acceptance*.

How you feel about something is no substitute for the hard, anxiety-producing and, often, mechanical work required for problem-solving. Spontaneity develops after the conflict is resolved; it is seldom the medium for conflict-resolution.

Are you looking for yourself or the meaning in life? I hope so, because finding the meaning of life is a lifelong struggle which consists of trying to put together meaningful experiences. Getting it together is life itself.

"UNEXPECTED TRAVEL SUGGESTIONS ARE DANCING LESSONS FROM GOD."
— Kurt Vonnegut

FOR PEOPLE WHO SUFFER FROM BEING A MINORITY

A minority is someone who feels different from most people or who feels abused because of circumstances s/he has no control over.

In this sense, women are a majority who are a minority.

In a way, just about everyone is a minority — but that fact doesn't help people who are discriminated against. Neither does that fact do much good for people who are the victims of circumstances even though there may be a rational reason for their situation (as with children who are upset and confused after their parents separate).

Another example: There are some Jews who don't like the fact that they are Jewish and they become like the anti-Semites. They identify with the aggressor. That is, they operate — perhaps unconsciously — as though the accusations by the bigots were generally true.

(It just goes to show that, no matter who you are, if you think in stereotypes it's very easy to "prove" any point you want.)

On the other hand, Jews who accept their Jewishness — whether because of parents, Jewish culture, or identification with Israel — generally feel better about themselves and have a fine sense of self-acceptance.

What we are getting at is that the best way to *start out* with coping with being a minority is to accept, rather than fight, your background. This goes for handicapped people too. People who are worried about their handicap are a burden on themselves and others. What happens then is that the poor self-image and depressions become even more of a burden than the disability itself.

Any experience can be turned to your advantage (after you've had it). The way to do this is to get involved in the background of your group and find out what the experience of it means.

So . . .

If you're black, learn about the history of the black experience.

If you're a woman, know your rights.

If you're Jewish, think about the good points of Jewish mothering and Jewish history.

If you're blind, accept that *other* blind people are as good as people who aren't blind.

If you're gay, discover that you're a person.

Once you know these things, *then* you are able to decide whether to be or not to be an activist or whatever . . .

FOR PEOPLE WHO DON'T THINK THEY ARE ATTRACTIVE

People who are self-accepting are sexually attractive to *some* other people — period. It doesn't matter what the cosmetic and toothpaste industries have to say about it.

It's not that short, fat or "unattractive" people can't "find" a mate; it's that people who hate themselves and express it in being (not looking) unattractive, short-sighted or fatuous tend to repel rather than attract others.

Believing that certain perfumes, hair tonics, vaginal sprays or selective techniques or positions will make you attractive will get you nowhere. *Being* a real person is what is attractive to other people. You'd be surprised; more and more people these days are into being real. We are in a "let's stop playing games" era.

 THERE IS SOMEBODY
FOR EVERYBODY

FOR PEOPLE WHO ARE ESPECIALLY BRIGHT OR SENSITIVE

If you want to expand your mental health, your positive weirdness, your intelligence, your skills, you will have to put up with a lot of abuse and snubbing from people who are less ambitious. However, once you have established your own identity and have your own circle of friends this won't matter at all.

By the way, people who are exceptionally sensitive and intelligent often go to great pains to hide these qualities. People get on to you anyway, though, and they will resent what they sense is a kind of reverse snobbery.

If you don't acknowledge high-level intellectual qualities in yourself, it is a very destructive experience. You tend to play down your abilities when talking with people; thus you might miss out on someone who is interested in you, rather than afraid of you.

When you repress an important part of your personality, there's only one thing to do: Fake it. Putting up this artificial front causes a lot of strain and diverts energy that you might use more profitably elsewhere.

Besides, it's really a drag for people who sense your tension, and don't

> **Beware of people who are self righteous, especially those who claim to have a monopoly on what constitutes the Judeo-Christian morality.**

know how to relate to you. In our sexist culture, this pitfall is especially true for women.

None of this means you should be a "typical" arrogant intellectual. (Arrogance is basically an irrational form of defense which blocks possibilities for intimacy.)

You just have to find some way to be a real self-expressing person.

FOR PEOPLE WHO HAVE BEEN INSULTED

The fear of being humiliated is one of the biggest blocks to being the way you want to be.

A lot of people are more afraid of being shamed and ridiculed than they are of being beaten up.

Some pointers:

● Don't take seriously the opinions of people you don't respect.

● Some people enjoy provoking and taunting others into getting flustered. They usually do it when they have an audience.

One very effective way of handling this form of abuse is — believe it or not — to ignore it. Your antagonist will generally try to get a rise out of you for awhile, until he starts to look silly in front of his audience because you aren't responding.

Sometimes playing along a little with the attack will neutralize it. If someone calls you stupid, maybe you can agree, "Yup. I'm so stupid, you wouldn't believe how stupid I am." Then, go on with your business and don't dwell on or drag out the exchange. By agreeing in an exaggerated — but controlled — way, you have blocked your opponent. At any rate, whatever your reply, it should be conscious and calculated.

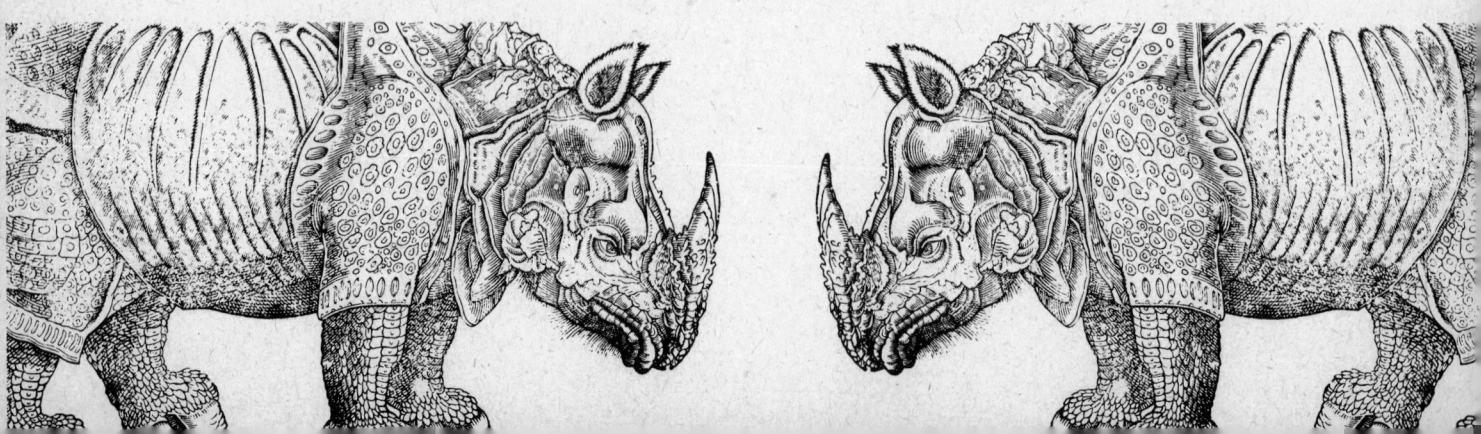

- Try to figure out the reason for the insult. For example, possibly you were a little too thin-skinned and the "insult" was basically good-natured ribbing, or well-deserved and well-intended criticism that might be helpful for you to accept.

Of course, some snipers are habitually nasty. The cutting remark is perfectly timed to deflate your ego. Even if the criticism is true, ask yourself how much it really means. Some people inflate their overly insecure egos by deflating others: Why should other people be hung up in your "faults" or problems? Possibly because you remind them of things they are worried about in themselves.

- What do you do about this classic insult: "You'll never amount to anything"?

    The best answer: "I know it, and that's what worries me about myself."

    They say: "So why don't you *do* something about it?"

    You answer: "Like you often say, it's easier said than done."

    If that doesn't end it, say that you need to be alone for awhile.

The point is not that you agree that you won't amount to anything, but that you are using a strategy to shut off a fruitless argument.

- If an insult comes from someone you don't know very well, the hell with it. If it comes from a good friend, a relative, or someone you love, don't let it eat you.

Be concerned only if their insults are habitual. Then figure out: What are you going to do about it?

FOR PEOPLE
WHO DEMAND EVERYTHING
— OR NOTHING

All-or-none type people typically want everything — or nothing at all. If their room can't be completely organized and tidy, they leave it a complete mess. If they can't be in complete control of a relationship, they break it up. If they can't do a job all in one session, they give up. If they don't think they can get the Gold Medal, they don't enter the contest.

They are basically unrealistic people, easily intimidated by phrases like: "If a job is worth doing, it's worth doing right." That's a nice idea, as long as you don't use it to block yourself from doing anything at all.

If perfectionism is a hang-up of yours, here's a tip:

> LOWER YOUR STANDARDS
> SO YOU CAN INCREASE
> YOUR PERFORMANCE.

Some people feel they are not qualified to help anyone else because they are not together enough themselves. Sure, you should try to get it together. That's life. But part of getting it together is realizing that the stronger should help the weaker.

If you want self-confidence, try taking some responsibility for someone else's welfare. For example, do volunteer work at your local crisis center or free clinic. Or find outlets in which you can share yourself with children.

Becoming an active carer may not solve all your problems, but — if you're lucky — you'll find that they aren't nearly as overwhelming as they used to be. When people are relying on *you* to get something done that really needs doing, you shouldn't have time to be overly hung up on your personal problems.

FOR PEOPLE WHO SMOKE, SMOKE SMOKE . . . SMOKE THAT CIGARETTE

Some people are so insecure about their image that they'll try anything that might give them a little boost of confidence.

Kids who have recently taken up cigarettes almost always "enjoy" smoking when others are around to see them. Smoking *looks* tough, or cool, or adult, or whatever. And, best of all, adults don't like it when teenagers smoke.

It's so dumb. Is the small bit of pleasure you get from tobacco worth risking addiction? Addiction sneaks up on you and you don't even know you're hooked — until one day you run out of cigarettes and you go crazy trying to get some. Some teenagers suffer from the screwy idea that being addicted to cigarettes somehow makes them more grown up. Actually, after awhile it is really degrading to be a slave to nicotine. Blah . . .

Notice that the people in the cigarette ads are almost always young, attractive, hip, suave, carefree, sexy, successful, manly, and so on. These ads are aimed at *kids*. Once a person gets past age 20 or so s/he won't ordinarily start smoking, no matter *what*.

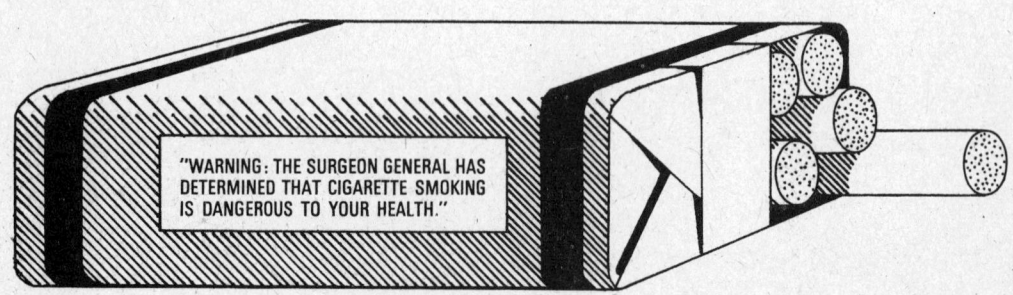

GUT NEWS
For Modern Eaters

Zing Comix

"mmm... not bad..."

CHOMP!

"HE REALLY EATS THIS STUFF UP"

"DOESN'T HE KNOW THIS COMIC IS IN BAD TASTE?"

I.M. CALORIE

O.U. CALORIE

TODAY'S SPECIAL: This book is for teenagers between 12 and 18 who have not been put on special diets by their doctors.

Text by Sol Gordon and Roger Conant
Nutrition consultant: Marjorie V. Dibble
Humor consultant: Marlene Conant
Facilitator: Kathleen G. Everly
Distribution: Del Cusmano
Illustrations and design by Roger Conant
Published by Ed-U Press, 760 Ostrom Ave., Syracuse, N.Y. 13210
Ed-U Press is the publishing arm of Syracuse University's
Institute for Family Research and Education

Other titles in this series of educational comic books include: *Ten Heavy Facts About Sex*, *V.D. Claptrap*, *Protect Yourself From Becoming an Unwanted Parent*, *Drug You -- A Survivor's Handbook*, and *Juice Use -- Special Hangover Edition*. These booklets and *Gut News* are available for 30 cents each from Ed-U Press. Bulk rates are available on request.
© 1974 by Ed-U Press

WHY DO YOU GET HUNGRY WHEN YOU DON'T NEED TO EAT?

Here are some of the things people do in order to relieve tension, anxiety and boredom:

Eat, drink, smoke, take drugs, watch TV, listen to music, b.s., masturbate, screw, get violent, take a hot bath, take a healthy dump, work hard, laugh...

It's OK to have a bite to eat when you are a little edgy or when you are depressed -- as long as you aren't eating because you "can't help it." If a behavior is compulsive (beyond your control), it is almost always bad for you.

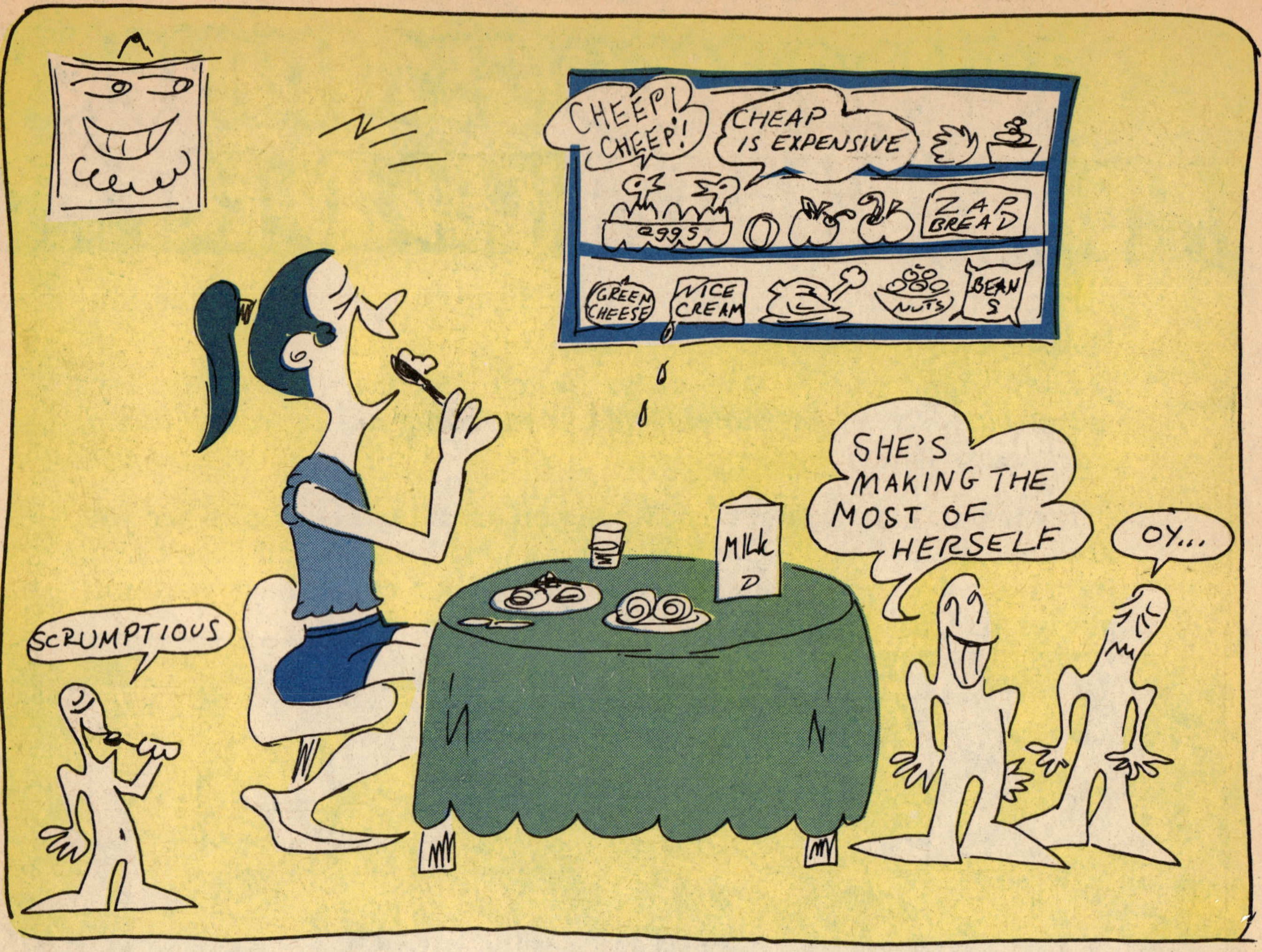

If you want to stay healthy, you need to stoke up regularly on foods like these:

WHAT YOU NEED TO KEEP FIT

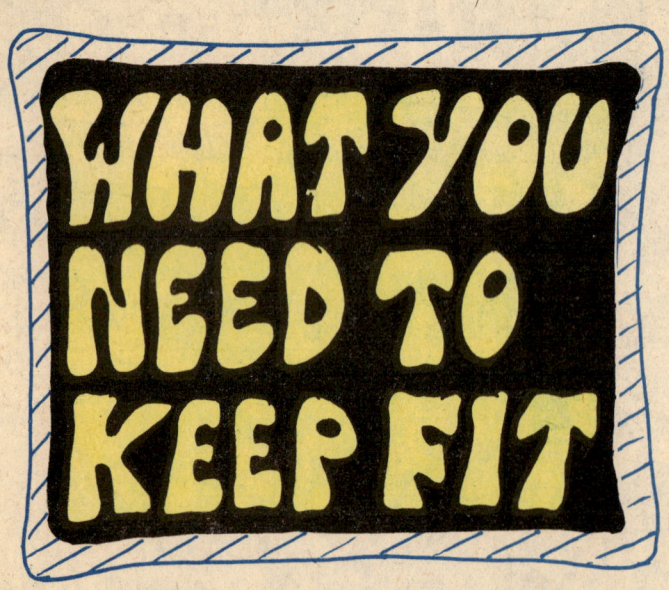

- **Milk, cheese, milk shakes, yogurt, ice cream, and other dairy products.**
- Oranges, grapefruit, melons, bananas, mangoes, strawberries and other fruits. If you don't like fruit, drink real fruit juices (not fruit flavored juices).
- Peas, string beans, carrots, tomatoes, sweet potatoes, corn, potatoes, spinach and other green and yellow vegetables. If you don't eat many vegetables, eat more fruit.
- Either whole grain or enriched breads, rolls, cereals, rice, macaroni, spaghetti. . .
- **Beef, liver, poultry, pork, lamb, seafood, eggs, peanut butter, dried beans, and nuts.** You don't need big slabs of meat to stay healthy.

Teenagers need plenty of protein. (Good sources of protein are shown above in bold type.) Did you know that most American adults get twice as much protein as they need?

Most Important Fact:

The more *variety* of good foods you eat, the less chance you have of being poorly nourished.

"I CAN LEAP TALL BUILDINGS IN A SINGLE BOUND, TOO."

"HOLD ON, I'LL MAKE YOU A HERO SANDWICH."

CAN YOU EAT YOUR WAY TO WEALTH AND HEALTH

Some people make a religion out of eating. While a good diet is important, it isn't "the answer." For example, isn't a meaningful relationship more important than a bowl of crunchy granola?

You don't necessarily need three squares a day to stay healthy. What counts is the quality of the food you eat. However, breakfast is important. People who don't like to eat breakfast might try eating just a small amount of food (a piece of toast, a bagel, some fruit, last night's hamburger...). They may find that they have a little more energy during the morning.

IF YOU'RE SICKLY

Did you know that many people eat a lot and are still poorly nourished?

There are plenty of fat people who are miserably undernourished. There are also plenty of people who are "thin as a rail" who are energetic and healthy.

No matter what your weight, you may not be eating right if you get colds easily, if you nearly always catch the bug that's going around, if you are run down and sluggish a lot.

Bad nutrition can hurt your mental alertness, your ability to work, and your sex life -- among other things.

Try being careful to feed yourself a healthy variety of high quality foods (even at snack times) -- and see whether it makes a difference after a week or so. Lay off the pretzels, potato chips, candy, donuts, cookies, soda pop.

MAYBE IT'S YOUR DIET...

WHAT'S WITH HARRY?

HE'S BEEN SWALLOWING TOO MUCH OF THE SAME OLD BALONEY

ANYBODY FOR A RED HERRING?

EVERYTHING IS A CONSPIRACY!

> HE CRASHED IN A FAST DIET

> DIET 500

> NO-NOTHING REDUCTIONS CORPS.

> SHOULD WE GET HIM SOME CHICKEN SOUP MAYBE?

If you go on a crash diet, you may put your bod through more stress than it's ready to take, and you may miss out on some of the things in foods that you need to stay healthy. In other words, you might get pretty sick.

The safest diet is to eat the types of food mentioned on page 2 -- in smaller amounts.

"Diet pills," no matter what kind, are risky. You can get really strung out -- mentally and physically -- if you use them daily. Amphetamines ("speed") and anorectics (such as Plegine) suppress your appetite, but they also give you a lot of fake energy and they screw up your judgment. Diuretics ("water pills") make you urinate a lot and lose water that your body needs.

Some fat-clinics offer "hormone shots." These shots are worthless.

CRASH DIETS

When you stop taking the drugs or you stop your weird diet, you are very likely to gain back any weight you lost.

The challenge is to change your life style so that less calories and more physical activity become normal parts of living -- and not just something you do for short times.

5

No matter what method of losing weight you try, *you will have to put up with a lot of tension and anxiety.*

However, if you can hold out for a few days, the tension that comes from starting to change your eating habits will usually become easier to handle.

The best way to take your mind off the tension is to find interesting and exciting things to do with your time.

If you're a boob tube junkie, you may have to cut down your viewing time gradually. (The more TV you watch, the more bored/boring you become.)

LOSING WEIGHT

HOW DO YOU LIKE BEING WEIGHTLESS?

HEAVY, HEAVY

People who are trying to lose weight often give up -- sometimes because their goals were too high. For example, they may not know that once you lose the first few pounds, it starts getting harder to lose more weight. (Anything you lose over about 2 1/2 pounds a week is water, not body fat.)

Sometimes people think that "all is lost" when they go off their diet. However, if your usual way of dealing with anxiety is to eat, then when you become super-nervous, you'll go off your diet. OK -- so have that piece of chocolate cake. But don't let feeling guilty about it knock you out: Go back on your diet tomorrow.

If you are also a heavy smoker and you stop, you'll probably have a very powerful urge to eat. If you have to stuff yourself, try carrots, celery and water. (Please don't use weight gain as an excuse for never trying to quit smoking.)

JUST AIN'T EASY

WEIGH THESE WORDS

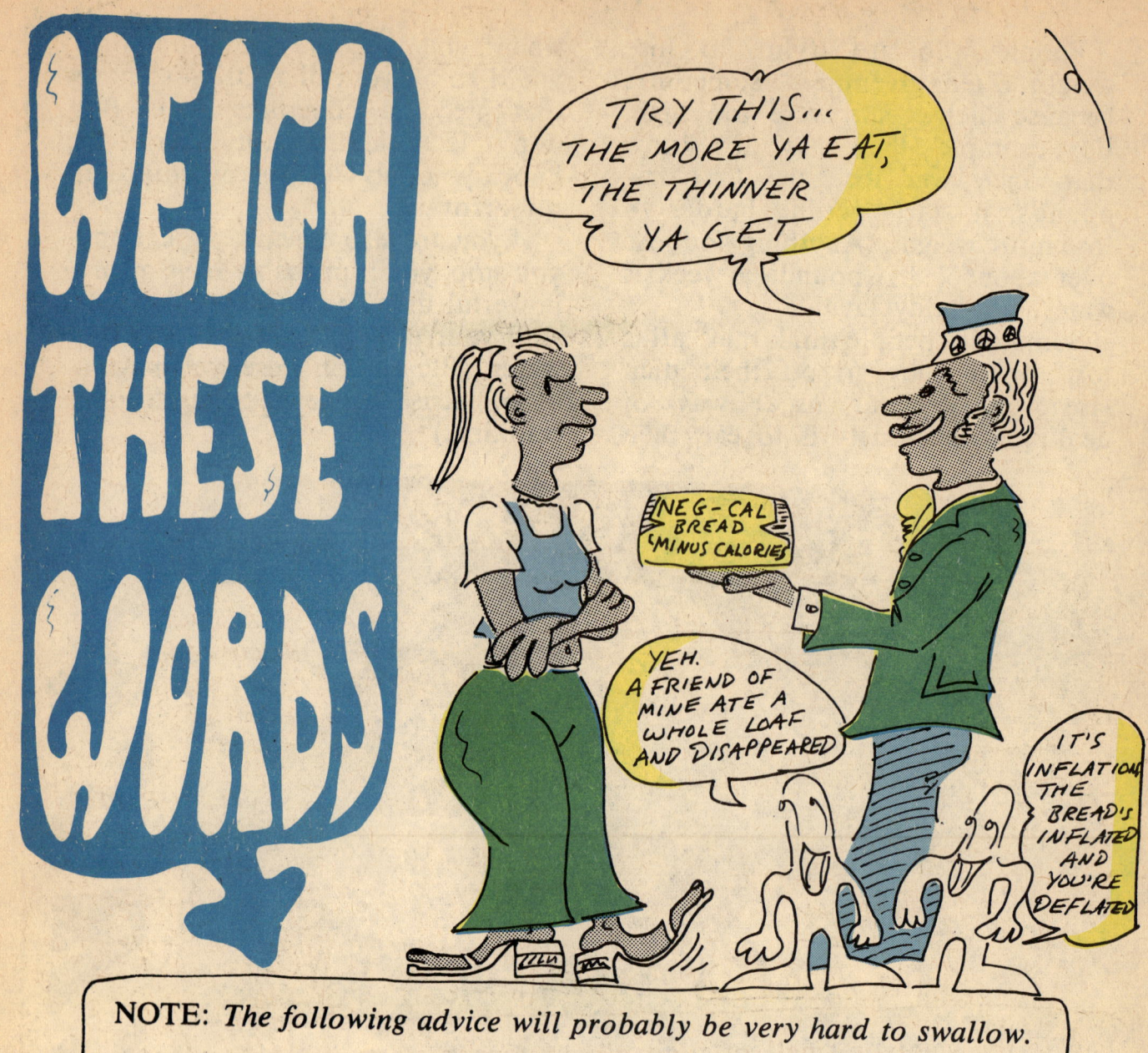

TRY THIS... THE MORE YA EAT, THE THINNER YA GET

NEG-CAL BREAD – MINUS CALORIES

YEH. A FRIEND OF MINE ATE A WHOLE LOAF AND DISAPPEARED

IT'S INFLATION. THE BREAD'S INFLATED AND YOU'RE DEFLATED

NOTE: *The following advice will probably be very hard to swallow.*

- If you're a fast eater, put down your fork between mouthsful.
- If you eat more than you need just because the food is there, ask the family cook to prepare less of it. (Ask that he or she stop pointing out, "There's more.")
- If there is a certain type of high calorie food that you usually eat (such as greaseburgers or chocolate frosting sandwiches), do without it.
- If you're the calorie-counting type, get a calorie chart and eat what you like, without going over the day's calorie limit. (Your doctor can tell you how many calories you should be taking in.)

"WHAT ABOUT YOUR DIET, HON?"

"JUST BUILDING UP MY STRENGTH, DEAR"

"IN THAT CASE, YOU OUGHT TO TURN INTO SUPERMAN ANY MOMENT NOW"

Super Corn Fakes

"CAN YOU BELIEVE ALL THIS CORN?"

"YUP. IT'S HARD-CORE CORNOGRAPHY ALRIGHT"

- If the sight or smell of food almost always starts you drooling, turn your head. If the munchies won't go away, immediately leave the scene and do something that needs doing, call up a friend, take a walk, look up a word in the dictionary -- anything, to help you past the temptation.

"HOW ARE YA, FRANK?"
"NOT SO HOT"

- If you get very little exercise, try taking *daily* walks and doing other activities (such as bicycling, gardening, working on the car). If you're really out of shape, the best exercises are the ones where you can go at your own pace. Some women think that exercising is not feminine. Not exercising is not healthy -- that's all. Also: The great majority of people with physical handicaps can and should do exercises specially suited to their needs.

OTHER WAYS TO OVERDO IT

"AN APPLE A DAY KEEPS THE DOCTOR AWAY"

BONK!!

Overeating isn't the only way to overdo it with food. How you are eating now will influence your future health.

I JUST HAD A BOWL OF UPDOC

WHAT'S UPDOC?

Some examples:

- If you don't control your sweet tooth, you may develop a gut. Too much candy, cake, ice cream, soda pop, and the like, can also crowd out the kinds of food you need for good health. By the way, the "energy" that this kind of sugar is supposed to give doesn't last more than two or three minutes. And don't forget what the dentist has been telling you since you were knee-high to a popsicle (how *could* you forget it?).

- If you eat a *lot* of fatty stuff (fatty meat, lard, eggs, butter, whole milk, cheese), you may be setting yourself up for heart trouble in your middle age. Did you know that many Americans eat much more meat than they need?

- If you eat mostly one type of food (such as mostly meat or brown rice or potatoes or milk or corn) without eating much else, you may get sickly from not eating foods with other stuff your body needs.

- If you drink a lot, you may gain weight and lose out nutritionally. As a food, alcohol is worthless -- but it is high in calories.

If you are a super-finicky eater, you are really a drag to have as a guest. Some people use finickiness as a way to express hostility (especially against people they live with).

There is not much point in forcing yourself to eat foods you don't like. But, on the other hand, there is no point in "deciding" that you hate and will always hate certain foods. (Some people go through life trying to get back at their parents by not eating vegetables or other foods.)

Anyway, it's boring to eat the same old stuff all the time if you don't have to. Use some imagination when you prepare food. After all, isn't variety the spice of life?

FOOD YOU CAN'T STAND

FACTORY-MADE FOODS

When food is ready-made in the factory, much of the good stuff (like vitamins, minerals and protein) is often lost. Even if they put some of these things back in, you can usually get a wider variety of nutrients from fresh food.

Also: The food industry dumps a lot of additives into foods to keep them from spoiling, to color them, to create a flavor that wasn't there, to form a tempting texture...

In our hungry world, it's necessary to add stuff that keeps food from spoiling. However, the more factory-made foods you eat, the more additives go into your system. Nobody really knows what some of these extra chemicals might do or not do to your body...

Besides, these foods often cost a lot more than fresh foods.

TV DINNERS AGAIN, HUH?

THEY'RE CHEAPER THAN HAMBURGER

We're not suggesting you do without factory-made food entirely, but it's hard to get a balanced diet if nearly all your food is ready-made.

How often do you eat factory-made foods like these:

WHAT'S HE GRINNING ABOUT?

I THINK HE JUST ELIMINATED ANOTHER MIDDLEMAN

ANYONE FOR MONOPOLY?

Instant potatoes, instant coffee, instant breakfast, instant pudding, instant cocktail mix, TV dinners, ready-to-eat breakfast cereals, canned potato salad, powdered soup, soda pop, cake mix, ready-made cookies, quick-cooking rice, non-dairy creamer, artificial sour cream, meat tenderizer, steak sauce, ketchup, hot dogs, bologna, potato chips, pretzels, cheese doo-dads... (Can you think of more?)

DON'T GET RIPPED OFF

*LET'S SEE HERE... **INSTANT HASH** CONTAINS: PANAMA RED, ACAPULCO GOLD, EYE OF TOAD, TAIL OF NEWT, 2 WHISKERS FROM A SHARK'S MUSTACHE, THE KITCHEN SINK, THE DEVIL TO PAY*

CALORIES: HIGH

Labels are often very sneaky and confusing -- especially when they talk about how "nutritious" the food is.

However, a new law has been passed to get food companies to make labels clear and complete. There's a chance that some of the new labels may actually be for real. In that case, maybe people will actually bother to read them.

At any rate, it is worth your time to check out the label so you can get some idea of what the product contains and how much it *really* costs. For example, a 5-ounce packet of frozen peas might cost more than a 7-ounce can of peas. But, there may be more peas in the frozen packet than in the can, which may have a lot of water in it.

Ingredients on the old-type labels are listed in order from the most to the least. So, if it says "water, beef, potatoes, carrots," then there is more water than beef, more beef than potatoes, and so on.

VITAMINS, MINERALS

By eating a variety of foods -- vegetables too -- you should get enough of the vitamins and minerals you need.

It's important that vegetables be cooked properly so you don't lose the vitamins and minerals. Use a small amount of cooking water, cover the pot, and don't overcook. Or, even better, steam them. If they're crunchy, they're good. If they're soggy, the vitamins and minerals are in the cooking water. (Drink it or use it in gravy.)

We can't tell you whether you should take vitamin pills or whether big doses of vitamin C cut down on colds or whether vitamin E makes you horny. Some experts swear by vitamin pills. Others say that, unless you have a special problem, they are a big rip-off.

One thing is sure: **Vitamin pills can't take the place of a well-rounded diet.**

SHE'S TAKING HER ONE-A-YEAR, YA KNOW

For Megavitamin Freaks
Huge doses of vitamins A and D can be very harmful.

IF YOU MIGHT BECOME A MOTHER...

How you eat during your teen years can make a difference in the outcome of all your future pregnancies.

During pregnancy, the trick is not just to eat more, but to eat better. For example, plenty of protein (see page 2) during pregnancy will help your baby's growth. Pregnancy is not the time to put yourself on a reducing diet.

WHAT DO YOU MEAN, YOU HAVE ALL THE IRON YOU NEED?

NO WONDER SHE'S GOT A MAGNETIC PERSONALITY

...AND EVEN IF YOU MIGHT NOT

Girls are big targets for anemia caused by lack of iron (which is lost during menstrual bleeding). Without enough iron, you are tired and listless a lot and you get sick easily.

Foods with lots of iron include liver, lean meat, egg yolk, dried fruit, whole grain and enriched breads and cereals, and dark green, leafy vegetables.

Since most women don't get enough iron these days, you might ask your doctor about iron pills.

(MUNCH!)
MORE TENDERIZER, PLEASE.
(URP!)
COOKOO COOKOO

IS HE OUT OF HIS TREE?

NO. HE'S JUST GETTING INTO IT.

FOR VEGETARIANS

Vegetarians can make it so long as they eat a *wide variety* of vegetables, fruits, nuts, rice, barley, dried beans (limas, kidneys, lentils, soybeans, peas. . .) and other non-animal foods.

Some experts suggest that vegetarians take multiple vitamin pills daily. For example, vegetarians who won't touch eggs or milk products don't get vitamin B-12. Nor do they get certain types of protein.

AND NATURAL FOOD TYPES

It's fine to eat "natural" or "organic" products – if that's what they really are. You may be paying a lot of money for a label that means nothing.

For example, rose hip vitamin C is mostly man-made vitamin C added to a rose hip base. Did you know that many "natural" breakfast cereals are one-fifth sugar or more?

Also: Even if the food you get really is grown with manure instead of artificial fertilizer or even if it has no additives -- can you afford it?

HELP YOURSELF

YOU NEVER HEARD OF LIFTING YOURSELF UP BY YOUR OWN BOOTSTRAPS?

REMEMBER: MAN DOESN'T LIVE BY BREAD ALONE

NOR BY ENTERTAINMENT EITHER

If you are poor, and even if you aren't, find out whether there is a grocery-buying cooperative in your community.

If you are pregnant, it is very important that you find out about a pre-natal diet. Check with your doctor, Planned Parenthood, your local free clinic, your local women's co-op.

If you have been unable to control your eating -- even with the help of a good doctor and even after trying to follow the advice in this book -- call your local hotline or free clinic and see whether they can refer you to group therapy for overeaters.

Check into TOPS (Taking Off Pounds Sensibly), Diet Workshop, and Weight Watchers.

WARNING: Stay away from the "fat" doctors who are more interested in your money than in your health.

Fat Lib

Our society puts a lot of stress on looking slim, trim and sleek. Don't go by the latest style -- go by what's good for you.

Anyway, not all fat people overeat (a few people are fat because of physical disorders). And whether or not they eat too much, fat people have rights -- including the right to genuine respect.

A GALLERY OF CALORIES

MILK 8 OZ. 160 CALORIES

POTATO CHIPS 10 115 CALORIES

SODA POP 8 OZ. 95 CAL.

CHOCOLATE 1 OZ. 150 CALORIES

FRENCH FRIES 10 125 CALORIES

DOUGHNUT 1 125 CAL.

ICE CREAM 8 OZ. ~ 1 CUP 295 CAL.

ICE MILK 1 CUP 285 CAL.

HOT DOG 1 155 CALORIES

APPLE 1 70 CALORIES

CELERY 1 STALK 5 CALORIES

CHOCOLATE CAKE 1 PIECE (WITH ICING) 445 CALORIES

HAMBURGER 3 OZ. 245 CALORIES

COOKIE 1 120 CAL.

CARROT 1 20 CALORIES

TOMATO SOUP 1 CUP 75 CALORIES

ORANGE 1 60 CALORIES

"I DON'T KNOW MUCH ABOUT IT, BUT I KNOW WHAT I LIKE"

Here's a line to watch out for: "*Real* smokers inhale."
Who needs to be a real smoker?
It's better to be a real person.

FOR PEOPLE WHO'D LIKE TO KNOW

HOW THE COMIC BOOKS WERE BORN

by Roger Conant

Sol Gordon had come to the conclusion that there are only a few things about sex that are really urgent for young people to know. He had in mind a leaflet with "attractive graphics." I said OK, I'd work on it. But when it came down to doing it, I just couldn't stand the idea of graphics. It seemed to me an uninteresting, boring project and, to tell the truth, I really didn't know how to go about it.

But I did know how to draw cartoons, although I wasn't a professional cartoonist. So I played with doodling the drawings and I came up with some dumb jokes.

When Dr. Gordon saw what I had done he didn't say, "That's *not* what I wanted." He said, "Far out." And he went bananas putting in more ideas, improving his wording, and promoting a wild new thing: a sex education comic book. He also pushed me and tortured me until I had wrapped up every detail and the result was: "Ten Heavy Facts About Sex."

I knew nothing about commercial illustration, or lettering, or paste-up, or any of the other stuff that I needed to know. But I could draw a cartoon and I did have an artistic sort of eye (even though some people don't think so). I learned the mechanics (and a lot of other useful things) *in the process* of getting the booklet ready for printing. *In the process* of undertaking a new venture, I learned a whole new set of skills.

TEN HEAVY FACTS AT THE N.Y. STATE FAIR

In 1971 we were stopped from distributing our comic book at the N.Y. State Fair; in 1972 and 1973, they wouldn't even let us in. In 1974, the state's highest court ordered fair officials to let us sell the comic book.

Following are a few clips from local newspapers. Can you believe all the fuss?

Bishop protests sex comic

"*The comic book itself is in very bad taste. It encourages unnatural acts and arouses in them (young children) a curiosity that is bad for them morally and which offends the community.*" — The Most Rev. David F. Cunningham.

Professor Sol Gordon
Syracuse University

For your Eternal Salvation do not distribute those sex books at the State Fair.

God has created every one of our souls to the Image and Likeness of God, Himself. If through your writings you cause any souls to sin and offend God, God will hold you responsible, and, "What does it profit a man if he gains the whole world but loses his soul." This would mean burning in Hell for all Eternity. God wants you and everyone else in Heaven with Him.

Teach your readers to follow God's Ten Commandments, especially the Sixth, which forbids all impurity, such as fornication adultery, premarital sex, sexual abuse etc. You will never stamp out gonorrhea, syphilis, and other venereal diseases, unless people live according to God's moral laws. These diseases come from sexual abuse.

God bless you and enlighten you to use the talents He has given you in the right way.

Cites Parental Right In Sexual Morality

Youngsters Sharp

To the Editor:
I consider it unwise to stop Dr. Gordon from distributing his sex comic books, relics from the days of "relevance" and the "Greening of America," at the Fair. This would only confirm his chosen role as an infallible prophet and martyr and reinforce his apparent theory that anyone who disagrees with him is either ignorant, bigoted, benighted, anti-semitic or, worst of all, a conservative.

I agree with his detractors, in that slogans, half-truths, and facile banalities might affect the young mind, but most of our young people are much sharper than we think. They will take Dr. Gordon's "heavy" facts for what they are worth.

Post Scripts: Sex 'facts

By MARIO ROSSI

A court ruling notwithstanding, the battle continues to rage over Dr. Sol Gordon's sleazy comic book, "Ten Heavy Facts about Sex."

Will Boycott Fair

To the Editor:
We want to go down on record as one Catholic family (fairly large) that fully intends to boycott the State Fair in protest of the distribution of the comic (?) book, "Ten Heavy Facts About Sex."

Change Moral Climate?

Youngster Asks

To the Editor:
Regarding the letter in Thursday's paper (Aug.8) from the regional director of Catholics United for the Faith, Mr. Charles R. Pulvek:

Mr. Pulvek criticizes the State Court of Appeals for refusing to ban Dr. Sol Gordon's "horrid little comic book, 'Ten Neavy Facts About Sex" from distribution at the New York State Fair, and makes an appeal to parents and citizens to create pressure against it. Mr. Pulvek argues that parents should have the right to educate their children "in the sensitive area" of sex and claims this right will be invaded by making Dr. Gordon's booklet available at the State Fair. He also claims that Dr. Gordon is crusading to "to brainwash our children" and that the State should exercise its power "to protect the morals of its citizens" by acting against him.

I would ask Mr. Pulvek — what is your objective? To stop "outsiders" (teachers, physicians and professional educators) from teaching young people about sex? To stop all talk about sex? To stop all sex completely?

At the beginning of your letter you state that Dr. Gordon's comic book is not technically obscene. But then you go on to call it "trash" and "filthy literature." Why is it filthy, Mr. Pulvek? Because it's in comic book form? Because it is written by Dr. Gordon and not the reader's parent? Or is it filthy

Would Not Boycott Entire State Fair

To the Editor:
A previous letter states a family is boycotting the State Fair due to distribution of "Ten Heavy Facts About Sex." Instead, we suggest finding out the location of the booth from the Fair office and simply avoiding this building or immediate area.

Since the university includes the comic in their packet for incoming freshmen and some case workers give it to children in foster care, chances

'Is Sex Filthy?'

because it is about sex? Is sex filthy, Mr. Pulvek?

I ask — how can a pamphlet at the State Fair invade a parent's right to teach his or her child about sex? If you wish to teach your child you may do so. Does the pamphlet prevent you? But what about those children whose parents are either too embarrassed ot too ignorant to give them the whole story? Ignorance is a dangerous thing in "this pleasure-minded hedonistic age" as you put it.

You imply that Dr. Gordon is teaching values — values different from your own and therefore wrong. On this point I cannot argue. You have the right to your own values. But, you claim that Dr. Gordon is "brainwashing" or forcing his values on "our youth". Here, I disagree. Right to Life also has a booth at the fair and no one is protesting because they are "brainwashing". But you seek to ban Sol Gordon from the fair and eliminate the right of free choice. With this you would be the one brainwashing or forcing your values on others.

Wake up and look around you, Mr. Pulvek. In these days of Watergate, "a lack of morality" means something very different and much more serious.

Are the Catholics United for the Faith planning to have a booth at the fair? If so, I doubt that Dr. Gordon is working against it.

are the kids will be exposed to it. Our copy was brought home by a foster daughter who obtained it at Hutching's Adolescent Program (710).

We feel the best method is to teach our children the facts ahead of time, i.e. advocation of abortion up to five months in the comic can easily be refuted by the findings of New York Medical Association, recent law signed by Gov. Wilson, or by viewing slides at Right to Life Booth, also at the Fair.

It's pathetic that something as beautiful as sex has to erroneously be presented as a form of cheap recreation to deprive them of the many fine displays at the Fair.

SYRACUSE, N.Y., FRIDAY, JUNE 8, 1973

Fair Booth Denial Upheld

ALBANY (AP) — The Appellate Division of State Supreme Court ruled Thursday that the state was justified in trying to limit the distribution of a sex-oriented comic book at the State Fair.

In a 3-2 decision, the court ruled that State Agriculture Commissioner Frank Walkley was justified in refusing to give space at the fair to a birth-control group unless the group agreed not to distribute the comic book to minors without their parents' permission.

In an opinion by Associate Justice Robert G. Main, the court said, "We are reluctant to characterize or even describe" the comic book, which bore the title "Ten Heavy Facts about Sex."

The birth-control group, the Family Planning and Population Information Center, had distributed the comic book from its rent-free booth at the 1971 fair even when asked to stop doing so, the court said.

It was denied rent-free space at the 1972 fair and was not allowed to rent space unless it agreed to conditions on the distribution of the book.

False and Crude

To the Editor:

I would like to comment on Peter Arneson's letter of Aug. 19. Like Peter, I too take exception to the description of Dr. Gordon's Ten Facts as "filthy." It is deliberately false and unbelievably crude — but not necessarily filthy.

I infer from your letter, Peter, that had Mr. Pulver, as the regional director of Catholics United for the Faith, advised people to brush after every meal, you would have objected to a pressure group forcing its values upon you. I agree with you. This is why I resented Dr. Gordon urging girls to join NOW, on the last page of his Ten Facts. And his recommendation of Planned Parenthood literature for further reading.

At sixteen, you are old enough to apply for a driver's license. You are expected and required to exercise control over yourself and your car. By virtually ignoring self-control in his booklet, Dr. Gordon denies its effectiveness and your ability to use it.

If Dr. Gordon and his followers insist upon promoting "Heavy Facts about Sex," then their adversaries must be doing all they can to offset the effects of this pamphlet which, at best, is a dangerous oversimplification and at worst, a destructive force.

Who was it said, "We've just begun to fight"?

SYRACUSE POST-STANDARD, August 28, 1974

Sellers of Sex Book Receive 1 Complaint

Protests 'Sex Facts' at Fair

To the Editor:

An open letter to Mr. Norman Rothschild, New York State Fair Director:

This is to protest the distribution at this year's Fair, of "Ten Heavy Facts About Sex," written by Dr. Sol Gordon, published by Ed-U-Press, the publishing arm of the Institute for Family Research and Education, College for Human Development, Syracuse University. Since it is not judged obscene, this book, which retails for 30 cents a copy, will be offered free to all teen-agers and their parents.

In the preface, the author states that the book contains ideas and ideas are more important than facts. In spite of this, he proceeds to list 10 facts, the first four of which are assurances that certain information available in the medical columns of daily papers, and the fourth states that pornography is harmless. Fact number nine gives practical information about birth control and ten informs that most practical people believe abortion to be moral and having a medical abortion before the 20th week is safer than giving birth.

Although Dr. Gordon mentions self-control as a means of dealing with problems of sexuality, he has also stated publicly, that it is not a realistic solution.

If you believe Dr. Gordon, he is a humanitarian seeking to stamp out VD and unwanted pregnancy by removing ignorance. He categorizes his opposition as "isolated and unimaginative adults." I resent his pontifical stance; I challenge him to prove his "facts," and I wonder who is paying for the free pamphlets to be given out at the Fair. I will further register my opposition by avoiding the building in which his propaganda is dispensed.

Going to Fair

To the Editor:

To Mr. and Mrs. John P. Barrett and family (Aug. 21):

This is a free world and being a Catholic family does not mean you can rule the world. If you don't want to go to the State Fair, that is your business. Stay away.

There are many people who will enjoy it the same as I have for years. I personally will enjoy the booth that distributes Ten Heavy Facts about Sex. (I believe you already have.) I am also a Catholic.

Opposes Sex Book

To the Editor:

At the 1972 New York State Fair a "comic book" entitled "Ten Heavy Facts About Sex" was distributed free to teenagers from a booth operated by Family Research and Education.

Now when this year's State Fair is about to open (Aug. 27) Dr. Sol Gordon's book will once again be available. I hope all concerned mothers will take the necessary steps to see that this degrading material is not made available to their children.

Will be at State Fair
'Ten Heavy Facts About Sex'

Sex Is Not 'Filthy, It's a Gift from God

ROME DAILY SENTINEL, ROME, N.Y., THURSDAY EVENING, JULY 11, 1974

Ruling overturned on sex comic book

ALBANY, N.Y. (AP) — The state Court of Appeals has overturned a ban on the distribution of a sex-oriented comic book at the State Fair, over the dissent of a judge who said it condoned homosexuality and perversion.

The court, the state's highest, ruled 6-1 Wednesday that Agriculture and Markets Commissioner Frank Walkley acted arbitrarily in banning the book, entitled "Zing Comix—Ten Heavy Facts About Sex," at the 1972 fair.

Judge Dominick Gabrielli dissented, arguing that "this so-called comic book" encouraged youngsters "to engage in homosexual experiences, to discard any thoughts to the evils of pornography and that finally there is nothing really wrong with oral or anal sex."

Gabrielli said that children are sent to the fair "obviously with the understanding on the part of their parents that their children will engage in healthy and wholesome activities, and certainly not be exposed to some of the activities encouraged and espoused by this so-called comic book."

FOR PEOPLE
WHO WANT TO PLAY
A SNEAKY TRICK

Here's a test you can try whether you are pro-astrology, against it, or neutral. Select, at random, an astrology book that provides fairly detailed passages interpreting various zodiacal signs. Find someone who knows little about astrology but is curious about it and ask for his or her sign (as indicated by date of birth). Then tell your friend you are reading the interpretation for her/his sign—but actually read out the interpretation for a different sign, substituting words here and there as may be necessary to avoid giving away the game. (Tell her/him of your subterfuge afterwards.) During the reading, note her/his reactions. Do many suggestions strike a sympathetic or responsive chord? Does s/he seem at least partly convinced? Ask her/him immediately afterward, "Would you say that this was pretty close to the mark?"

What conclusions do you draw from the experiment?

FOR PEOPLE
WHO ARE ALLERGIC
TO IDEAS:

FOR PEOPLE WHO THINK THEY CAN'T WRITE A POEM

Think of words . . . any words . . . that you like or that you find interesting. If you can't think of any, look in a book or magazine and pick out words that strike your fancy or that you like the sound of.

When you have written down 10 or 20, shuffle them around in any order you like and divide them up into several groups. Play around with the words in each of these groups until you get an image, a sound or an idea that interests or pleases you. Feel free to take out any words you don't want and to fit in new words (including words like "the," "that," "but," "and," "then" and so on.)

Once you've gone that far, it's not too hard to arrange these different groups of words to make up the verses of a non-rhyming, free-style poem.

When you finish, turn the page to learn something you will be very interested to know. (Don't look ahead before you finish your poem, or you may spoil the experience.)

A Poem*

_____
_____
_____
_____
_____
_____
_____
_____
_____
_____
_____
_____

*an original by_____.

SO, YOU WROTE THE POEM...

Congratulations! You have revealed something very important about yourself to yourself. Try to figure it out.

Are you confused? Don't be. Enjoy your new creation instead.

WORDS FOR SURVIVAL

I

Why travel heavy
When you can
  travel
    light

II

Anything
        you can do
once
        you can do
twice
       once over
lightly

III

  is there
    an inner self
no
    one else
is there
    an inner self
no
    one else
is there
    an inner self
no one
    one self
no
    one

IV

love is
  not
  always
  always
  always

V

How much
is
too much?

Once
is
too much

If
you don't
enjoy it

VI

who speaks
for
Gertrude
  Stein
does

VII

I feel younger
  as I get
    older
I get younger
  as I feel

VIII

cheap
is
expensive

IX

write poems
when you
are sad or happy
inbetween poems
stink

Which of the two "I am I" poems strikes your fancy?
This translation from the original German version:

> I am I and you are you
> Who can know another's inner turmoil and inner peace
> Each of us must travel alone
> Learn it early and remember it well
> Nothing remains shared forever
> Love is the urgent rushing from blood to blood
> Soon even the hottest embers die down
> And your demise is lonely
> Search for no home, build no nest
> Aim to serve no wanderer
> Preserve and hold on firmly to your heart's wretched rest
> Desire has sightless eyes
> This is knowledge and deepest repose
> I am I and you are you

or Fritz Perls'

> I do my thing and you do your thing.
> I am not in this world to live up to your expectations
> And you are not in this world to live up to mine.
> You are you and I am I
> And if by chance we find each other it's beautiful.
> And if not it can't be helped.

RANDOM THOUGHTS ON ROSH HASHANA* 5735

We all have some areas of vulnerability. Not everything in life can be understood or resolved.

I feel that just about everything really worthwhile in life involves some risk and some sacrifice of time, energy and patience.

I suspect that really meaningful experiences are of brief duration (albeit repeatable) and rarely occur on schedule.

Even tragic events offer us opportunities for review and renewal.

Some people are strange. If they don't understand something they haven't heard about it, they think it either doesn't exist or it isn't worthwhile.

If God wants to test you, what will you do?

*The Jewish New Year

Where Have All the Heroes Gone?

Since there are no more heroes, you have to be your own.

No, you don't agree? You can think of some heroes?

List some people you admire who struggled against overwhelming odds for a worthy cause:

1. _____
2. _____
3. _____
4. _____
5. _____
6. _____

or more

Perhaps you know some antiheroes (or as we say in Yiddish "Schlemiels"*):

1. _____
2. _____
3. _____
4. _____
5. _____
6. _____

or more

*It goes without saying—A schlemiel is the kind of person who falls on his back and breaks his nose.

THIS PART IS FOR MY 17-YEAR-OLD SON

This is a portrait by Howard Siskowitz of my son, Josh, who is still looking for himself and therefore has not found me. He will find his way. He is pretty cool.

On the next pages are a "conversation" he had with his friend, Howard, and an invitation to you to write your own. Then follows

(1) Four love poems of mine

(2) A drawing given to my son by Howard Siskowitz entitled: Standing On the Verge of Getting It On

(3) Some underwater photographs by Josh Gordon, whose current search for himself is at sea.

CONVERSATION FOR ALL TIME

Tell it like it was	up town
man, like it was	I hear you man
what it is, what it is	I hear you
heavy duty	Together
heavy	right on
laid back; down	man this is
fly man	beat
what it is	really
what it is	

WRITE YOUR OWN TIMELY CONVERSATION

i

COUNTER HEROES

This is the last year of
my youth
I want to make
a thing of it.

Too bad the world is
black and white
color TV can't help us much

What are you waiting for
Indeed
death is not

I'm not ready
my Lord
ready or not
my Lord
I'm not

I'm looking for
salvation
and when I
find
it
I'll look for countersalvation

I'm looking for
you
my love
and when I
find you
I'll look for
counter you

I'm looking for
a hero
my salvation
my love
and if I find you
I won't see you
for the forest
has become

a tree
and the
tree is not
free
to move about
like an anti hero
sandwich

Amen.

ii

KADDISH

What are you
waiting for

What force
propells you

to destroy your

beautiful body

with my perfect mind

where is your
mind

eating away

all the cream cheese
in the
neighborhood
until one
day
  it was
clear
  after all the anger
and
  despair
    and the cream
cheese
  and the milk and
the beer

and the
shoes and the shirts
and all the money
turned
   to hate
and all the love
   returned with love
and after
   all the sleep
and the TV
   and the lies
and the contempt
   and all
      the four o'clocks in
the morning
   and the heavy drunken
climb
   up our despair
you turned into
a cream cheese
sandwich

delectable and
charming

and you said good
morning and thank you

and we flipped
with joy

and said Kaddish
to our despair

and we asked you to
clean your room
and you did.

iii

TOMORROW

What are you waiting for
my love
is not always kind

30

my mind
travels
in airplanes
searching
for
fame and acclaim
which I'd
gladly exchange
for your
love

iv

UNTITLED

Name: The Heart of the Matter
Place: Can we pass thru?
Intermission
End: Come back when you can linger.

32

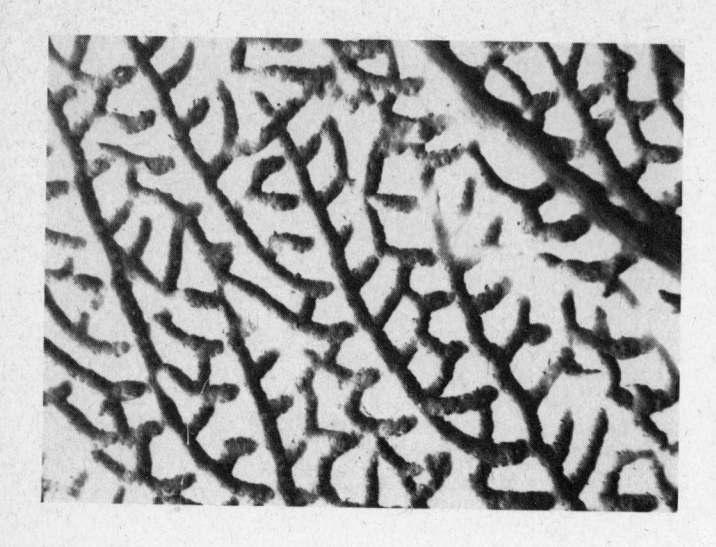

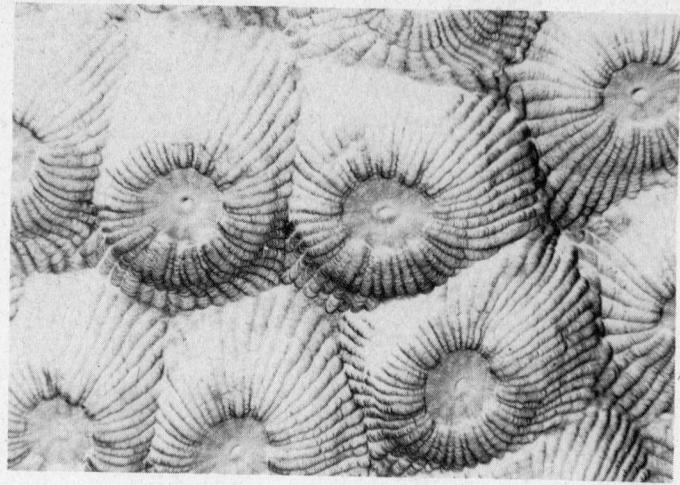

Put your own favorite photos here!

THE PSYCHOLOGY OF A REACTIONARY*

Not many people are
responsive to other people
(most react)
When you
Respond
you care about what
another person thinks
or feels
When you react
you care only about
how you feel or think

Responsive people are a joy
to be with
Reactive people are boring
or hostile

Risk letting people know
who you are
or want to be
by
Responding more and
reacting less

Even though many people do not
care about
who you are
or want to be
but have a tendency to
react more or less
reactionary.

LET IT BEGIN WITH YOU

Being unselfish
    really
      is
rarely possible
without
Getting it together
Selfishly for yourself
Really
really
Often

*This is a non-poem with an incongrous title. It is an homage to responsive people, presented in poetic form as a tribute to my friend Craig Snyder, who started me thinking about my own reactionary tendencies.

POEMS BY PETER GOLLOBIN

LOVE TO MEET A GIRL

Love to meet a girl
about as sweet as summer turning into spring
Walking down the street
like a bird in the wind
Passing the day
flying away
Singing a song, as free as the morning
and lovely

Take her in my arms and pick her up
Swinging her high above the ground
Hugging each other as hard as we can
laughing with me,
laughing as we
fall in the grass, alone at last
kissing

love to meet a girl
that would love to meet a boy,
Someone like me

SOMETIMES I feel like I'm not going to make it

    I'm gonna fall like a house of cards
    come tumble down on top of me

waste away like a dried up leaf

An' there ain't nothin' I can do to stop it!   !

    And you tell me to be cool

I remember my brother
He did me good
He was my brother

And there was mom
She did me good
She was my mother

And there was always dad
He did me good
He was my father

And through it all
no one knew

POEMS BY JERRY MANNHEIM

    Yesterday I Walked Down
    The Street and Didn't
    Step On An Ant.

Yesterday I walked down the street and there
    Was an alleyway ahead
And a lot 'o noise came outa there
    (and I wondered why)
And suddenly into that plain, unoccupied
    Space, that clear transparent space,
Suddenly a nigger took that space
    (not as much as a "By your leave")
And he was bleeding all over that space,
    Just as if it were his space
And he were yellin just as if he were
    The dispenser of quiet and spent it all
And he were staggerin like he were
    A walkathon
And he were grabbin for me to hold him up
    Just like he were a white man
The three shots finished him off
    But I was late for church

    THE UNIVERSAL CLOWN

On top of the hillock
    This way and that
Stars and comets
    Spitter and spat

On the horizon
    Upside down
Lazily lolls
    The Universal Clown

He winks an uneye
    Shut and open
Watching the cosmos
    Along its lopin

Was there a tick
    Before a tock
Was there time
    Before a clock

Will seconds cease
    When the clock runs down
Don't ask me
    Ask the clown

FOUR AD VICES
(for people I really care about)

1. If you have a really far-out goal or even a near-in one, don't tell anyone. Work for it; don't subject it to prior review or criticism from anyone.
2. Don't think of yourself as lazy (ever). Laziness is a description, not an explanation. It's better to think of yourself as unmotivated (for the moment).
3. Repeat to yourself over and over again: Cheap is expensive; until it is clear to you that anything worthwhile (in life) is expensive.
4. If you find yourself negative and angry most of the time, it's because you feel that way about yourself. Try being nice to people. It will rub off on you (after a while).

Write your own Ad Vices for someone you care about.

WISH YOU COULD BUT KNOW YOU WON'T

I wish I could knock the shit out of people who are
    rude, like those who talk at movies or won't stop even when you ask them to
    crude, like those who throw litter around and mess up beautiful parks
or   lewd, like those who talk only in dirty jokes.

I wish I could knock the shit out of people who are
    cruel and hateful and especially those who
    mug and steal and murder because they can't get what they want.

I wish I could
    to all the mean people in the world
    but I'm afraid to try it because of what *they*
    might do to me.

☞ TURN IMMEDIATELY TO THE NEXT PAGE ☜

Make up your own wish-you-could list (no holes bared)

_____

_____

_____

_____

_____

_____

_____

_____

☆ ☆ ☆ ☆ **ELEVEN LAST MINUTE SURVIVAL* IDEAS** ☆ ☆ ☆ ☆

1 Risk intimacy by telling people about yourself. You thus become vulnerable to being abused and rejected, embraced and accepted.

2 If you can't be anything you want to be, at least don't be anything you don't want to be.

3 If you have a tendency to be self-deprecating, don't tell anyone. It's really boring to be with anyone who is down on him/herself.

4 If you have advice to give, don't expect anyone to follow it easily (or at all). When was the last time someone told you "not to worry" and you stopped worrying?

5 If you do something wrong, you should feel guilty. Mature guilt is organizing, but not long-lasting. You will either make amends or you won't do it again.

6 If you feel guilty about something that doesn't make sense—like having "evil" thoughts — your guilt will disorganize you and be the energy for repeating the unacceptable thoughts (obsessions) or behavior (compulsions) over and over again.

7 If your love for another person is mature, this love will energize you and contribute to your feeling optimistic about yourself. If your love is immature it will exhaust you, generate feelings of depression, anger and jealousy.

*We mean survival—not salvation.

8 If you want to change a *behavior* of yours (for example, talking too much or not enough) your initial efforts to change must be forced or mechanical. This is because you are trying to counteract unacceptable behavior which has become a habit—in a sense a spontaneous, "natural" response to tension. Upon forcing an alternate response (e.g. not talking so much) you will be "rewarded" by enormous rushes of anxiety. If you are able to tolerate the "mechanical" changes and the related tension, you will be able to change to a more acceptable "habit." (Number eight is heavy; read it over several times.)

9 If you notice that you are intolerant of someone else's behavior—like a person who is boasting a lot—and that person is not hurting you, it means that you are reacting to something about yourself that you don't like.

10 The process of not doing what you are supposed to do is much more tiring than doing and getting the most boring tasks over with. The ultimate creative busyness is when you have time for almost everything you want to do.

11 The criticism of someone you don't respect should have no impact on you. Life is too precious for you to be offended by or react to anybody's ridicule. Remember too, not everything you say or they say—or happens—is important. Select, don't settle.

WHAT ARE YOU WAITING FOR?

ENJOY
PROTECT *YOUR-*
KNOW *SELF*
DISCOVER
BE

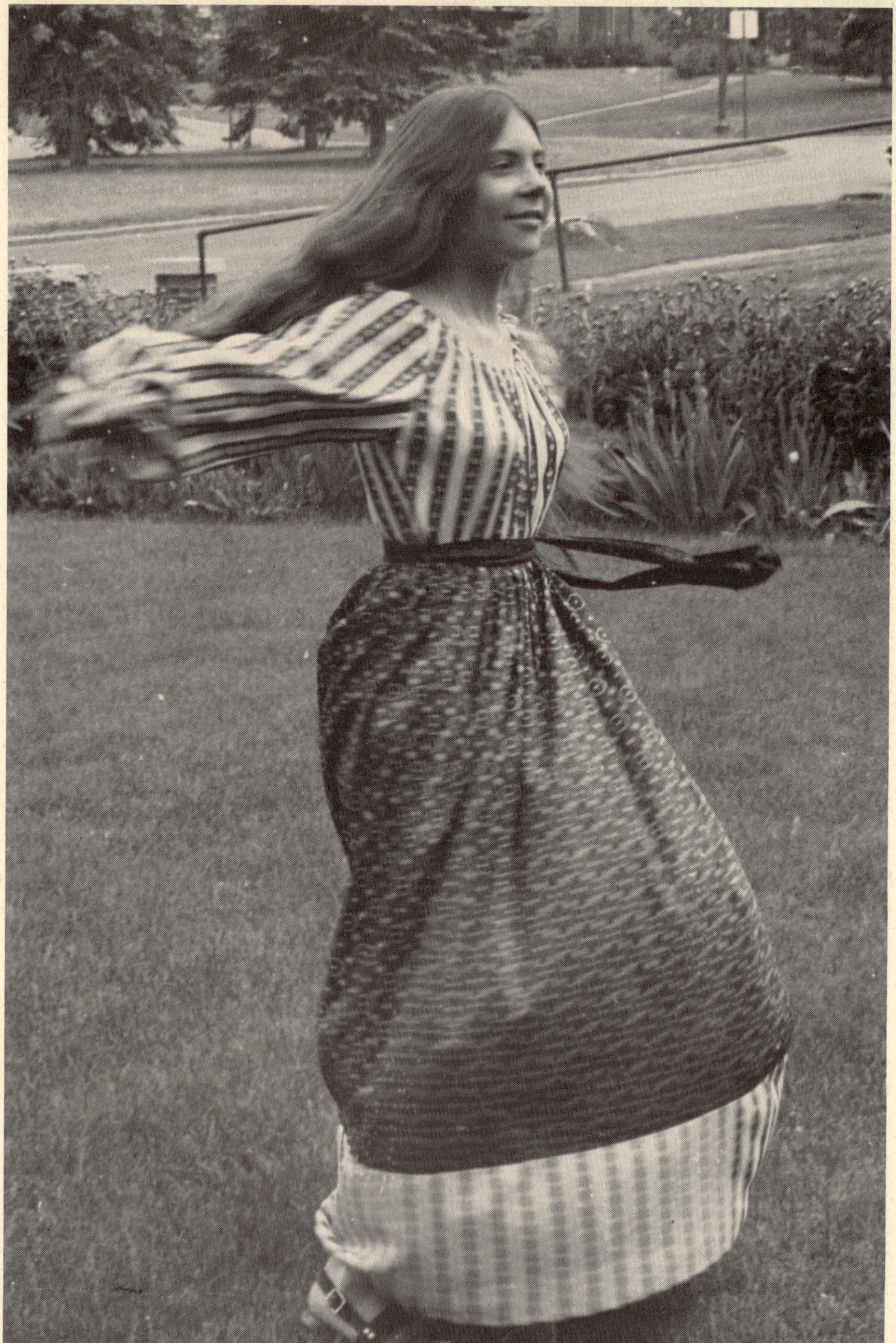

new experiences

Sometimes I think our world is full of "experts" who claim to have solutions for everybody else's problems. With all the people offering us happiness by reading certain books, eating certain foods, believing certain prophets, or watching certain stars, it's little wonder that life remains full of uncertainties. Often I wonder if human beings aren't so mixed up that they must put a lot of energy into getting themselves together. The less together they are the more of their time is spent unproductively being angry. They are too angry for love or new experiences.

Life is funny sometimes. If you want something done, you ask a busy person to do it. If you need support, don't ask for it from people who can't support themselves.

People who hate themselves hate a lot of people in the process. It took me a long time to discover this. I remember a day of terrific insight—sitting around a pool rapping with a friend. What a time we had. We spent four hours talking about all the people we hated until it dawned on us: All the people we hated were having a good time swimming and loving while we were talking about them. What a waste of time!

Psychology opens up the world—our dreams, our fantasies, our wishes, and our experiences help us in the never-ending process of defining ourselves. If our definition excludes fantasies or the awareness of the infinite number of possible events and opportunities, our life is boring and tiring. If our life is dominated by self-doubts, fears or compulsions, we become too busy protecting, hiding or kidding ourselves, to do our own thing. The

If you are not controversial, you have nothing to offer.

> **If you don't do things when you can't afford them, you don't do them when you can.**

things we do tend to be self-destructive or exploitative. And if people also have to worry about being poor or being victims of discrimination, it really is rough.

Life is complicated. Life is not a meaning but an opportunity (at least it should be) to make life into meaningful experiences. But getting your life together does not mean that you can't enjoy contradictions, or unrelated and isolated experiences. Sometimes I meet someone for a brief moment and it's love at first sight, knowing full well I'll never see that person again. Sometimes I think about being a poet—and even write a lot of poems, knowing that I may not be a poet. I sense that poets write poetry and are serious and I write poetry and I am not sure I'm serious.

I don't know much about photography, but the idea fascinated me and I set out to express the fascination by taking fascinating pictures. The result: a new experience. Now I take photographs for pleasure. But does it mean that I am not a photographer because no one will buy my pictures or will give me a diploma?

I never thought I could write. But after a "civil rights" Mississippi interlude some years ago I wrote about it. Here is an excerpt:

> I have been around enough psychologists to know that most of us have three main (secret) ambitions in life. The first is to write a novel; the second is to be a hero; and the third is to be able to exchange, at will, one set of neurotic symptoms for another. Any psychologist who would like to enjoy an instantaneous illusion of realizing all three ambitions should spend a civil rights summer in Mississippi.
>
> Upon arrival in Jackson, you feel like a hero (albeit in search of an heroic situation) and on your way to the Delta, your mind is pregnant with your novel. (I remember the first sentences of my "autobiographical" novel. I thought about writing something that psychologists would enjoy, something that would lend itself to "interpretation" and would readily be misunderstood.) Within twenty-four hours (unfortunately and whether you like it or not), whatever symptoms you start out with are traded in for paranoia.

I got a lot of praise for the thing I wrote. I'm not sure why—but suddenly I write. Maybe I am not a writer, but who cares?

I remember surviving my high school days by daydreaming a lot. It was the only relief I had from hating everything. (I was really messed up when I was a kid.) But, you know, I feel younger now than I did in those days. I do a lot of things and I am very seldom tired—it's weird in a way. In those days I hated:

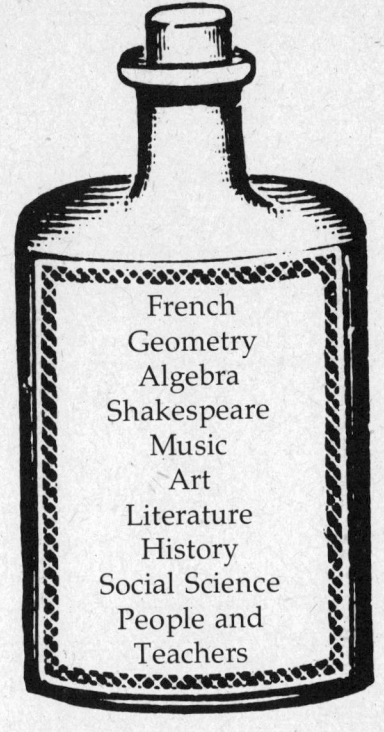

> French
> Geometry
> Algebra
> Shakespeare
> Music
> Art
> Literature
> History
> Social Science
> People and Teachers

I daydreamed and read a lot of books that had sad endings.

Later, much later, when I was in France, I was angry that I didn't know French. Later, even later than I care to admit, I was tricked into seeing a Shakespearean play and I loved it. A new experience!

Now, whenever I can, I trick people into having new experiences. When I was teaching high school I assigned new experiences. Get a load of this assignment:

- **You are required, in order to pass this course, to have several new experiences (sheer blackmail).**

- **Write a brief psychological report on three new experiences. Choose from the following list.**

1. Read (not just look at) *Playboy* or *Viva*
2. If you are a conservative, read from cover to cover *The New Republic*.
3. If you are a liberal, read from cover to cover the *National Review*.
4. If the only time you've ever been to an art museum is when the school dragged you along—visit a large art museum and spend your time trying to figure out why people visit art museums voluntarily. Even go so far as asking a stranger who seems to be enjoying the experience.
5. Go to a ballet.
6. Listen to an entire opera like *Aida*.
7. Get the Sunday *New York Times* and spend four hours finding out why it is America's most prestigious newspaper.

> **8** If your everyday personality is grumpy, spend a whole day being nice to people.
>
> **9** If you have the philosophy that people should love you for what you are and not how you dress or act—try acting and dressing conventionally for a week and note carefully the responses you get from people you assumed shouldn't care.

Got the message?

Whatever you decide to do with your life—decide on the basis of a wide range of alternatives. New experiences help you make your choice. Don't decide in advance about all the things you hate and will always hate.

Look at all the new things you can try if you feel stuck:

1. Keep a diary.
2. Remember dreams.
3. Learn a new word each day.
4. Photograph trees.
5. Write one poem.
6. Write two poems.
7. Fly a kite.
8. Say hello to a person you think you should hate.
9. Decide on a country to visit in Europe. Read all about it first and then figure out how you are going to get there.
10. Read a short book like *Jonathan Livingston Seagull*. Try to figure out why you liked such a corny book.
11. Write me a letter.
12. Write a letter to someone you owe a letter to.
13. Go see a foreign film.
14. See a Chaplin film.
15. Figure out why some people think Andy Warhol is a genius and some people think he is cracked.
16. Imagine yourself in love with someone. Dream or write about it.
17. Read "Public Works."
18. Try transcendental meditation.
19. Practice Yoga.

LIVE A LITTLE

HERE ARE SOME THINGS I LOVE IN LIFE:*

The Declaration of Independence
Marc Chagall
Chocolate cake
Some students
The Sunday *New York Times*
Money that's for spending, and not saving in the bank for my old age or my wife's old age or my son to inherit
My wife (who is Danish)
T.S. Eliot
Leonard Cohen
The New York City Ballet
Mozart
Elie Wiesel
What used to be the Beatles (but since they broke up and began to act like *people*, I have second thoughts. So I really should have written the old Beatle records)
Syracuse (the University, not the climate)
San Francisco, but Jerusalem even more
Israel in general
London in particular
A bunch of people who remain unnamed
Getting high
Chicago when the wind doesn't blow

*And see how I've revised my list by the time I reached the end of the book.

Remember when the air was clean and sex was dirty?

People often ask me at parties if I read minds. I always answer, "Yes. I don't."

**MAKE UP YOUR LIST
OF SOME THINGS
YOU LOVE IN LIFE.**

"There is absolutely no inevitability as long as there is a willingness to contemplate what is happening."
— Marshall McLuhan

WHEN YOU ARE BORED, YOU ARE BORING TO BE WITH

Everyone is bored, upset or depressed now and then. That's of no particular significance. It's only when boredom or depression becomes a style of life that you have to get off your dead end.

There is nothing more uninteresting than a bunch of people standing around talking about how bored they are—which often ends up with them agreeing to go out and pick up somebody. Maybe one day you'll get the chance to see the film "Marty," which immortalized what a drag the pick-up trip really is.

☞ Here is a list of the most boring things you can do: ☞

1. Run yourself down. Tell yourself and others how worthless and rotten you are.
2. Similarly, when people ask you how you feel, tell them the details of your rottenness.
3. Tell people you're horny.
4. Boast about things that everybody knows you haven't done.
5. Watch more than an hour and a half of TV a day. Have you noticed: the more you watch, the more bored you get?
6. Masturbate not because you enjoy it, but because you have nothing else to do. Have you discovered that if you feel guilty, you hardly enjoy it at all?
7. Talk about only one subject (sports, girls, boys, etc.). It's OK to have one main interest, but if that's all you talk about, people won't listen.

8. Come across as pollyannish (oh, everything is wonderful!); or cynical and sarcastic.
9. Relentlessly tell people you're tired.
10. Talk too much. It's not as boring to talk too little—as long as you participate by listening.
11. Complain a lot (ugh!).
12. Be paranoid and suspicious of everyone's motives. You're always thinking: "What do you want to know for, anyway?"
13. Relate to people without ever risking being intimate (which also means risking rejection).
14. Be super-dependent on what other people think of you. They get the message that they can't talk frankly with you.
15. Begin your approach to people by saying, "I don't want to trouble you—bore you—take up too much of your time . . ." It's fake humility.
16. Not be open to new experiences.
17. Be a super-miser. You don't want to do the most interesting things because "you can't afford it." It will be forever before you can afford it.
18. Persistently analyze the motives of everyone's behavior.
19. Be a gossip. (Super boring.)
20. Nearly always wait to be asked; hardly ever ask.
21. Almost always be serious and humorless; or almost never be serious, and kid around all the time.
22. Relieve tension *mainly* with drugs or alcohol.
23. Almost never tolerate being alone at times.
24. Lead an unexamined life.
25. Spoil other people's stories (because you've said, thought, heard it before).
26. Trust no one; or trust everybody.
27. Announce how self-sacrificing you are and
28. What ungrateful slobs the rest are.
29. Complain that there's nothing to do, or talk endlessly of future plans that usually don't pan out . . .

If you're bored
turn to page 144 and look at
a fabulous picture.

Never take to heart the opinions of people you don't respect.

HOW CAN YOU MOVE OUT OF BOREDOM & DEPRESSION?

The process of not doing anything is exhausting. A big disadvantage of being bored is that it's very tiring. It's no accident that when employers really want something done, they ask their busiest employee to do it. The more you are doing, the more alert you are and the more time you have to do all the things that you want to do.

By the way, when you are bored or depressed you need to be especially careful about taunting, tormenting, and hurting younger brothers and sisters. Boredom is often one of the biggest factors in senseless delinquent acts, and other evil.

The best medicine for *just getting out* of boredom or depression is to do or learn new and different things. This will give you a first-class rush which you can then seize on and keep going. You'll become alert, energized, stimulated—and more confident too. Now is the time to do things. It doesn't matter whether it's clean house, get a ball game going, finish a homework assignment, bake a cake, do all the odd jobs you've been putting off, finally start the big project you've been dreaming about doing . . .

JUICE USE

IT'S JUST A CASE OF GRAPE RAPE

HIC

SPECIAL HANGOVER EDITION

UNDER THE INFLUENCE

We are trying to put you under the influence...of your own good sense. That's all.

We are not for or against drinking.

But we *would* rather see people fulfill and enjoy themselves than see them get into some down bag.

Still, if you don't agree with all our opinions, that's cool, too.

IS HE UNDER THE INFLUENCE?

MORE LIKE UNDER THE TABLE

YEH, AND TOMORROW HE'LL BE UNDER THE WEATHER.

Text by Sol Gordon and Roger Conant
Illustrations by Roger Conant
To Mark Matthews
Published by Ed-U Press, 760 Ostrom Ave., Syracuse, N.Y. 13210

Ed-U Press is the publishing arm of Syracuse University's **Institute for Family Research and Education**

Other titles in this series of educational comic books include *Ten Heavy Facts About Sex, What Do You Do When You're All Drug Doubt?, Gut News for Modern Eaters, V.D. Claptrap,* and *Protect Yourself From Becoming An Unwanted Parent*. These booklets and *Juice Use* are available for 30 cents each from Ed-U Press. Bulk rates are available on request.

© 1974 by Ed-U Press

IF YOU ARE BORED, YOU ARE BORING TO BE WITH

LIVE A LITTLE

Almost everything in life is risky.

Since you **must** take risks, why not take risks that might get you something meaningful? Why take risks that can't get you anywhere?

A few risks worth taking:

- Reveal yourself to another person and risk rejection (and acceptance).
- Learn something NEW and risk liking it or not liking it.
- Smile at people and risk their not smiling back.
- Risk excelling at something. (The first step is to get away from the T.V.)
- Are you an ordinary person? Don't settle for "average." Risk being yourself.

LIVE A LOT

HOW MUCH IS TOO MUCH?

EASY, EASY...

LEMME AT HIM... HE'S STICKING HIS TONGUE OUT AT ME.

MOOOooo

Too much is when you've had a few and you show one or more of these signs:

- You feel fantastically confident, but
- You are drinking more and more and faster and faster.
- You can't walk straight, but
- You're sure you can drive.
- You insist you can walk straight, but you can't.
- You're making others very uncomfortable, but
- You insist you can handle more.
- Your normal fears and anxieties become exaggerated.
- You tell the people who are worried about you: "Leave me alone -- I'm all right."
- You are easily offended, especially by people who care about you.
- You are unconcerned about your own safety.
- You really don't give a damn about anyone else (but you're not usually like that).
- You are the most spiteful and hurtful to the people who have loved and cared for you the most.

SEX

Yeh. Gimme a screwdriver

"LIQUOR SURE IS QUICKER"

ZZZZ

"THAT THERE WAS SOME FAST ACTION"

"HE'S FEELING NO PAIN — AND SHE ISN'T FEELING ANYTHING"

The magician -- not his wand -- works the magic.

- The person who needs a drug -- like alcohol -- to get aroused must feel really uptight inside.
- Alcohol may increase the desire, but it decreases the performance (and also the meaning).
- Heavy drug users quickly lose interest in meaningful sex.
- Drinking heavily for many years usually kills a person's sex life. Men can't even get a hard-on.
- A person who spends a lot of time in bars trying to score is a person who just can't handle an intimate relationship.

LOVERS ALERT

Are you in love, or going out, with someone who drinks too much?

If you really care about your lover, you will try to get him or her to slow down and (if that doesn't work) to get help.

But, be careful - go by actions, and not by words.

If you are not succeeding, you'll know by these signs:

- Does your partner often lie to you?
- Does he or she easily get jealous for no good reason?
- Does your lover become impulsively angry and make unreasonable demands?
- Does he or she say "Don't worry" and get angry if you push it?
- Is your partner's first love you -- or alcohol? Test by seeing how much time and energy he or she gives you compared to how much time and energy goes into lies, boasts, drinking, and drinking friends.

IF YOU PLAN TO MARRY

Just be sure you're not about to wreck your own life by marrying someone who is moving toward destruction.

You don't need to marry someone whose own selfish needs always come first (like a baby).

You don't need a partner who finds intimate relationships to be so heavy that she or he avoids responsibility by drinking.

A lot of people think that their love is strong enough to change another person. It doesn't usually work that way. Changes can take place when *two* people love each other.

If you're really in love, it's energizing; if your love is immature, you're tired a lot.

COMMON SENSE SURVIVAL

Society tries to lay on you what's cool and what isn't. For example, when people come over it's considered cool to whip an alcoholic drink right on them.

Actually (and this goes for adults, too), we are giving our guests the message that without drinks they won't be interesting company. If you want to serve drinks, offer them but don't push them. And have munchies available.

WHAT HAPPENED TO HER?

SHE WAS DYING FOR A DRINK — SO SHE GOT SMASHED.

SHE HAD REAL CLASS... IN FACT, SHE STUDIED CLASSINESS UNDER ONE CAT WHO HAD SO MUCH STYLE THEY HAD TO PUT HIM IN A MUSEUM — THE HIP HALL OF FAKE.

Another screwy idea: "Real men" gulp hard stuff straight. It's sort of like the wham-bam-thank-you-ma'am type of sex. At any rate, how can masculinity possibly depend on whether you drink pink ladies or boiler-makers?

And, of course, if you drink because something or someone is bugging you, you'll still have the problem and you'll be drunk to boot. People who are drinking in response to a problem put things off a lot. After relaxing with a drink, they somehow don't get around to doing the things that really need doing.

HANG-UPS...

Some people enjoy their juice now and then without much trouble. Beautiful.

But other people use booze as their main way of handling head hassles. Maybe they know that booze never solved a problem. Maybe they've just given up. It could be that they aren't really aware of what they are doing.

What a drag...They probably don't know that they might easily get hooked.

A lot of people are hooked — addicted, that is. If an addicted person's body doesn't get alcohol, he gets sick. The sickness can be anything from the jitters to horrible hallucinations (the "D.T.'s").

It's possible that some people are born with a body make-up that leaves them easy targets for addiction. Even so, **chances are high that if you drink heavily for several years, you will wind up addicted.**

People who want to stop a bad habit must have the gumption to put up with the tension that follows.

...THE ALCOHOLIC

"I CAN TAKE IT OR LEAVE IT"

"I'VE SEEN THE 'TAKE' PART, BUT NEVER THE 'LEAVE' PART"

"SHE'S REALLY A GOOD MOTHER WHEN SHE'S NOT DRUNK"

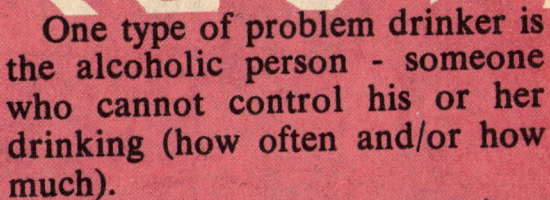

One type of problem drinker is the alcoholic person – someone who cannot control his or her drinking (how often and/or how much).

Out of 96 million American drinkers, 9½ million are alcoholics. That is, *one out of every 10 people who drink at all cannot control his or her drinking.*

One definition of an alcoholic is someone whose drinking frequently interferes with his or her family, social life, or work.

It is hard to tell who will become an alcoholic and who will not. **People who are becoming alcoholics usually don't know it, or won't admit it to themselves.**

Most alcoholics are addicted or soon will be.

Once you've been addicted to alcohol and you stop, it's very hard to start drinking again without losing control again.

Teenagers can be alcoholic.

WHY DO PEOPLE DRINK?

- **Many people are (when you get down to it) shy and tense.** *Some people use juice to help them b.s. more easily at parties or among friends.*

- **Some people drink to impress others.** *When you think on it, what's the real payoff to you?*

- **Some people don't want to drink much, but don't want to be left out.** *Sometimes a person just has to have the guts to risk being left out. Or to change crowds, if necessary.*

- **Some people rely on booze to get others to have sex.** *They are sexually hung-up.*

- **Some people use getting drunk as their main way of feeling free and having fun.** *If that's your bag, you're in trouble. Get help immediately.*

- **Some people drink because they are bored.** *You'll feel much worse afterward. Do something else. Go for a walk, call up a friend, say hello to someone you don't even know.*

- **Some people drink in order to express their hostility.** *If you are not able to tell people how you feel when you're sober, then the next best thing is to work off your frustration by exercise — bowling, jogging, fixing the thing you've been putting off....*

100 VIPERS

PINK NIPPLE

OLD BUZZARD

CRUDDY SNARK

HIGH-LOW

"HI-LO TO YOU TOO"

"YOU CAN GO SOLO"

Alcohol (juice, that is) is a mind drug.

It can relax you and make you feel high.

It can also relax your coordination and your judgment. Your judgment is that inner you that says, "This is important -- this is not," "This is real -- this is fantasy," "This is OK -- this is not."

"AND HE 'ONLY' DRINKS BEER"

"I'M A LITTLE HIGH"

"THEN WHY YOU DOING THE LOW-CRAWL?"

A greatly weakened judgment is why some people who are mentally healthy sometimes act like they're crazy when they have been drinking too much.

It's common for a drunk to feel super-cocky. For people who are usually unsure of themselves this can be a nice feeling -- until they get into something they can't handle.

ALCOHOL IN ACTION

"OK FOLKS— BOTTOMS UP!"

Alcohol is fast-acting stuff.

Once the alcohol is in the blood, it's a matter of moments before it reaches the brain. That's when you start getting high.

Things like bread, milk or a good dinner help you hold your liquor. They slow the alcohol from going into the blood all at once. But nothing will stop you from getting drunk if you have a lot to drink.

People can build up some tolerance to alcohol. It takes more and more for them to feel the high. This can be a danger sign. The body may be building up a physical need for the stuff.

Also, heavy drinkers may after awhile develop a reverse tolerance: One drink sends them into orbit.

THE INSIDE STORY

Q: *What would you have if you gave a drunk black coffee and a cold shower?*
A: *A wide-awake, freezing-cold drunk.*

No matter what you do, you can't speed the body's way of getting sober.

If you weigh 150 pounds, your body needs two hours to use up the alcohol from two 12-ounce bottles of beer. If you drank a half-pint of whiskey, your body would need 10 hours to get rid of the booze.

HQ. GEN. DeCAY

CAN YOU GIVE US THE LATEST BLAST FROM THE BOTTLE-FIELD, SIR

PRESS

WHAT A SET OF JUGS

HERE'S THE INSIDE DOPE: I WENT DOWN IN A VOLLEY OF SHOTS

The liver can only burn up small amounts of alcohol at a time (how much depends on your weight). The rest of the alcohol stays in your blood and goes through your brain until the liver is ready to take a little more.

When even a little bit of alcohol is in the blood (and brain) you are considered intoxicated. This can be anything from a mild high to out-and-out drunkenness.

The faster you drink and the stronger your drinks, the longer it will take the body to sober up.

MIXED UP AND OVERLOADED

Mixing alcohol with other drugs and medicines is risky. You might make the medicine useless. You might end up with a bigger punch than you expected. Many people have died after mixing alcohol and sleeping pills.

People who take ups (like amphetamines) and/or downs (like barbiturates) risk temporary insanity. Suicide is not uncommon.

Enormous amounts of alcohol swallowed quickly can kill you. The brain's breathing center is knocked out and you just stop breathing.

Heavy drinking for even a few years can cause a lot of damage inside -- including to the liver and brain. Brain damage is permanent.

HEY! WHY DON'T YOU TAKE A COFFEE BREAK!?

YOU PLAYED SPIN THE BOTTLE WITH ME... NOW I'M PLAYING SPIN THE BED WITH YOU.

LET'S NOT MESS UP OUR OWN CHILDREN

THAT'S MY DAD. HE'S A BAR-HOPPER

Sheese...

Women who drink heavily during pregnancy run a risk of giving birth to a baby with a defect. Mental retardation is a common result.

It's true that some children are more adequate than their parents. Still, if one or both parents are alcoholic, the children should be extra careful not to use alcohol or other drugs to handle their problems.

Parents who are always super-uptight about other people's drinking may be doing harm when they want to do good. Their kids may turn to hard drinking as a reaction to such rigidity.

THE GREAT AMERICAN NIGHTMARE

Who needs to be another victim?

- One out of three people who drinks at all will get into trouble because of booze.
- One in seven drinkers often gets into serious trouble because of drunkenness.
- Half a million American teenagers have drinking problems.
- If you smoke and drink heavily, your chances of getting cancer are 15 times greater than if you do neither.
- Drunk drivers are involved in about half of all the traffic deaths every year.
- Every summer alcohol use plays a big role in large numbers of drownings and water tragedies.
- Alcohol was tied into two-thirds of the murders committed last year.
- Alcohol abuse often triggers mental breakdowns.
- Alcohol poisoning kills thousands every year.

LET'S HAVE ONE FOR THE ROAD!

NO THANKS. I'M NOT THIRSTY.

THAT DOESN'T EVEN MAKE SENSE. OF COURSE, A DEAD DRUNK MAKES NO SENSE EITHER.

BEER, WINE

Most *beers* and *ales* contain 4 1/2 to 6 1/2 per cent alcohol.

Most *wines* contain 12 to 14 per cent alcohol. Fortified wines, such as sherry or port, have brandy or straight alcohol mixed in. Fortified wines hold 18 to 21 per cent alcohol. "Pop wines" may taste like soda but they pack the same punch as fortified wine.

OR LIQUOR?

Distilled spirits (also called "hard liquor") include whiskey, gin, vodka, rum, brandy, and many others. The alcohol content is high -- from 35 to 50 per cent. *Proof* is roughly double the alcohol content. Thus, 80 proof whiskey contains about 40 per cent alcohol. Sometimes the moonshine made in the stills in the hills is as much as 80 per cent alcohol (160 proof).

15 SIGNS THAT YOU NEED HELP, QUICK!

1. Reading this booklet makes you really uptight.
2. You're drinking more, because you "really enjoy it." Actually, there is something eating you which you feel powerless against.
3. You get drunk almost every weekend.
4. You need "one or two" nearly every day.
5. You keep "going on the wagon."
6. You think about booze a lot.
7. You arrive at parties and social affairs already well oiled.
8. You begin to lose friends quickly even if you make them easily.
9. You have blackouts. That is, the next day you can't remember what happened while you were drinking.
10. You drink to get rid of a hangover.
11. Once you take a drink you find it hard to refuse another. In fact, you hardly think about it.
12. You make excuses about your drinking.
13. Your family makes excuses about your drinking.
14. You get into trouble because of your drinking.
15. Once you start drinking, you can't stop. You go on long binges which you can't help.

¡15 SEÑALES QUE NECESITAS AYUDA RAPIDAMENTE!

1. Al leer estas lineas te pones muy nervioso.
2. Estas bebiendo más porque "te gusta mucho." Actualmente hay algo que te esta molestando y no puedes luchar en contra de eso.
3. Te emborrachas casi cada fin de semana.
4. Necesitas "uno o dos" tragos casi todos los días.
5. Intenta de controlarte en el licor por un tiempo.
6. Piensas mucho en la bebida.
7. Al llegar a fiestas o alguna reunión social ya estas casi borracho.
8. Encuentras amigos facilmente pero los pierdes rapidamente.
9. Tienes momentos en que te encuentras ausente, por eso al próximo día no te acuerdas que occurrio cuando estabas tomando.
10. Tienes que tomarte un trago para quitarte el malestar.
11. Al tomarte un trago encuentras que es difícil rechazar otro. En realidad casi ni lo piensas.
12. Encuentras excusas para tomar.
13. Tu familia busca excusas de tu manera de tomar.
14. Te enredas en problemas por estar tomando.
15. Al empezar a tomar no te puedes controlar. Tienes que estar tomando por días sin parar.

WHERE TO TRY FOR HELP

It is difficult to break the habit, but it is possible and has been done by many people. If you have the support of even one friend whom you really care about, your chances are good. If there is one person whom you *really* love, your motivation to stop will be stronger.

In many places it is hard for a problem drinker to get good medical and psychological care. Good places to check (see your phone book) are:

-- Your local medical association.
-- Alcoholics Anonymous. They will bend over backwards to provide their own help or get you other expert help. Yet they won't badger you or chase you.
-- A.A. also sponsors groups for members and friends of an alcoholic's family: Alateen and Al-Anon. Check with your local A.A.
-- Free clinic or crisis center.
-- Hotline.
-- Marriage and family counseling service.
-- The Rescue Mission and the Salvation Army.
-- Your local council on alcoholism.
-- Try transcendental meditation.

You may also write the National Clearinghouse on Alcohol Abuse and Alcoholism, P.O. Box 2345, Rockville, Md. 20852.

BULL-EATER'S FAMOUS GIN

so you too can be full of bull

Try...
"The Bull Buster"
5 jiggers of Bull-eater's famous gin
1 glass of milk
3 toad's tails
2 bat's eyelashes
1 bull's eye
3 sheets to the wind

BULL-EATER'S FAMOUS GIN

The way the booze ads, TV and the movies make it out, drinking is a sign of hipness, heroism, sexiness and success. Bull.

While it may seem difficult to get out of a bored state, if you are willing to take a chance and follow the suggestions below, it may not be as hard as you think.

● Try this: Go to the refrigerator or cupboard (many of you do this anyway when you are bored or upset) and eat or drink something with sugar in it.* You'll feel better, but the physical effect will last only about two minutes. Ordinarily, you might want to eat more and more, but you might end up feeling worse than when you started. Here's the gimmick: Once you have taken something sweet, you have two minutes to learn or do something new or different.
● Call up a friend and say: "What's new?" If the answer is "Nothing," hang up and call another friend. But seriously,
● Read an article in a magazine that would give you some new information.
● Prepare a dish you haven't made before and try it out on somebody.
● Buy something you can't quite afford but that you've been wanting for a long time. We are not talking about going on a buying spree, which is useless and will usually result in guilt feelings, or about compulsive buying (which is a neurotic symptom, like compulsive overeating).
● Renew a friendship you've neglected for a long time. Risk its working or not working.
● Go out to an interesting place to eat.
● Let people know you are in a good mood.

The Most Boring Conversation

Any of these responses to the question:
"What would you like to do?"

I don't know.
It doesn't make any difference to me.
What do *you* want to do?
There is nothing *to do*.

If you have nothing to do....
don't do it 👉 here

Don't do it of course, if you are on a sugar-free diet for medical reasons.

51

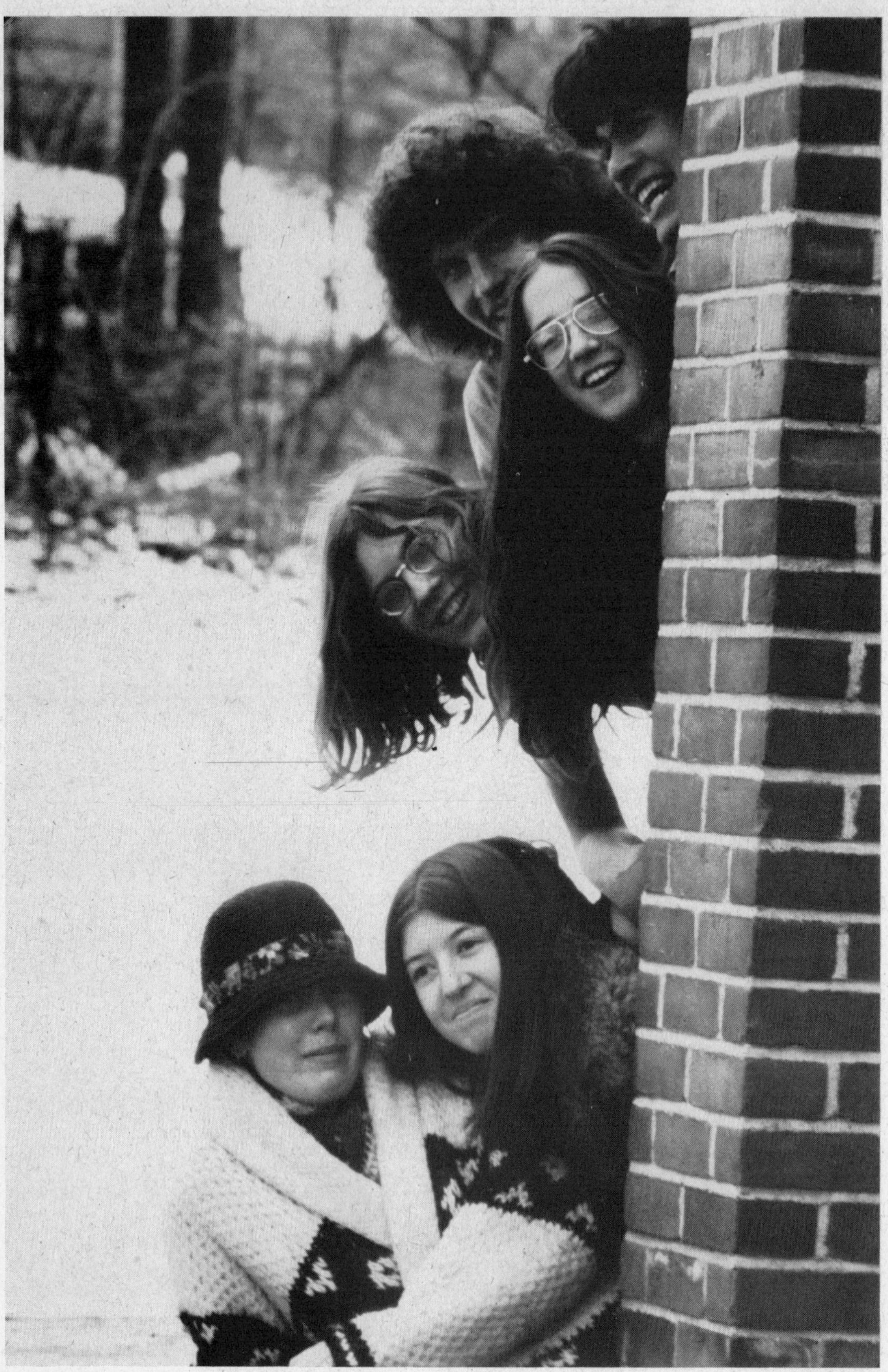

STAYING SANE
✯ DESPITE SCHOOL ✯

NOTE: If you are studious and into school, skip this section. You don't need it.

SURVIVING HIGH SCHOOL

"You could do better if you applied yourself."

Sure, you could do better if you applied yourself. But maybe you *can't* apply yourself. Once, in desperation, I said to my son—an underachieving student—"Why don't you pay attention to your teacher?" He replied, "But, Dad, it's boring to pay attention."

I must confess that I survived my schooling by daydreaming. But my grades were so bad that I couldn't talk my way into a college for quite a while and then not even to one of my choice. If you can't pull off the daydreaming, get involved in something that's exciting and interesting to you. It doesn't matter what—drama, sports, religion. Perhaps the inspiration and the energy you acquire that way will rub off a little and give you enough patience to apply yourself to the routine, boring stuff that most schools call the compulsory curriculum. Just the same, keep in mind that the future can be counted on to provide the penalties for today's self-neglect.

"You'll never get a good job if you don't go to college."

A well-paying job is not the answer to life's challenge. And besides, a college degree doesn't guarantee a good education. It doesn't guarantee anything, really. On the other hand, we must recognize that there are certain jobs in this country that require a college degree. Now is the time to start asking yourself: "What kind of skills do I want to learn? Is college where I need to learn them?" Maybe you should work a few years, then go to college. Maybe not. But whatever the case, don't assume that not going to college is by itself some kind of awful failure. But don't evict yourself either. Most "interesting" jobs require a college degree before you can even apply for them.

"Because of your report card, you're grounded for a week."

Look, the most important thing about grades is what they can get you (and can't get you). It's tough when your parents put the pressure on, but your grades are really your business. As long as you achieve in other areas, have friends, and have lots of different things to do, bad grades don't mean that

---

If you can't risk failure, you won't be successful.

The process of not learning is exhausting.

there is something drastically wrong with you. If you are an all-around underachiever, have no friends, and also have lousy grades, you need to risk making a friend and risk achieving in some area that interests you.

"I just can't understand why you can't learn (English, algebra, science)."

The best way to deal with a subject you are blocked in is to lay off it for awhile and to develop skills in other areas. When people keep harassing you to learn a particular subject or skill, they may be making it harder for you. Try asking them politely to let you work it out yourself. It might not help, but then again it just might. Anyway, it is not the end of the world when you can't learn something.

"When we were kids we took our studies seriously. We knew it was a privilege to go to school."

In classes that are so boring that you can't handle them, sit in the back of the room and do something creative—doodle, write poems, read comic books, anything to get you through periods of meaninglessness. Sometimes (not always) you must put up with regulations and controls you don't like if you are to eventually get what you want.

★

Going to school shouldn't mean "going along with the system." Systems are just not where it's at. Meaning is what is important.

Still, it is certainly true that many faculty members are basically disrespectful of students while insisting that they be bowed down to (no matter what they say). All right, so many adults are immature. Some aren't. Take the good things you are offered and throw out the bad.

If you are to hold on to your self-respect and independence it is essential that you maintain a somewhat skeptical attitude. (But that doesn't mean you have to be a cynic.) Just because some High Muckamuck says something is so doesn't make it so.

Remember this: *Real knowledge is SELF-taught*.

Sure. Some students are narrow-minded; some teachers are unbelievably boring; some parents are hypocritical when it comes to school or college.

What you learn doesn't have to be relevant.

Just the same, don't let bad classroom experiences turn you off from learning anything much. How can you fulfill yourself if you are opposed to expanding your mind (and your skills)?

Get into something. Sports, drama, even politics. So few schools permit students power such as control over student papers or even optional courses.

If nothing works, try talking your parents into paying for alternative or "free" schools or colleges. For example, point out that as it stands now, you are doing badly, so would they be willing to help you prove yourself in a different type of environment. Most parents find "unstructured" learning distasteful, but it's worth a try.

For those planning to drop out of HIGH SCHOOL

Look at the box of income potentials below. Keep in mind that the lowest-paid work is usually the most dull, dehumanizing work. A system which punishes people who can't hack school isn't right, but that's the way it is.

The high school drop-outs who make good are usually very remarkable people with a lot of other things going for them. That doesn't mean you aren't a remarkable person. If your self-esteem is high, you may make it without that diploma. But don't count on it. Most employers require a high school diploma even for the most ordinary work.

If you still feel compelled to quit school, check out your state's high school equivalency program.

A LIFETIME'S EARNINGS: THE IMPACT OF EDUCATION

Estimated total income from age 18 to death for males* with varying levels of education

Less than 8 years	$280,000
Grade school completed	$345,000
High school—1 to 3 years	$390,000
High school completed	$480,000
College—1 to 3 years	$545,000
College completed	$710,000
College—5 years or more	$825,000

Note: Earnings are in 1972 dollars

(Source: U. S. Census Bureau)

*For females, the figures in each category are several thousand dollars less.

?¥£$¢%0

SURVIVING COLLEGE

For those planning to go to college and for those already there:

Half the people who start college drop out before finishing. *Their reasons for quitting have little to do with intellectual ability.* (Plenty of semi-literate, badly educated, poorly trained people are graduated from our universities every year.)

College can be an *opportunity* to teach yourself in an environment of concentrated intellectual resources and stimulating company. But people who haven't discovered that they must dig out the gold themselves from the vast mountain of slag that is also part of college are easily disillusioned and discouraged.

The biggest reasons for quitting are unhappiness due to not making friends and to uninteresting courses.

The person who is not used to being out of his/her crowd and away from family will have a rough time if s/he tends to be lonely and isolated anyway. Listen, if you have no friends and you aren't the super-studious type and you can't hack the sorority/fraternity trip—what's left? Without the stimulation of good company even your few interesting courses tend to become meaningless. You need to go out of your way to take chances to make even one or two friends (apart from chatting with the people in your dorm). Get off your duff and make a point of going out for the evening. At the campus flick or at the local hangout sit near someone else who is alone. You'd be surprised how conversations can develop out of a remark about the flick or the food. An excellent method of finding meaningful relationships is to *volunteer* at the campus crisis center, health service or student association. Everybody is always pleading for volunteers. Make yourself useful and discover people.

FRESHMEN BEWARE

After you go through the agonizing experiences of getting organized and registered, you are likely to find—if you attend an ordinary college—that freshmen are systematically frozen and manipulated out of all the interesting courses.

As a psychologist and a professor, I can tell you, for example, that on most campuses the introductory psych course has almost nothing to do with what psychologists actually do when they work with people. I sometimes

If you take everything literally, you are spiritually illiterate.

suspect that, since psychology is attractive to many students, the first courses in psych are made as boring as possible to eliminate everyone but the super-studious types.

Other people-professions are the same. For example, the reason there are so few humanistically oriented physicians around is that aspiring doctors have to go through a tedious dehumanizing curriculum.

There are exceptions, of course. For example, several psychiatrists I know hardly ever use anything from their early training, but they feel that they had to pay the price.

The price? If you want to get into psychology or medicine or social work or some other allied profession and you basically care about people even though you are a scientist, *you just have to suffer*.

DON'T FORGET:

You can always try transferring. There are lots of colleges with considerable curriculum freedom which is reflected in a more liberal atmosphere.

Many people who have failed at one school have made good after they were fortunate enough or clever enough to make an appropriate transfer.

WORK

WHAT YOU SHOULD KNOW ABOUT ROUTINE WORK YOU HATE

We all have to do varying amounts of tedious, mechanical and often, unfulfilling, work.

Here is one way to tell whether you should do it: If you don't do it, will you feel bad (like less of a person)? Or will you feel better?

If you are having a hard time getting the work done that you need to do, maybe you need to develop endurance. Endurance is what keeps you going despite pain and fatigue. If you want to learn about endurance, try setting yourself the goal of walking, or jogging, twice as far as you've ever walked or jogged, and then do it, allowing yourself no excuses. (By the way, have you ever noticed how easy it is to get aches and pains and upset stomachs when you face doing something you don't want to do?)

Sometimes you can do something that you hate doing by not fighting it and getting into a rhythm. Usually you get the rhythm as you move along, not before you start.

If you have a big pile of monotonous work to do, schedule it in stages. If you leave it all for one big session you probably will end up not doing it at all. Even so, doing it in one big all-nighter is better than not even trying.

There may be some types of work that you shouldn't be doing. Suppose you go to work for a boss who is almost always ruthless and dishonest with his customers. The work you are doing is helping your boss be a crook. Maybe you should take a stand.

Remember: *If you don't do the monotonous work that needs to be done, all your pleasurable experiences are reduced to cop-outs.* (Of course some people use work as their main way of avoiding their problems. That's a drag, too.)

WHAT YOU SHOULD KNOW ABOUT JOBS

If you want to get a devastating picture of work, read Studs Terkel's *Working*. He shows that almost nobody likes his/her job. And of the few people who do like their work, most of them had to wait years before they found such a spot.

The point is that there are *very few* entry points into the work world which give *real* job satisfaction. The fact is that most jobs are a drag.

But it is really good if you can get work that you like. Yet, if you can't, you have several options:

(1) Take advantage of your leisure time by being with friends and family and by accomplishing things that don't have much, if any, financial payoff.

(2) Work extra hard to get money. However, be sure to think this over: How important is money in your life? What exactly do you plan to use it for? We're not against making money, but too many breadwinners have sacrificed family, friends and leisure for an extra buck. In this regard, when you get older be cautious about making a change which might look good, but not be worth it. Many marriages have been shaken and some have been wrecked after a promotion tied to transfer to a new community with a different, high-pressure life style. Additionally, that new promotion may turn out to be a completely inappropriate place for someone with your skills, talents and inclinations. People have stayed in one job for years, and then, two or three months after being promoted, have quit or been fired.

(3) If you want to improve your job situation, be aware that once you have a position, your chances of success most often hinge on enthusiasm, your own initiative (ideas), and—many people don't realize this—your willingness to take care of details. "Idea" people are a dime a dozen, and so are "details" people. Whether you work on your own or for an employer, your services are usually highly prized when you are able to get things done by not only thinking something up, but also by wrapping up the hundreds of uninteresting details. (It doesn't always turn out this way, of course. You may end up under a boss who feels threatened by your competence.)

UNEMPLOYMENT

If you just can't get work, consider self-employment. It has its ups and downs and insecurity but at least you have more opportunity to make up some of your own rules of the game.

Of course, if you think that you can or should do only one type of work, you narrow down your possibilities to freelance.

Whatever you do, don't let "unemployed" time become dead time. After all, working or not, it's still your life going by. Rather than sitting around thinking (or complaining) about how rotten life is, or going from bar to bar or from bed to TV set, use the time to learn a new skill, to read, to catch up on all the little things you've been putting off.

COMPETITION

Finally, understand that competition is somewhat important, but don't let it drive you into a mental hospital or the grave.

You'd be amazed at how worried and obsessed people get about "success." Certainly you need to succeed. But first, you simply must ask yourself what that word means *for you*. If you constantly compare yourself to what others are doing and making, you will be unbelievably miserable.

Really, you need to be thinking about what are and what should be the most important elements in your life.

62

SEX

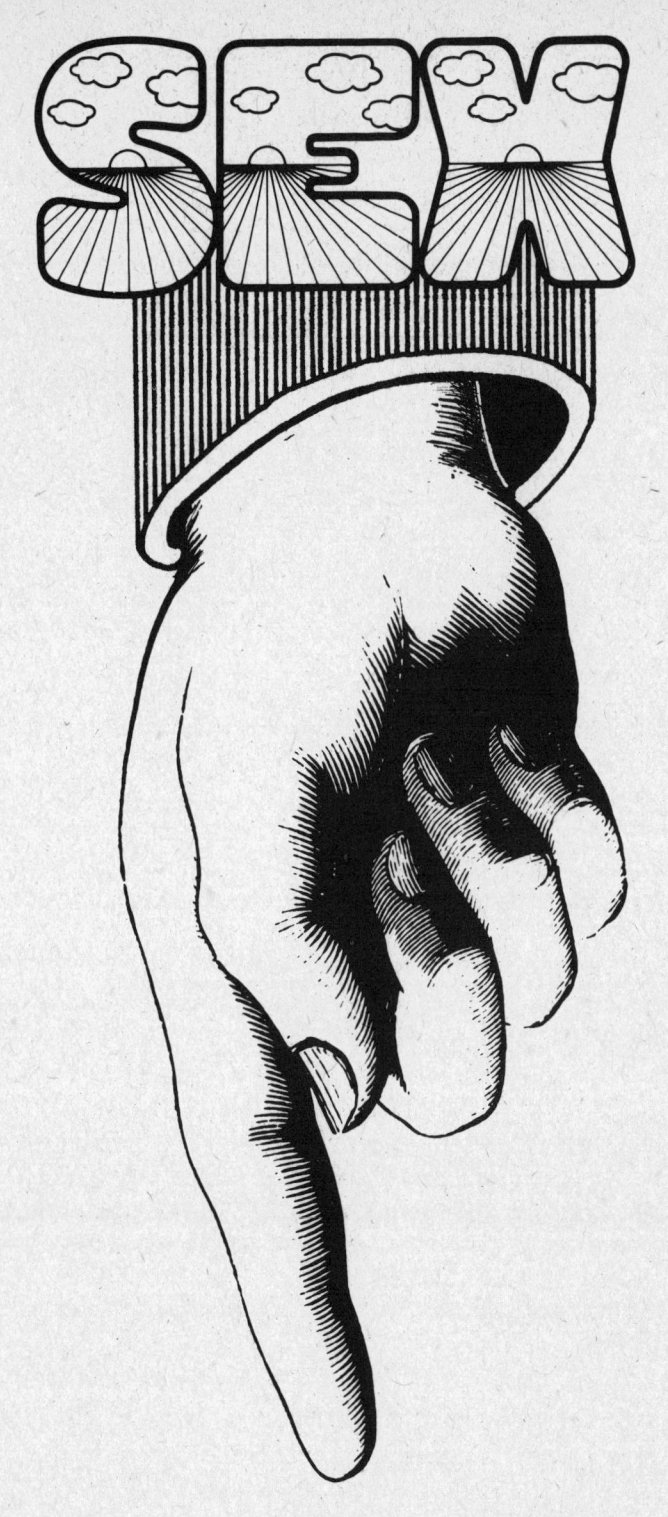

is a good thing, and important.

It looms very large and menacing in a life that is empty and frustrating.

It is an exquisite part of a life that is developing, searching and striving for harmony.

Here are a few thoughts about sex that we feel could be helpful to young people who are still into life:

    If you don't feel like reading much
        but still want to know more than you do (maybe), turn immediately to the comic books. You can always come back to this section later.

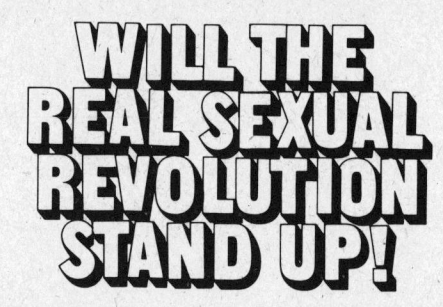

WILL THE REAL SEXUAL REVOLUTION STAND UP!

People have become so performance-oriented, so preoccupied with the number of times they've scored, with orgasms and with positions that they avoid intimacy and become sexual acrobats or, more likely, bored with life itself.

    Who knows what this revolution means anymore? Except that:

☞ **One in four pregnancies is still unwanted. The birth rate is going down in every age group except among teenagers.**

Some 500,000 adolescent girls gave birth to largely unplanned, unwanted children in 1974. About half married to "cover" the pregnancy.

☞ **There were three million new cases of V.D. in 1974.**

Our studies reveal that young people are having sex earlier and more frequently than in the past. Also, the younger they have sex, the less they know about it. We have also found that the average teenager must pretend (at least in public) that he or she knows everything there is to know about sex.

    It's really odd how a lot of people think the reason so many girls are sexually active these days is because of the pill. Yet research has shown that only about 10% of teenage girls having intercourse use effective birth controls. If only they *would* use the pill!

IS BED-ED DEAD?

You can rarely rely on schools or even colleges for an adequate sex education. If they give a course at all it usually deals with "plumbing." It turns out to be a relentless pursuit of the fallopian tubes.

In one school the high school gym teacher introduced his *course* to a segregated male audience like this: "Hey fellas, that *thing* between your legs is not a muscle, don't exercise it."

In another school the students complained that the teacher taught sex so clean it came out dirty.

The following letter appeared in a New Jersey high school newspaper:

To the Editor:

As a male who has finally obtained the privilege to learn about sex, I am most disappointed. I thought that senior sex education would provide the answers to my sexual hang-ups. Instead, I learn that the proshate (?) gland is underneath the bladder and above the testicle, and that a woman's larynx is smaller than a man's. In addition, a certain film left me with the impression that holding hands leads to pregnancies. I won't argue with the importance of this information, but how is it relevant to sex education? What happens when the teacher refuses to call "sexual intercourse" sexual intercourse and refers to it as, "it" or "that", and other indefinite pronouns? We do not lack the maturity to discuss the various aspects of sex (love, percussions, marriage, morals, etc.), so why are these topics avoided? Perhaps an improvement in the subject matter taught might awaken the growing number of boys to whom the term "bed-ed" has come to mean just that — a period of sleep.

SEX, READY OR NOT!

Most young people will have had sexual intercourse several or many times during their adolescence. When young people have sex they don't ask their parents' consent. They simply know that their parents will say no. Teenagers also don't ask me or any other counselors, because we all have a tendency to say "no!" But who's listening? So, I quickly add, "Look, if you are not going to pay attention to me, at least use birth control."

The main problem is that *most* young people experimenting with their first intercourse do not use birth control. Many girls think it is not romantic to be prepared. Irresponsible boys feel it's the girl's job to worry about birth control. Some girls fall for lines like, "Don't worry about it, I'll pull out in time," or, "I don't get any feeling when I use a rubber (condom)" or, "It's too expensive." Girls should respond, "What about my feelings when I'm pregnant, need an abortion, or give birth?" or, "All the boys I know enjoy it with a condom on. What's wrong with you?" Or even your own line.

There are other problems when young, immature people have sex. The first experiences, often due to unfortunate circumstances and/or lack of knowledge, tend to be disappointing or without pleasure and are frequently misinterpreted by the people involved to mean that there must be something wrong with them.

Many adults who have consulted me because of sexual problems have been able to trace them to bad sexual experiences they had as teenagers. Of course, many people can also recall that their only good love and sexual experiences took place in their teen years.

So the best I can say to young people is that if you want sex, it's better to wait at least until you are older (in college or working) but if you are going to anyway, use birth control and join the campaign against absurd state laws which prohibit teenagers from getting birth control information and services without parental consent.

VIRGINS HAVE RIGHTS TOO!

SOMETIMES A YOUNG MAN WILL SAY TO ME, "I WANT TO MARRY A VIRGIN."
I REPLY, "I HOPE YOU'LL MARRY A PERSON, NOT A HYMEN."

It is safe to assume that if about 60% of females who marry have sex before marriage, then about 40% wait until marriage. And notwithstanding the figure for males who wait (about 20%) we must emphatically declare that virgins have rights too even if they are a minority.

Despite "official" support for virgins, this group is rapidly becoming more ridiculed and more vulnerable.

And because everybody who is anybody supports virgins, there are no "pressures" for virgins to organize to protect their rights. Can you imagine an organization called the Virgin Activist League with the slogan "Power to the Virgins" and a button declaring "Virginity is Beautiful"?

Now I happen to believe that committed virgins should stick to their guns and not be intimidated by peer pressure. Just because some of the worst elements in the Establishment support (often for people other than themselves) the virginal state is no reason to question its validity. Some of society's best people also support virginity. Our society, for its very survival, needs more people who have the courage of their convictions.

It is no accident that in my 25 years as a psychologist no young person has ever asked my consent for sex. Yet I am frequently asked if it is normal to wait until marriage, I, of course, reply "yes." I could be very sanctimonious and stop there, but I add: "If you are going to wait, I trust that you won't expect simultaneous orgasms on your wedding night. Otherwise you might ask yourself the question 'For this I waited?' " ("For this I waited?" is an effective comment only with a Jewish accent.)

SEXUAL PREFERENCE

It is no longer believed that homosexuality is caused by any one thing or special combination of factors. Homosexuals exist in every culture and society. The ancient Greek culture found homosexuality acceptable; our culture has frowned upon it.

Homosexuality is not hereditary, biological, chemical or constitutional. I suspect that few people would be exclusively one way or another if we were more open about our sexual attractions. As an example, men in our society are especially frightened by normal desires for intimacy with other males because of their fear of being diagnosed as homosexual.

In any case, we now know that homosexual experiences are not rare during childhood and adolescence. These experiences do not necessarily mean that a person will embrace a gay life style as an adult. One (and even some) homosexual experience doesn't make a person homosexual any more than one (or some) heterosexual experience makes a person heterosexual, any more than one (or some) drink makes a person an alcoholic.

It is completely untrue that if you have homosexual thoughts or dreams you must be a homosexual. Mature people are aware that they have both homosexual and heterosexual feelings, even though the majority of them

Sex is a good thing. Don't offer it to someone you don't love.

Risking rejection is also risking acceptance.

prefer sexual activities with members of the opposite sex. In this connection you should know that it is not easy to judge whether a person is a homosexual. Some feminine-looking men or masculine-looking women are heterosexual, and some highly "masculine," muscular, "all-American" types of men are homosexual.

There is no such thing as latent homosexuality in the sense that it is, by itself, a problem. Everyone starts out with latent bi-, homo-, auto-, and hetero-sexualities. People who are afraid of their healthy sexual impulses have a problem no matter what expression it takes.

The gay liberation movement has made it abundantly clear that homosexuals are, in fact, just as healthy or unhealthy as heterosexuals. Sexual preference does not determine whether a person is mature or "normal."

Some activist gay people have criticized me because of my notion that people can, in fact, choose the sex life they want. I agree that after many years of conditioning it is very difficult to choose another way of life; but we must not, at the same time, insist that just because people have been turned on to members of their own sex they cannot learn to turn on *if they wish* to members of the opposite sex or to both sexes.

People should be free to choose the sexual life they want. I hope there will come a time when people's sexual preferences will be of little or no interest to lawmakers and certainly none of anybody's business (unless that body is an unwilling partner).

Being "with it" doesn't mean you have to like anal, oral, auto, homo or group sexuality. But having fixed, powerful emotions like "revolting," "disgusting," "perverse," "obscene," or "unnatural" in response to behavior which is enjoyable *to others* often means *you* have a problem. It's especially serious when you make a big deal out of your aversion. For example, we occasionally hear men say, "If any faggot so much as comes near me, I'll kill him." This, of course, means that the person who makes the threat is immensely threatened by his own homosexual impulses (which, of course, we all have).

A heterosexual person can respond to a homosexual advance by saying (or feeling): "That's your preference, but it's not mine." A homosexual can say the same thing to a heterosexual.

Other responses could be (not necessarily verbal):

> Bug off.
> Not this time.
> I'm faithful to my partner.
> You are not attractive to me.
> I'm not promiscuous.
> I'm straight/gay. I don't enjoy the idea of a relationship with a man/woman.
> I'll try it and see what it is like.
> No, thank you.

Or, just walk away.

sexual arousal

Popular culture, especially the mass media, creates the notion that there are standard ways to get aroused. Men, for example, are "supposed" to be aroused by the pretty girl selling automobiles or by Playboy's bunnies. That's all right except that men who aren't aroused by the current fashion often feel compelled to fake it. The fact is that human beings are sexually aroused by an endless variety of stimuli.

And *not* knowing that *all* forms of arousal are all right is what causes trouble. The problem is somewhat more acute with men only because they sometimes can't hide obvious hard-ons. But men who are comfortable with their sexuality (in this case, who don't feel guilty about getting a hard-on) should be able to get rid of an erection about as easily as they can get one.

Some people feel guilty if they are sexually aroused when playing with children, roughing it with dogs, being attracted to their parents, sitting in moving vehicles, having sadistic fantasies, looking at pornography. If you can accept the arousal experience without guilt, no harm is done. And why not enjoy some of it? The only real problem occurs if you can get excited only by thoughts or acts you or your partner find unacceptable and exploitative.

DO YOUR SEXUAL THOUGHTS BOTHER YOU?

Sexual thoughts, wishes, dreams, daydreams, are normal, no matter how far out. *Behavior* is what counts the most. Thoughts, images and fantasies cannot, in themselves, hurt you or others. If your religion teaches that deliberately cultivating sexual or sadistic fantasies is immoral, that's your business, so long as it is something you can control. But to get hung up because of passing thoughts that you have little control over is not only pointless, it may even be harmful.

Guilt is the energy for the repetition of fantasies that are unacceptable to you. The people who massively repress their fantasies or become preoccupied with them because of guilt are the ones most likely to harm themselves and others.

AN EXAMPLE

A 15-year-old boy caught a glimpse of his 13-year-old sister taking a shower. The first thing that came into his mind was to have sex with her. He felt terribly guilty and could not free his mind from the image or the sexual wish. Nobody in his family could understand why he began to avoid his friends, became hostile to his sister and seemed to be getting more and more depressed.

Here, of course, guilt caused the sex fantasy to return over and over again. It became obsessive (involuntary repetition of ideas) and he was preoccupied with it. After a while he might "forget" (repress) the incident and only hostility to the sister would remain. What a pity that this boy didn't understand that his wish was normal. Had he known it, the thought would have remained with him for a brief time (whether he enjoyed it or not doesn't matter) and nothing would have happened.

Anybody with even the slightest bit of imagination has, from time to time, murderous, sadistic, incestuous or rape fantasies. That does not mean they are going to act them out. As a matter of fact, accepting as normal one's "unacceptable" thoughts is the best way to keep them under voluntary control.

"Close your eyes, Jeffy — I'm comin' in."

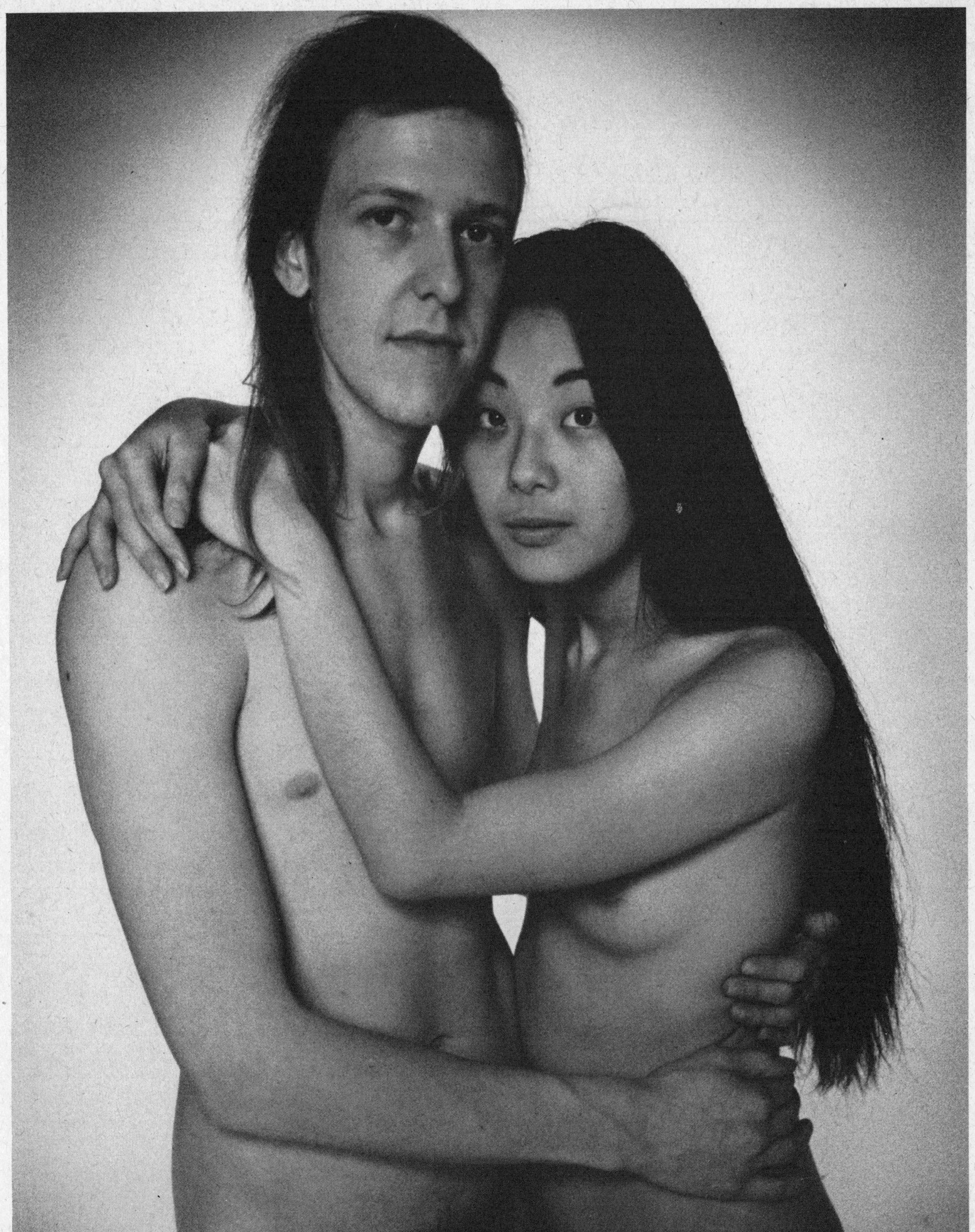

Fantasies

- It is common for people to have sexual thoughts when they are masturbating, having sexual intercourse, when they are daydreaming and at other, sometimes less convenient, times.
- No matter what you think about (even having sex with someone other than the person you are having it with), it's best when it is enjoyable. It's even all right if it's not enjoyable, provided you don't feel guilty.
- Almost all reasonably healthy people *at times* find their fantasies more exciting than the real thing.

AUTO-EROTIC OR SELF ABUSE

Nearly everyone these days says that masturbation is all right . . . a normal developmental stage (and then there is a pause) . . . "It's all right if you don't do it too much."

And nearly everyone is asking the question "How much is too much?" Once a year? Twice a month? After every meal?

The answer: Once is too much if you don't enjoy it.

In my day, it was simple. No question about it. From playing with yourself you got acne, tired blood, insanity and blindness (that's why I wear glasses). We were pioneers in those days!

Funny now—sad once

Those days weren't as far back as you might think. But even further back, this is the kind of advice kids were given. It's from *Safe Counsel* (Practical Advice About Sex, Sin and Sane Living), first published in 1873 and revised by Intext Press in 1973.

"There are some boys who are so strong that they can go on for some time, even two or three years, and do not show serious damage. There are others who give evidence of their loss of virility immediately and finally break in a pitiful way, but in general we are safe in saying that one or more of these results will follow the practice of self-abuse . . . retarded development of the body . . . another mark of the damage done by this secret habit is the weariness of the boy . . . another result of the abuse of the body is the weakening of the nerves . . . The discharge of the semen in the final act of self abuse is a severe strain for it brings with it the arousing of the whole body and ends in a considerable shock . . . Going along with the mental and physical damage is also the moral loss which comes from this habit."

Masturbation is a normal sexual expression for all people, no matter at what age or stage in life you happen to be—a child, teenager, young adult, middle-aged, elderly—and whether you are single or married.

PENIS almost PRONE
HALF MOON

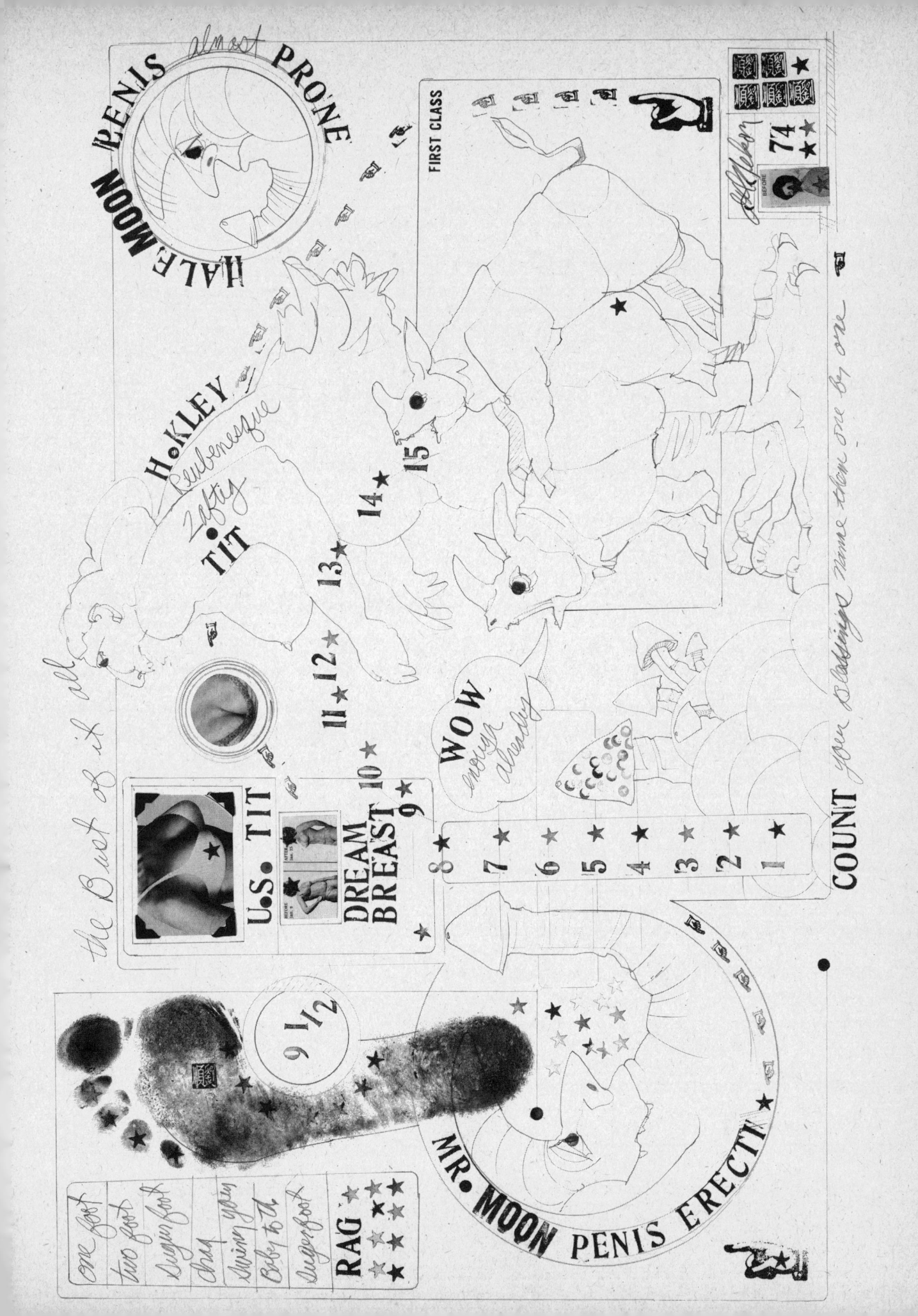

FIRST CLASS

74

H•KLEY
Reubenesque
Zoftig
TIT

★ 15
★ 14
★ 13
★ 12
★ 11

WOW
enough already

the Bust of it all

U.S. TIT
DREAM BREAST
★ 10
★ 9
★ 8 ★ 7 ★ 6 ★ 5 ★ 4 ★ 3 ★ 2 ★ 1

COUNT your blessings name them one by one

9 1/2

MR. MOON PENIS ERECTI

| one foot |
| two foot |
| sugarfoot |
| Chop |
| swing your |
| Baby to it |
| sugarfoot |

RAG ★★★★★★★★

Compulsive eating, talking, sleeping or masturbating is an example of natural behavior which can indicate problems. This does not making eating, talking, sleeping or masturbating unnatural. If I had to settle for one compulsive behavior to express my problems I would certainly select masturbation.

A lot of men and women don't often admit it, but they achieve their best orgasms by masturbating. A lot of married people with satisfactory sex lives masturbate. Some people (not many) masturbate hardly at all or not at all. That's all right too. Guilt about masturbation is about the only thing that's bad about it.

If You Have a Problem
or you are nervous about new sex experiences:

> ☞ CONCENTRATE ON THE RELATIONSHIP
> TALK ABOUT AREAS OF CONCERN AND MUTUAL PLEASURE
> TALK ABOUT WHAT TURNS YOU ON AND OFF
> DO ACTIVE THINGS TOGETHER (almost anything except watching TV)

Talk to the person you care about the most (or to the person with whom you most would like to improve your relationship). Start with how you feel. Speak about yourself *and* the relationship (not if only *you* could change); for example, "It would feel good to me if we could be a little more affectionate with each other at times other than having sex."

> ☞ HOLD OFF HAVING SEXUAL INTERCOURSE
> GET TO KNOW EACH OTHER'S BODIES
> GIVE EACH OTHER BATHS OR SHOWERS
> MASSAGE EACH OTHER (let your partner tell you what feels best)
> MASTURBATE EACH OTHER.

Advance in time to what feels good to you. Don't be so serious about it all. If you don't have a well-developed sense of humor yet, start by smiling. —And when you feel ready

> ☞ TRY INTERCOURSE, but without concern about the orgasm.

And if this doesn't work, seek professional help.

Whom to See for Help

(For Nonsexual Problems As Well)

The best places to try first for information are hotlines; free clinics (street clinics); Planned Parenthood; a professional, or a clinic associated with the American Association of Marriage and Family Counselors, Rational Emotive Therapists, Masters and Johnson clinics; humanistic psychologists. Don't remain with any professional who you feel after the first couple of sessions is not competent and really does not care about you. Remember the professional is your employee—you can fire her/him anytime. Don't be intimidated by credentials or affluence. The professionals to be on guard against are those who start out by saying that therapy is going to take a long time (years). There is no evidence that sexual problems need take a long time to cure or that analysts or psychiatrists are any better at it than clergymen or social workers. This is *not to say*, however, that for some people therapy should not continue for a long period—even years.

GETTING TO KNOW SOMEBODY IS THE ULTIMATE AROUSAL

If you want a little distance from someone you are supposed to be close to, be polite.

TOWARD A PSYCHOLOGY OF BEING SEXUALLY VERY HEALTHY*

To achieve healthy sexual adjustment, I believe
we must seek these basic freedoms:

FREEDOM *from sexual stereotyping*

Cultural definitions of masculinity and femininity are the key to sexual stereotyping. Our culture has insisted on the idea that men should be aggressive, worldly, strong, rational and dominant, and that women should be passive, domestic, weak, emotional and submissive. The destruction of these stereotypes is necessary to achieve honest human relationships.

We have also been led to believe that heterosexual love is the only legitimate and normal kind of love. We must recognize that homosexuality (whether male or female) and bisexuality are also valid sexual behaviors. We must also guarantee the right to reveal or not to reveal sexual interests and tendencies.

Furthermore, we have to break out of stereotypes, new and old, about marriages and living together, and recognize *both* as healthy arrangements for two people who respect and care about each other. Other stereotypes that need to be legitimized are such unconventional pairings as an older woman with a younger man, elderly couples, interracial couples and couples who decide not to have children. We must also eliminate discrimination against people who choose to be single and/or celibate.

FREEDOM *from sexual oppression*

The exploitation of women for the purposes of selling products and services reduces all women to sexual objects and creates narrow, stereotypical standards of beauty. Women are also exploited as workers, being underpaid for most jobs, and receive little recognition—and, usually, no pay—for being housewives and mothers. People must be made aware of this exploitation on all levels—economic, educational, social, and sexual—before any two people can relate with sexual honesty.

Men are also exploited because of roles they are supposed to play in our society. For example, men who are not interested in sports, or who like

*A manifesto developed by the author and several of his students at Syracuse University

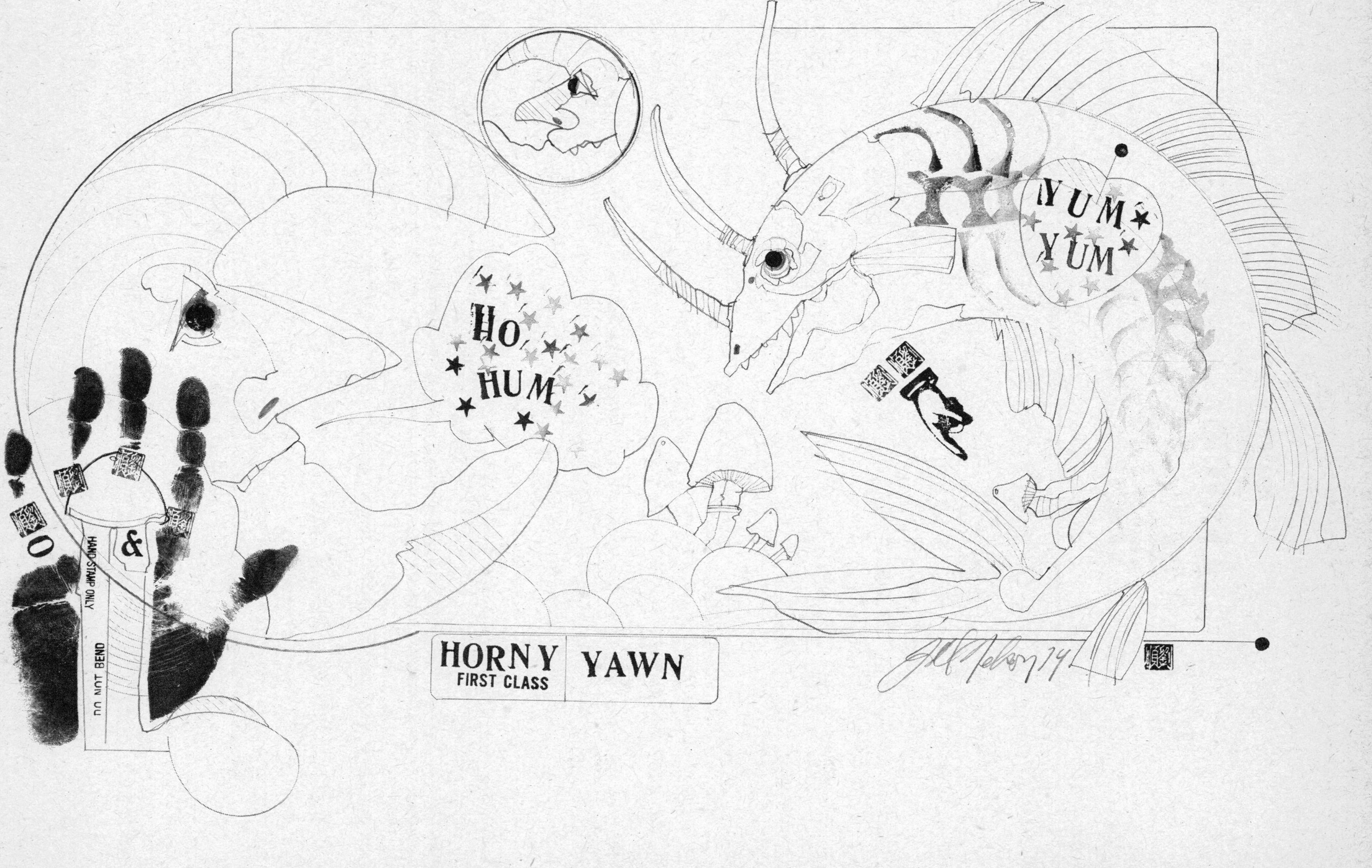

YUM YUM
HO HUM
HORNY
FIRST CLASS
YAWN
HAND STAMP ONLY
&
O

housekeeping, are ridiculed and often are deprived of economic opportunities because they do not fit into a company's image of what constitutes the male role.

Women, too, exploit men and expect them to fulfill roles such as "provider," "daddy" or "stud."

FREEDOM *of information*

Access to basic information must be guaranteed to all regardless of age, sex or intelligence. In the case of mentally handicapped people, special efforts must be made to give them the information they need in a way that they can understand. Freedom of information should also include the right to read pornography and all other literature that has been subject to societal restrictions. Only complete freedom of information can ensure an educated and enlightened populace.

FREEDOM *from repression of the last generation*

Young people must realize that many parents do not have adequate information about sexual behavior, or if they do, they are often unable or unwilling to communicate it to their children. Even parents who present the basic facts may find it difficult to deal with their child's feelings about his or her own emerging sexuality. Perhaps because of their own fears and misconceptions, many parents overreact to their children's questions or sexual behavior. Although parents are a good source for moral values and attitudes, we must recognize the possibility of their passing on misinformation, prejudices and personal problems concerning sexual matters. What is needed more than school programs is a massive sex education program directed at parents and newlyweds. Our feelings and knowledge about sex become exceedingly important when we realize that we may pass on unhealthy attitudes to *our* children.

FREEDOM *from research nonsense and sex myths*

Access to accurate information is crucial to a healthy sexuality. Unfortunately, not everything in print is reliable information. One "study" reported that males were "in their prime" at age 17, and females in their late 20's. Popular reports like these, and even more reputable studies, often confuse people seeking a common sense approach to sexuality. Some research is extremely valuable for debunking sexual myths (for example, some of the work of Masters and Johnson). However, a flood of popular articles on sex in magazines and newspapers actually creates new myths. We must find a sane perspective on research based on common sense and the basic facts about sexual behavior.

FREEDOM *to control one's own body*

We must be free from legal controls of our own bodies. This freedom would prohibit legislation restricting medical abortion, voluntary sterilization, consensual sexual relations among adults, contraceptive information and devices for minors, and privacy of sexual expression. Also implied would be the right to choose one's own life style and sexual partners. Inherent, too, is the right to proper medical care and access to contraceptive devices for anyone who wants them.

FREEDOM *to express affection*

Until we overcome our fear of expressing our affection for one another, regardless of gender, we cannot achieve full sexual adjustment. Our culture now suffers great anxiety even about *touching* another person (hugging, holding hands, etc.). We must be able to feel free to touch other people, even a member of the same sex, without fear of critical diagnosis and fixation. This is expecially important with children, who want and enjoy physical affection from adults and peers.

FREEDOM *of sexual expression for the handicapped*

We must recognize and facilitate sexual expression among the mentally retarded, emotionally disturbed and physically handicapped. Special educational efforts should be directed to helping these people find appropriate sexual opportunities.

While these freedoms are a necessary precondition for healthy sexuality, they are not without their corollary responsibilities. These moral or ethical standards also must be commonly accepted.

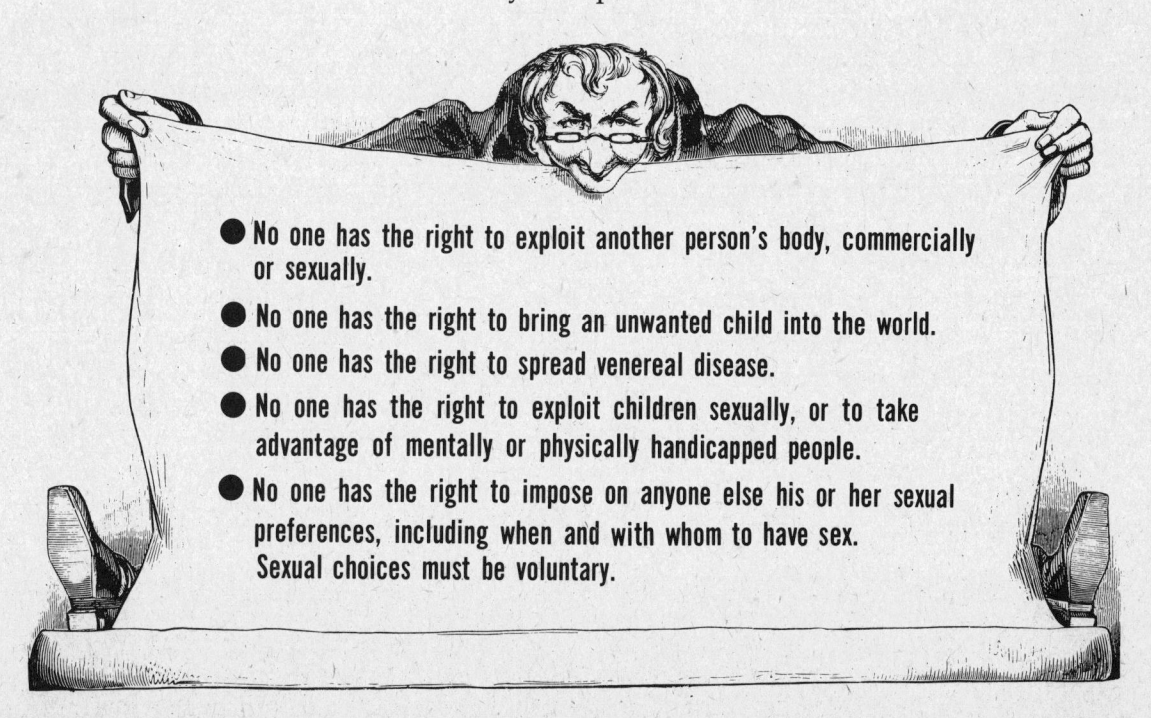

- No one has the right to exploit another person's body, commercially or sexually.
- No one has the right to bring an unwanted child into the world.
- No one has the right to spread venereal disease.
- No one has the right to exploit children sexually, or to take advantage of mentally or physically handicapped people.
- No one has the right to impose on anyone else his or her sexual preferences, including when and with whom to have sex. Sexual choices must be voluntary.

These freedoms and responsibilities cannot be guaranteed by the Constitution but will evolve gradually as people's consciousness about sexuality changes. The most important factors in effecting this change will be a willingness to communicate openly and to explore our preconceived notions about sexuality. Complete access to information will make the process of change easier.

Eventually, we will come to realize that any two adults have the right to voluntary non-exploitative sexual relations. Ideally, their relationship should lead to and enhance each other's personal growth.

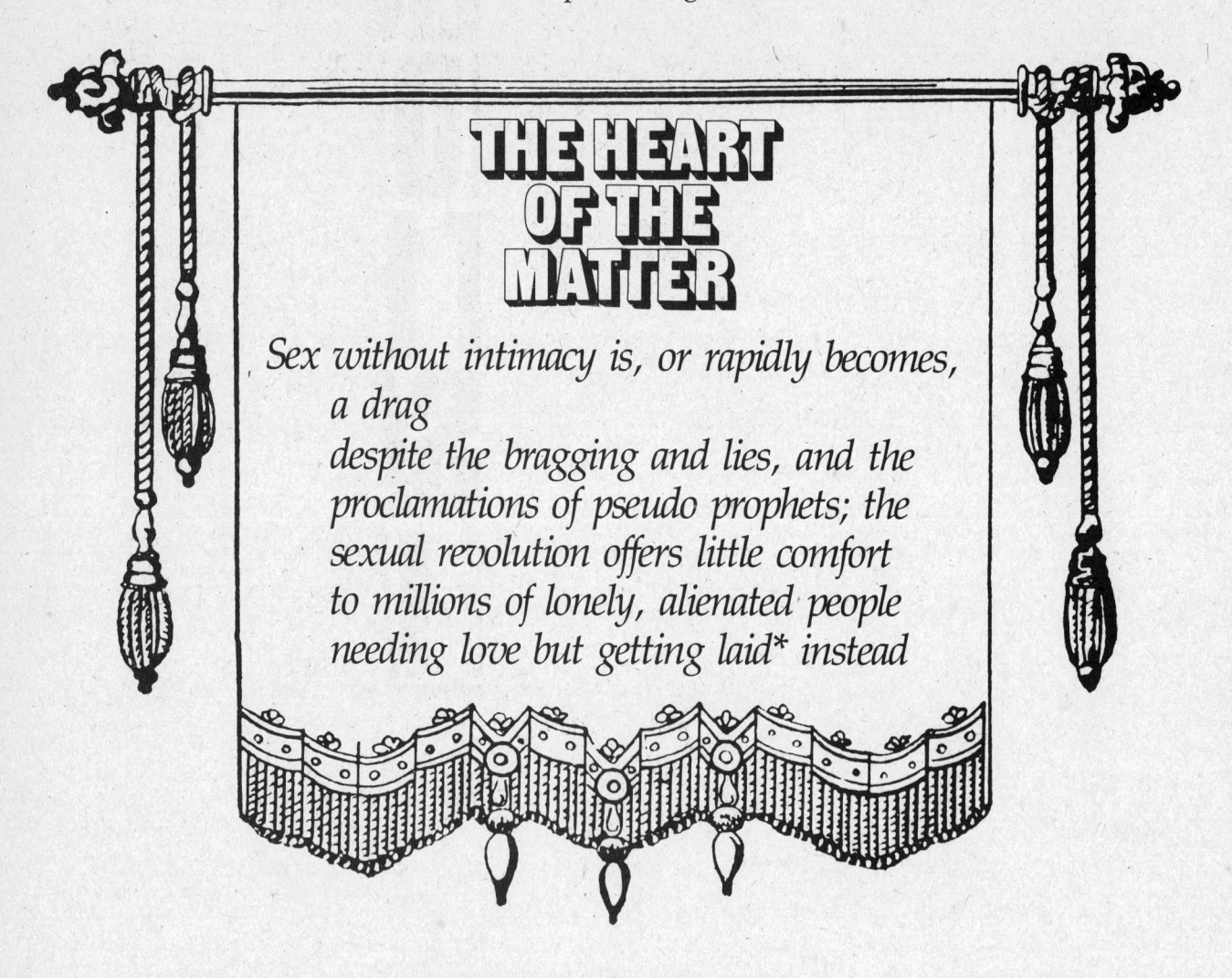

THE HEART OF THE MATTER

Sex without intimacy is, or rapidly becomes, a drag
despite the bragging and lies, and the proclamations of pseudo prophets; the sexual revolution offers little comfort to millions of lonely, alienated people needing love but getting laid* instead

WHAT'S MISSING?

What's missing is the fun and joy of sexuality that is shared with a person you love. It's not included because that part is up to you.

*An archaic term for having sex without intimacy

The women's liberation movement is also the best single force for the liberation of men. While women have suffered the most from lack of equal opportunities as well as exploitation and abuse, men, in the long run, will profit the most from being *forced* to relate to liberated women. Men, freed of the pressures of the double standard and aggressive, ulcerous behavior, will

THE WOMEN'S LIBERATION MOVEMENT HAS A LOT TO SAY TO ALL OF US

Here is what we have to say:

be able to share responsibilities and bring harmony to the most disquieting, sexist aspects of our society.

Many people have come to associate the women's liberation movement only with specific issues, such as abortion on demand, day care, sharing household responsibilities and equal opportunity in job employment. But liberation is much more than this. Liberation means that you are attempting to discover yourself in a realistic, rather than romanticized or culturally stereotyped, manner, and then are *acting* on your discoveries. Explaining

> What it means to be a male in America today is nothing that anybody should be fighting for.
>
> Karen Decrow

these new feelings and actions may be one of the most important bridges that men and women must build.

It is fashionable now for some women to say that they don't want to be liberated and for men to say that they want the old fashioned unliberated women to care for and endear in the manner of their worst impulses. It's too late to stop the most revolutionary movement of our times, and the men and women who struggle against this movement will suffer the terrible fate of boredom.

ON GIVING UP ONE'S CAREER TO SUPPORT YOUR MATE'S GETTING ONE

☛ DON'T DO IT ☚

Many people (mostly women) work their fingers to the bone (as secretaries, of course) to enable their husbands to complete their under- or post-graduate studies only to be abandoned, and "exchanged" for a woman with a comparable degree.

THE BOREDOM OF UNLIBERATED WOMEN AND MEN

It is boring to relate to an unliberated woman.

Can you imagine after five years of marriage she still responds to your question, "What should we do tonight?" with "Anything you want to is fine with me, dear."

The unliberated man, of course, may pretend he enjoys this response, or it may be he who acquiesces. Regardless of who plays what role though, it is exhausting to be with someone who constantly relies on you.

FOR THOSE OF YOU WHO SUFFER FROM SEXISM IN HIGH SCHOOL

The way to power is *organization*. One outspoken person is usually much more effective with a *group* behind her/him.

Young women can no longer afford to be routed into classes that exclude them from vocational skills, such as industrial arts. This is why: One

ZING COMIX

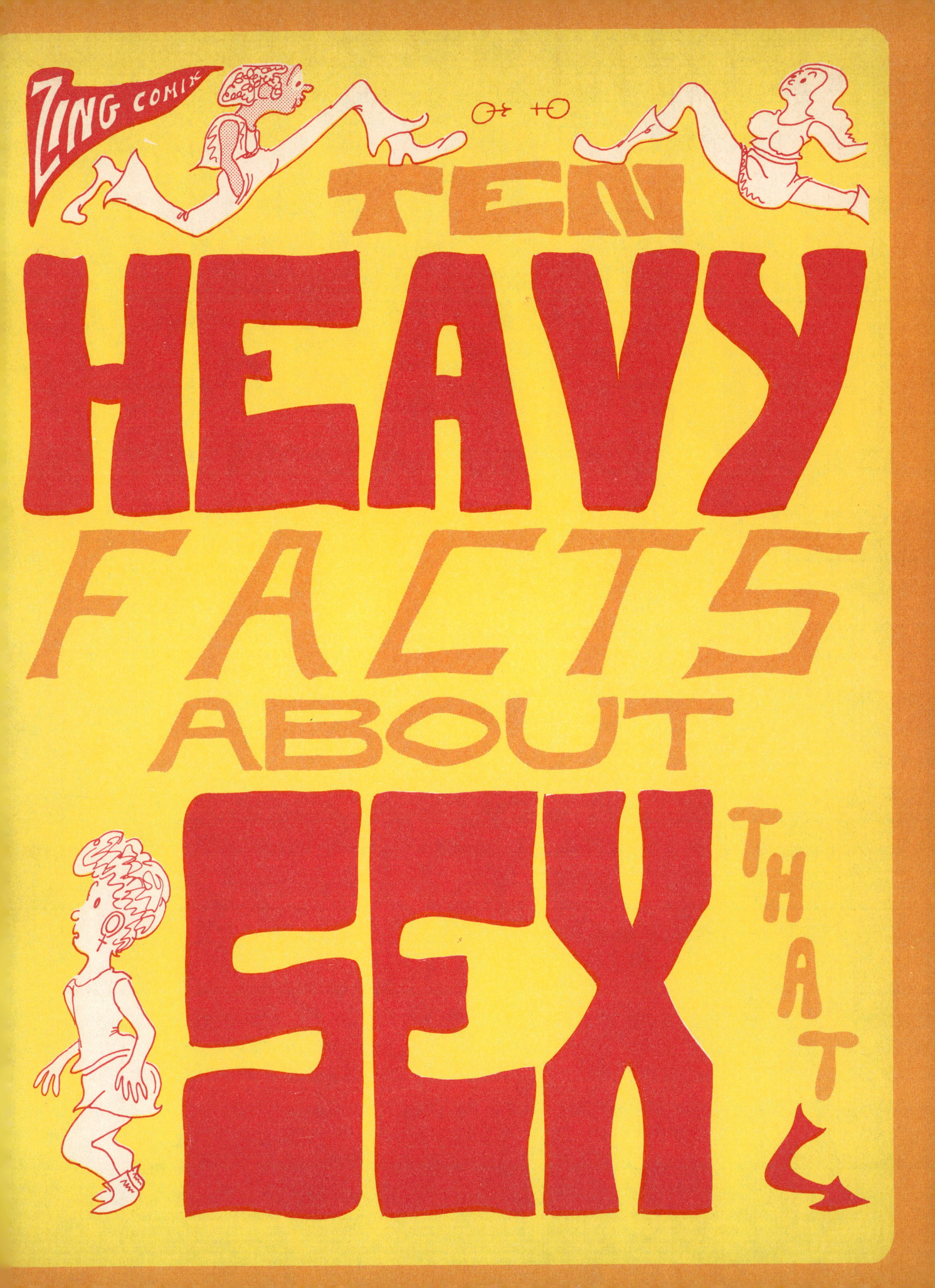

TEN HEAVY FACTS ABOUT SEX THAT

THAT...
YOUR FRIENDS DON'T KNOW

"LOOK HERE, WHEN IT COMES TO SEX, I KNOW ALL ABOUT IT"

"I BROKE MY ARM ONCE. DOES THAT MAKE ME A BONE SPECIALIST?"

Text: Sol Gordon
Illustration and design: Roger Conant
Facilitator: Kathleen G. Everly
Distribution: Del Cusmano
Published by Ed-U Press, 760 Ostrom Ave., Syracuse, N.Y. 13210
Ed-U Press is the publishing arm of
**Syracuse University's
Institute for Family Research and Education**

Other titles in this series of educational comic books include: *V.D. Claptrap, Protect Yourself From Becoming an Unwanted Parent, What Do You Do When You're All Drug Doubt?, Juice Use -- Special Hangover Edition,* and *Gut News for Modern Eaters.* These booklets and *Heavy Facts* are available for 30 cents each from Ed-U Press. Bulk rates are available on request.
NEW, REVISED EDITION
© 1971, 1975 by Ed-U Press

THAT... YOUR PARENTS DIDN'T TELL YOU

Panel 1:
MUMBO JUMBO BIRDS 'N' BEES! ZZZXX FLAPDOODLE ABCNYAM FM GIRLS! ahem ZZXKLP... MMM... YOUNG MAN'S FANCY THEREFORE... XXNXMLP SEE WHAT I MEAN? (ULP)

Heh heh

WHA....?

Panel 2:
DON'T!

?

THAT... YOUR DOCTORS and COUNSELORS AIN'T TALKING ABOUT

101 WAYS TO COP OUT OF TOUCHY QUESTIONS

"HOW MUCH IS TOO MUCH? WELL, UH, DUH AHEM..."

"SHEESE!"

BE NICE · WORK HARD · DON'T

THANK YOU!

THAT... YOUR SCHOOL IS STEPPIN' LIGHT AROUN'

SEX INFO FREE

HEH HEH

NEATO!

BUT THE FACTS ARE:

1 ALL THOUGHTS ARE NORMAL

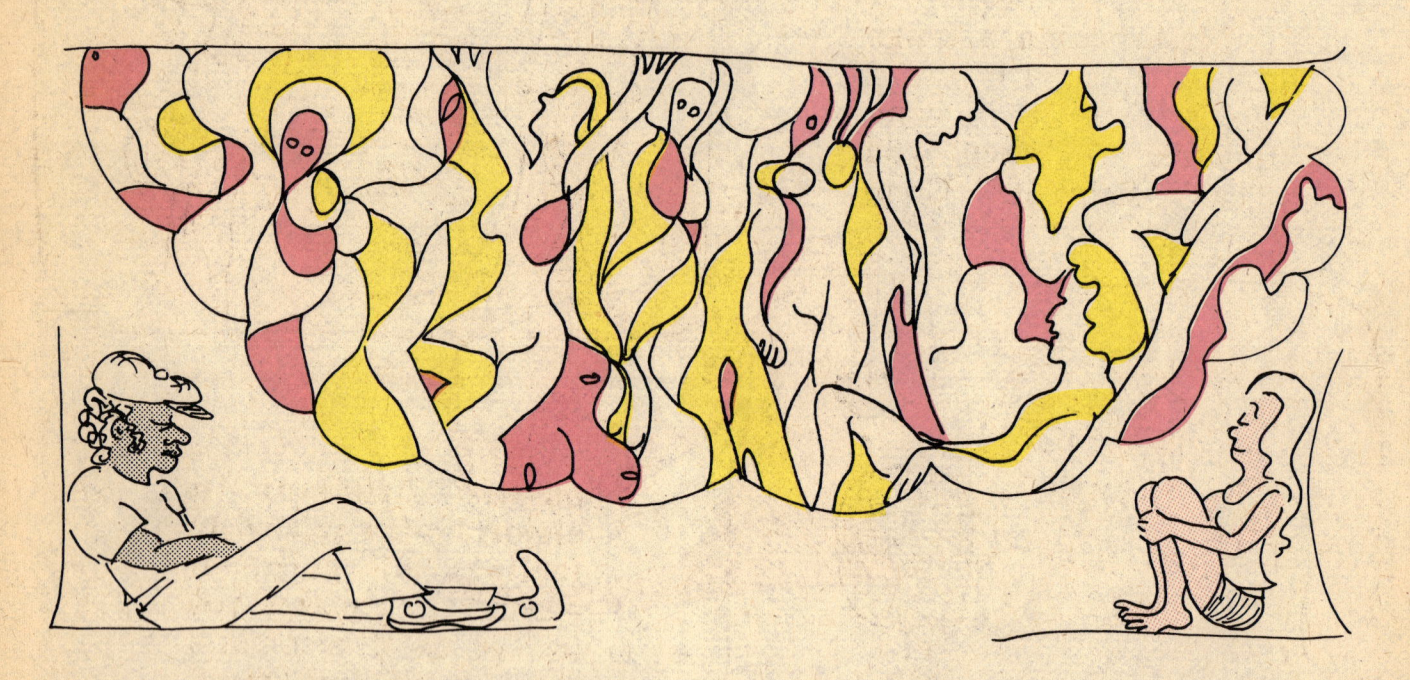

Sexual thoughts, wishes, dreams are normal -- no matter how far out. Thoughts, images, impulses and fantasies cannot, in themselves, injure you. Your actions are much more important.

However, if your religion teaches that it is immoral for you to purposely draw out sexual or aggressive fantasies, that is your business - so long as it is something you can control. But, to feel guilty about passing thoughts over which you have little control may be harmful.

If your fantasies make you feel guilty, you probably won't be able to avoid having them. Realizing that all thoughts are normal will let you have, for the most part, the ones you want. The thoughts you don't like will occur less and less.

2 MASTURBATION

Masturbation is a normal expression of sex for both males and females at any age. Enjoy it. There's no harm in masturbation no matter how often you do it.

Masturbation is a sign that something is wrong *only* when it is compulsive -- when you "can't help it." Compulsive behavior is almost always related to feelings of guilt. If masturbating makes you feel guilty, it becomes a form of self-punishment.

Psychologically, masturbation is fine as long as you want to masturbate and as long as you enjoy it. If it makes you feel guilty, don't do it.

3 HOMOSEXUAL

ARE YOU SOME KIND OF LONG-HAIRED FAGGOT?

MUSIC IS MY GIG, MAN

WELL, YOU WANNA COME UP TO MY PLACE AND LISTEN TO SOME RECORDS?

MOM

Most people, men and women, have occasional homosexual thoughts and many people have had homosexual experiences.

This doesn't make them homosexuals. A homosexual is a person who in adult life prefers and has sex relations with members of the same sex.

Homosexuality is not biological or inherited. A few homosexual thoughts or actual experiences don't mean you will become a homosexual if you don't want to. So choose the sexual life you want. Ninety per cent of the population prefer heterosexuality. That's their business. Ten per cent choose homosexuality or bisexuality. That's their business.

Letting yourself be bothered by fears of homosexuality is a waste of time.

Any type sex (hetero, homo, or auto) can be considered "abnormal" when it is involuntary and exploitative (using a person without caring for her/his interests). That's when sex is an expression of a problem rather than an enrichment of a relationship.

4 'PERVERSIONS'

A lot of people wonder about oral and anal sex, and some think it is "perverted." We think there is nothing wrong with any kind of sex if both partners are mature and it doesn't hurt anyone. It is, for some, a normal part of foreplay and it is also a way to have sexual pleasure when you don't want to have intercourse.

5 VD

> HOW DID YOU SAY YOU GOT THAT EAR INFECTION?

> D.O.C. (Doctor Of Course)

> WELL, IT ALL BEGAN AT THIS PARTY, WHEN SOMEONE SAID, 'STICK IT IN YER EAR, MAC'

Venereal disease (V.D.) is spread by having sexual contact (heterosexual or homosexual) with someone who has it. Besides intercourse, V.D. spreads through oral and anal sex (even open-mouthed kissing).

A fairly good way to cut down chances of getting V.D. is to urinate and wash your genitals with soap and hot water right after sex relations. This, however, is *no guarantee* against V.D. (Girls using contraceptive foam should not douche until six hours after relations.)

The two most common forms of V.D. are gonorrhea and syphilis. First signs of gonorrhea are pus and "burning" while urinating. First sign of syphilis is a sore on the penis, or in the vagina, mouth or rectum. Girls may not notice any signs when they have V.D.

Signs of V.D. go away by themselves without medical treatment. But the disease is still doing damage. You just don't know you have it.

You cannot get cured without treatment from a doctor. Most states have sensibly revised their laws to permit teenagers to be examined and treated without parental consent or knowledge.

The County Health Clinic is usually the best place to go. Or you can call on your local hotline, free clinic or Planned Parenthood.

6 PENIS SIZE

Boys often wonder about the size of their penis and girls help them worry by making remarks. But no matter how big or small, the sexual pleasure -- for either sex -- is not determined by penis size.

Besides, you can't tell the size of a penis by looking at it when it is not erect.

OH, NOW I UNDERSTAND — YOU WANTED TO SHOW ME YER BIG OLD CLOCK!

DONG! DONG!

WHAT A PAIR OF KNOBS

BREAST SIZE

Many girls are concerned about whether their bust is too small or too big, and boys who make comments don't help matters. Breast size is not an indicator of your sexuality. Mature people appreciate and value differences.

Also, during the teen years, a girl's breasts can grow at different rates. This is normal.

PORN

Pornography becomes boring after awhile. If porno is your main bag, you're not mature -- sexually or otherwise.

Some people think that if you look at pictures of nudes or read descriptions of sex acts, you might become corrupted. What is really corruptive is deliberate deception -- whether it has to do with politics, morality, sex, or anything.

Pornography, like beauty, is in the eye of the beholder. Would you believe that some people say this comic book is pornographic and corruptive?

LOOKING AT DIRTY BOOKS AGAIN, I SEE

NAW. I ONLY READ THE ARTICLES

THERE'S A GREAT PIECE IN THERE ON MUD-SLINGING

8 WHEN CAN A GIRL GET PREGNANT?

Nothin' to worry about—it can't happen if we do it standing up

There is no 100 per cent safe time when a girl can have intercourse without risking pregnancy. But, in general, most girls are not able to get pregnant during menstruation or in the two or three days after menstruation.

A girl can get pregnant the first time she has sexual intercourse. She can get pregnant if she has sex standing up, sitting down, or in any other position.

Two ways of avoiding unwanted pregnancy: self control or birth control.

9 BIRTH CONTROL
~PILLS & RUBBERS~

The Pill -- still the most effective. Take heed: just taking one or two is no help. Females must take their pills regularly under a doctor's care. (The Pill has not yet been proved safe for adolescents who are in the early stages of their physical development.)

Other good medical birth controls are the IUD (intrauterine device) and the diaphragm.

The best birth control available without prescription is a combination of the rubber for the boy and the foam (which is inserted before sex) for the girl. When buying rubbers, ask for a brand name, such as Trojan. Delfen and Emko are two names of contraceptive foams. They are available in drugstores.

Douching (washing out the vagina) -- no matter with what -- and the rhythm method are not trustworthy ways to prevent pregnancy. The same goes for withdrawal of the penis before "coming" (ejaculation) -- although this is better than no protection at all.

GALOSHES?

WARNING: The Pill does not prevent V.D. If you have intercourse with someone who has V.D. and he does not use a condom, your chances of getting it are greater if you are on the Pill.

Medical abortions are now legal in all states for women in the first 12 weeks of pregnancy. In the second three months, a state may impose regulations designed to safeguard a woman's health.

In the final 10 weeks, a state may limit abortions to protecting the health or life of the mother. (In any case, if you are pregnant and want to avoid giving birth or if you are having sexual relations and want to avoid pregnancy, contact your local Planned Parenthood, Family Planning, county or hospital clinic.)

We think having an abortion is more moral than bringing an unwanted child into this world. Having a medical abortion before the

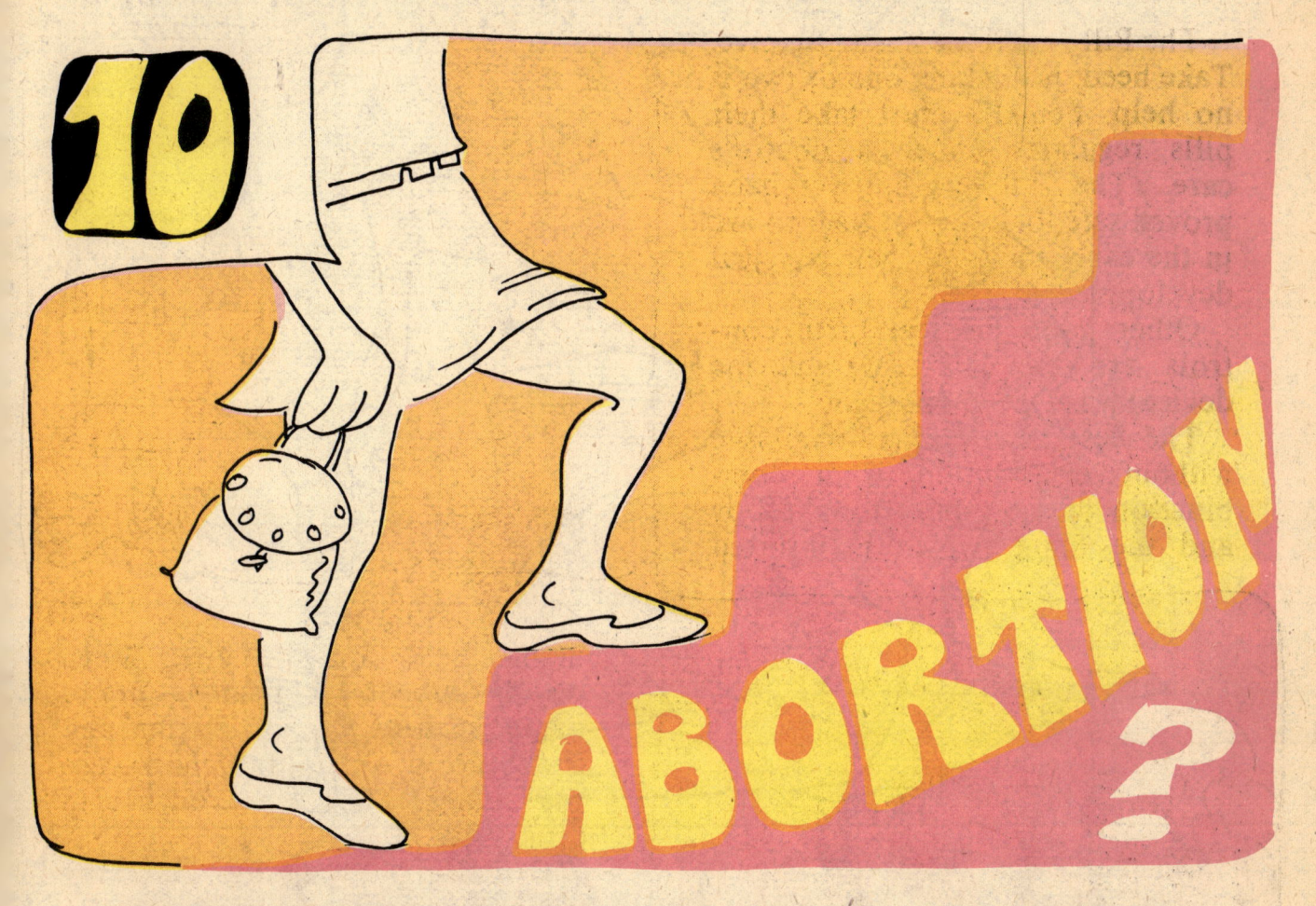

10 ABORTION?

twentieth week is safer than giving birth -- so don't let anyone tell you it is a dangerous operation.

During the early stages of pregnancy a medical abortion is safe, brief and relatively painless. It is *very dangerous,* however, when it is *not done by a physician.*

Some people consider abortion immoral and they have a right to think this way. Most people, as well as the majority of religious groups, believe that women should have the right to make their own decisions about their unintended pregnancies -- whether to give birth (keep the child or put it up for adoption) or have an abortion.

2 Extra Points

"What say we get together later for a game of, uh, ball."

"No thanx. I'm not up for grabs at this time."

"It takes two to tango."

VIRGIN RIGHTS

Males and females have a right to be virgins. These days there is a lot of pressure on guys to "prove" their masculinity by having sex and there is increasing pressure for girls to "get with it" and ball.

People who choose to be virgins should stick to their guns. Those who make fun of virgins reveal their own sexual insecurity. On the other hand, some boys who fool around themselves say they want to marry a virgin. We say, we hope you'll marry a person, not a hymen.

SEX PROBLEMS

If it turns out that your first few sexual experiences weren't enjoyable or satisfactory, don't assume that there is anything wrong with you. A lot of people have temporary difficulties when they first begin.

For example, some men find that they are impotent -- unable to have an erection when they want to have intercourse -- or that they have premature ejaculation -- coming before or immediately after the penis enters the vagina.

Some women are "frigid." They don't enjoy sex, or even if they do, they worry because they don't get an orgasm. (It is not necessary to have orgasm to enjoy sex.)

Such difficulties are usually solved in time when two people work at their problems with sympathy and understanding for each other. If problems persist, seek professional help.

SEX IS A DRAG WHEN...

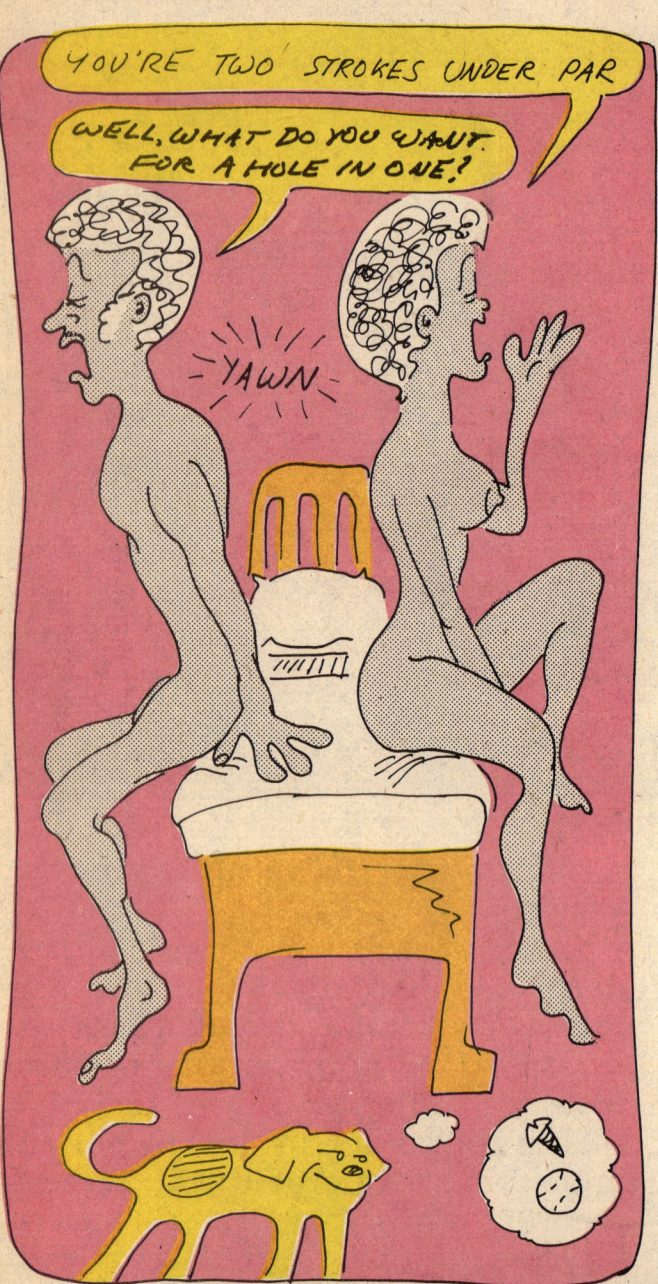

> YOU'RE TWO STROKES UNDER PAR
>
> WELL, WHAT DO YOU WANT FOR A HOLE IN ONE?
>
> YAWN

- You don't care about, much less love, your partner.

- It is compulsive. You do it a lot when you really don't want to and you get very little pleasure out of it.

- It is exploitative. You use sex against people as a way of trying to "prove" that you're not inadequate. (Frequency of sex has little to do with its meaning or importance in the lives of people.)

2 More Ideas...

SEX IS COOL WHEN...

- You are ready for it. (It is even normal to wait until marraige.)

- You are in love.

- You want a baby or, if you don't,

- You use birth control.

> BUT THERE'S NO SIGN ABOUT THAT...

Signs: NO PARKING / NO SINGING / NO HUNTING OR TRAPPING / NO DANCING / NO FISHING OR SWIMMING / NO! THINKING / NO SMOKING OR DRINKING / NO LOOKING CROSS-EYED AT HIGH NOON ON TUESDAY

MORALITY IS GOOD FOR YOU

FOR GUYS:

- No sex unless you are ready for it.
- Protect your lover; wear a rubber.
- Don't reveal your sexual inadequacy by boasting about your sexploits.
- Don't go around hurting girls because you feel insecure. (A guy who is always on the make basically hates women.)
- *Machismo* is when you're man enough to share responsibility for a pregnancy.
- No sex with anyone you don't care about or who doesn't really care about you.

FOR GIRLS:

- No sex unless you are ready for it. (Don't fall for lines like: "If you don't have sex with me, we might as well stop seeing each other.")
- No sex with a guy without a reliable method of birth control. (If the guy is too cheap to spend 35 cents for a condom, he shouldn't be allowed in.)
- No sex with anyone you don't care about or who doesn't really care about you. (Find out if he'll go out with you even if you won't have sex with him.)
- Support Women's Liberation NOW!

IF YOU WANT TO KNOW MORE:
Facts About Sex For Today's Youth
By Sol Gordon (John Day Paperback, $1.90)

IF YOU WANT TO KNOW MORE THAN THAT:
Understanding Sex - A Young Person's Guide
By Alan F. Guttmacher (Signet Paperback, 95 cents)

IF YOU WANT TO KNOW ABOUT THE COLLEGE SCENE:
Sex In A Plain Brown Wrapper by
The Student Committee on Sexuality at Syracuse University
(760 Ostrom Ave., Syracuse, N.Y. 13210, $1.00)

PROTECT YOURSELF

FROM BECOMING AN UNWANTED PARENT

GOOD REASONS FOR KNOWING HOW TO PREVENT PREGNANCY

Lying in bed one morning, Candy feels like she's just swallowed a frog. She thinks, "Wow, it's been six weeks since I had my period. But I *can't* be pregnant! I only made it with Tom a couple of times and for just a few minutes! It can't be *that* easy to get pregnant."

Add Candy to the more than 800,000 teenagers who become pregnant each year in the U.S. The next few months will probably read like a soap opera: heartache, embarrassment, maybe a forced marriage, dropping out of school or the hassle of an abortion, and a whole new set of responsibilities that neither Candy or Tom are ready for.

It's really too bad that so many teenagers have to go through all this when pregnancy can be easily and safely prevented nowadays.

I CAN'T UNDERSTAND IT. I THOUGHT IT COULDN'T HAPPEN TO ME.

GLUG GLUG

Whatever *you* do, can you accept the idea that it is wrong to bring an unwanted child into this world? Many children grow up emotionally disturbed, roughly treated, and poorly fed because their parents, whether they know it or not, are angry at them for being born.

Sure, sometimes a baby who starts out unwanted later becomes wanted. But still, if you're a teenager with one child, don't have another too soon. "Too soon" is when you feel you can't handle a second baby, emotionally, physically and financially.

If a girl has one baby and finishes high school, things may work out. But a mother who doesn't finish high school and has more babies usually stays on welfare and the kids don't have much to look forward to.

Text by Sol Gordon and Roger Conant
Illustrations and design by Roger Conant
Kiwi bird by Kieth Van Kirk
Published by Ed-U Press, 760 Ostrom Ave., Syracuse, N.Y. 13210.
Ed-U Press is the publishing arm of Syracuse University's
Institute for Family Research and Education

Other titles in this series of educational comic books include: *Ten Heavy Facts About Sex, V.D. Claptrap, Gut News for Modern Eaters, Juice Use -- Special Hangover Edition,* and *What Do You Do When You're All Drug Doubt?* These titles and *Protect Yourself* are available for 30 cents each from Ed-U Press. Bulk rates are available on request.

Revised 1975 © 1973, 1975 by Ed-U Press

SO, YOU WANT TO GO ALL THE WAY

- If you have sex before you're ready for it, you might have a confused, unhappy experience, which could harm your future sex life.
- If your partner doesn't care about you, or if you don't care about your partner, then sex with that person is a drag.
- If you use sex as a way of trying to "prove" that you are manly or womanly, then you are an exploiter, not a lover. An exploiter is a person who uses another person. The exploiter usually screws himself or herself up at the same time that he or she is not caring about someone else.

Of course, we know that a lot of teenagers will go all the way, no matter what any adults think they should not do. If you do decide to be sexually active, at least protect yourself from unwanted pregnancy (as well as unwanted V.D.).

HEY SUGAR, DO YOU WANT TO GO ALL THE WAY...?

SURE, HONEY POT, YOU CAN DRIVE ME ALL THE WAY HOME RIGHT NOW

HE TRIED TO PULL A FAST ONE WITH HER. NOW HE'LL HAVE TO PULL IT OFF WITHOUT HER

...BY THE WAY DID YOU KNOW...?

"YOU SHOULD'VE SEEN 'ER. I HAD 'ER DANGLING FROM MY STRING. BUT I LET 'ER GO. SHE WAS PROBABLY A COLD FISH, ANYWAY."

"YOU GOT ONE WITH YOUR POLE?"

"HOLY MACKEREL."

- A person who feels unsure about himself or herself may try to talk others into having sex - for his or her own selfish reasons. People like this don't really consider the other person's needs.
- People who brag about their sex experiences are usually lying and they don't enjoy sex much at all. If they enjoyed what they were doing, they would keep it private (once in a while they might talk it over with a close friend).
- People who are always "on the make" may not know it, but they hate the opposite sex. They really don't like themselves much, either.

WHY KIDS SHOULDN'T HAVE KIDS

- A high number of babies who die suddenly are born of mothers aged 15 (or younger) to 18.
- The younger the mother, the greater the health risks -- for her and her baby. The risks include prematurity, low birth weight, and difficult labor as well as serious illness in mother and child.

BUT WE TOO YOUNG TO KID OURSELVES, HON'

NO KIDDING?

- Teenage mothers have more retarded and brain-injured children than mothers in their twenties.
- Pregnant teenagers attempt suicide more than do people in other groups.
- About seventy per cent of teen marriages end in divorce or separation.
- Fathers of "unplanned" children also have a rough time. Some pretend that they don't care, but many feel guilty and suffer emotionally and financially.

If you enjoy your own growing-up years, then you're more likely to enjoy your own children later and have a good relationship with them. Parenthood should be more a satisfying responsibility, than a burden.

WHEN CAN A GIRL GET PREGNANT?

WE CAN'T GO ON DOCKING LIKE THIS, SAM!

DON'T WORRY, NATASHA, WE WON'T GET IN TROUBLE... I'LL BE PULLING OUT SOON.

THAT'S WHAT YOU AMERICANS ALWAYS SAY

After a girl has her first menstrual period, she is able to get pregnant. Girls usually start having periods between the ages of 11 and 15.

Almost from the time a boy has his first hard-on (erection) and comes (ejaculates) he is able to make a girl pregnant. Most boys have their first ejaculation between the ages of 11 and 15.

There is no 100 per cent safe time when a girl can have intercourse without risking pregnancy. ("Intercourse" is when a man's penis enters the woman's vagina.) But, in general, if a girl's periods are *regular*, she *probably* won't get pregnant if she has sex during her period or two or three days before or after it. However, *it doesn't take much to throw off her regularity -- even simple "tension" can do it.*

A girl can get pregnant the first time she has sexual intercourse. She can get pregnant if she has sex standing up, sitting down or in any other position. Whether or not a girl has sexual feelings during intercourse has nothing to do with whether she gets pregnant.

HOW DO GIRLS GET PREGNANT?

Sometime between one menstrual period and the next, a tiny egg is released from one of the ovaries.* It passes through one of the Fallopian tubes into the uterus (womb).

If a woman has intercourse within two or three days before or after the egg is released, some of the man's sperm cells can meet the egg cell in the Fallopian tube. One of these sperm cells may get inside the egg, fertilizing it.

The fertilized egg then travels the rest of the way down the tube and attaches itself to the lining of the uterus -- and pregnancy begins. If the egg is not fertilized, it falls apart in the Fallopian tube.

*The egg is released about 14 days before the next period is due, if the periods are regular. If a girl's periods are not regular, the egg may be released at a different time of the month. This also can vary from month to month. Some girls may release more than one egg during a month.

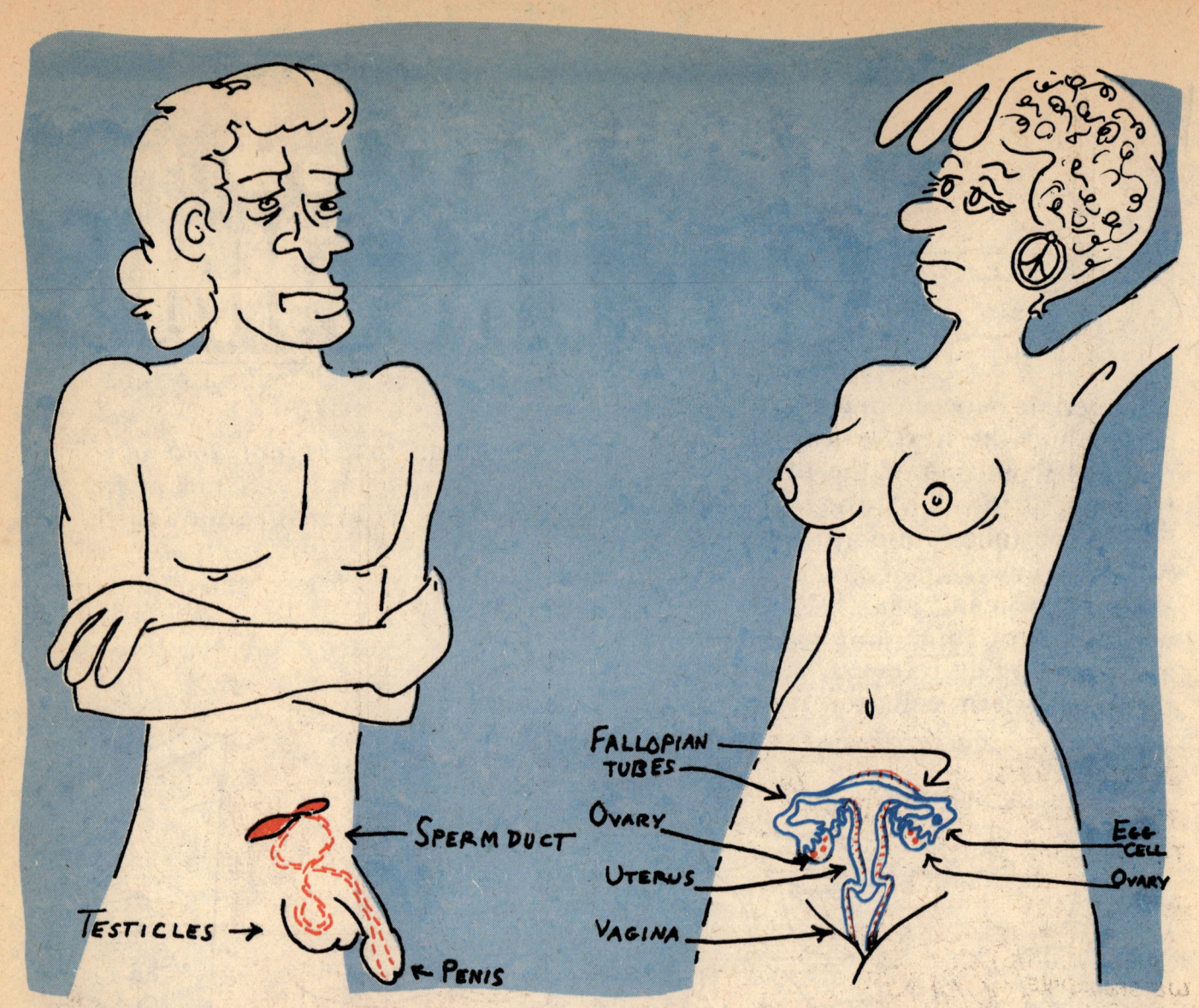

HOW CONTRACEPTION WORKS

The ways to prevent pregnancy while having sex are known as contraception (birth control). The best contraception works in one of these ways:

• The sperm can be blocked from reaching the egg cell if the boy correctly wears a condom (rubber) on his penis during intercourse, or if the girl has been properly fitted by a doctor with a diaphragm.

• Contraceptive creams, foams and jellies destroy the sperm cells before they can reach the egg.

• The Pill stops the egg from developing. No egg is released into the Fallopian tube where a sperm cell can fertilize it.

• Many scientists think that the IUD, a small device placed inside the uterus (womb), prevents the fertilized egg from attaching itself to the wall of the uterus. The experts aren't sure about this, but they do know that the device works very well in preventing pregnancy.

WHAT DOES NOT STOP PREGNANCY

Douching (washing out the vagina) after intercourse -- no matter with what -- doesn't work to prevent pregnancy, because it is already too late. The male sperm cells don't take long to get from the vagina to the Fallopian tubes. Douching before intercourse doesn't prevent pregnancy either.

Feminine hygiene sprays and suppositories -- like Norforms, Pristeen, Vespray, Feminique -- are mainly deodorants. *They are not contraceptives.* (And, since the vagina cleans itself naturally, they are not necessary for cleanliness.)

Anything that is *not sold as a contraceptive* (such as Saran Wrap, Coca-Cola, balloons) *is not* a birth control. Some kids are good at telling dumb stories about how to avoid pregnancy. Believe them and, if you are having sex, you risk becoming a parent.

I KNOW 'IT'S THE REAL THING, WHAT YER HOPIN' TO FIND,' AND ALL. BUT I STILL THINK WE SHOULD'VE USED SOMETHING ELSE.

SLURP SLURP

TASTE ME! TASTE ME!

IT'S WHAT'S UP FRONT THAT COUNTS

DORA

WINS

'RHYTHM' AND 'PULLING OUT'

- *Pulling out* (withdrawal). Don't trust it. Even if the male can control himself and stop himself from coming inside the girl, some of the sperm cells can leak out, before he comes, and fertilize the egg. Even if the male releases his sperm outside the vagina, it is still possible for her to get pregnant. If the sperm gets into the moisture around her vagina, they can swim right on up.

- *Rhythm.* The rhythm method is based on the idea that the woman can have sex except around that time when, supposedly, the egg is released. The old way of figuring when the egg will be released isn't much good, but there is a new, more accurate method that has worked very well in other countries. People who, for religious reasons, don't want to use ordinary birth control methods can get more information from Responsible Parenthood, 349 Cedar St., San Diego, Calif. 92101.

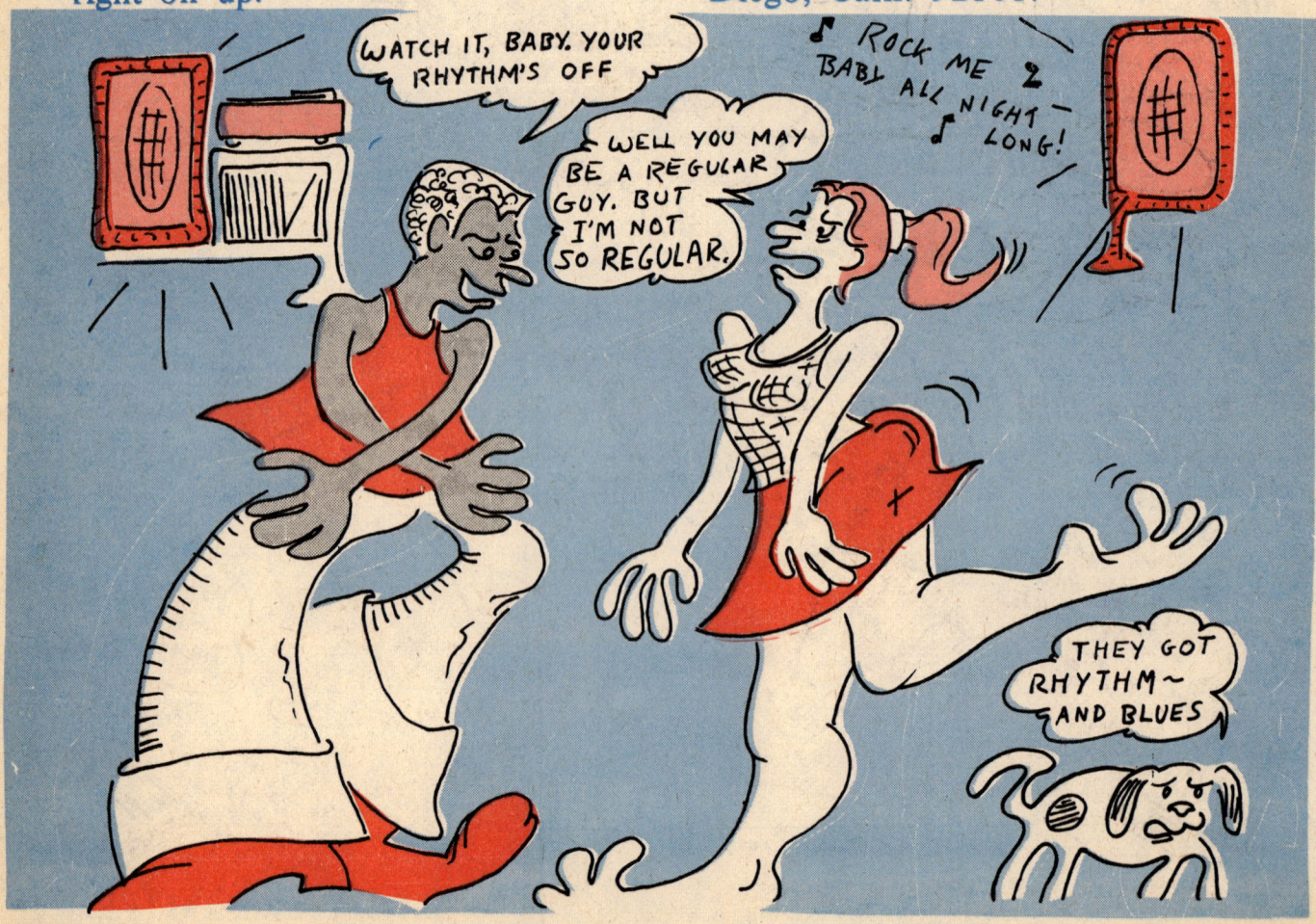

THE PILL

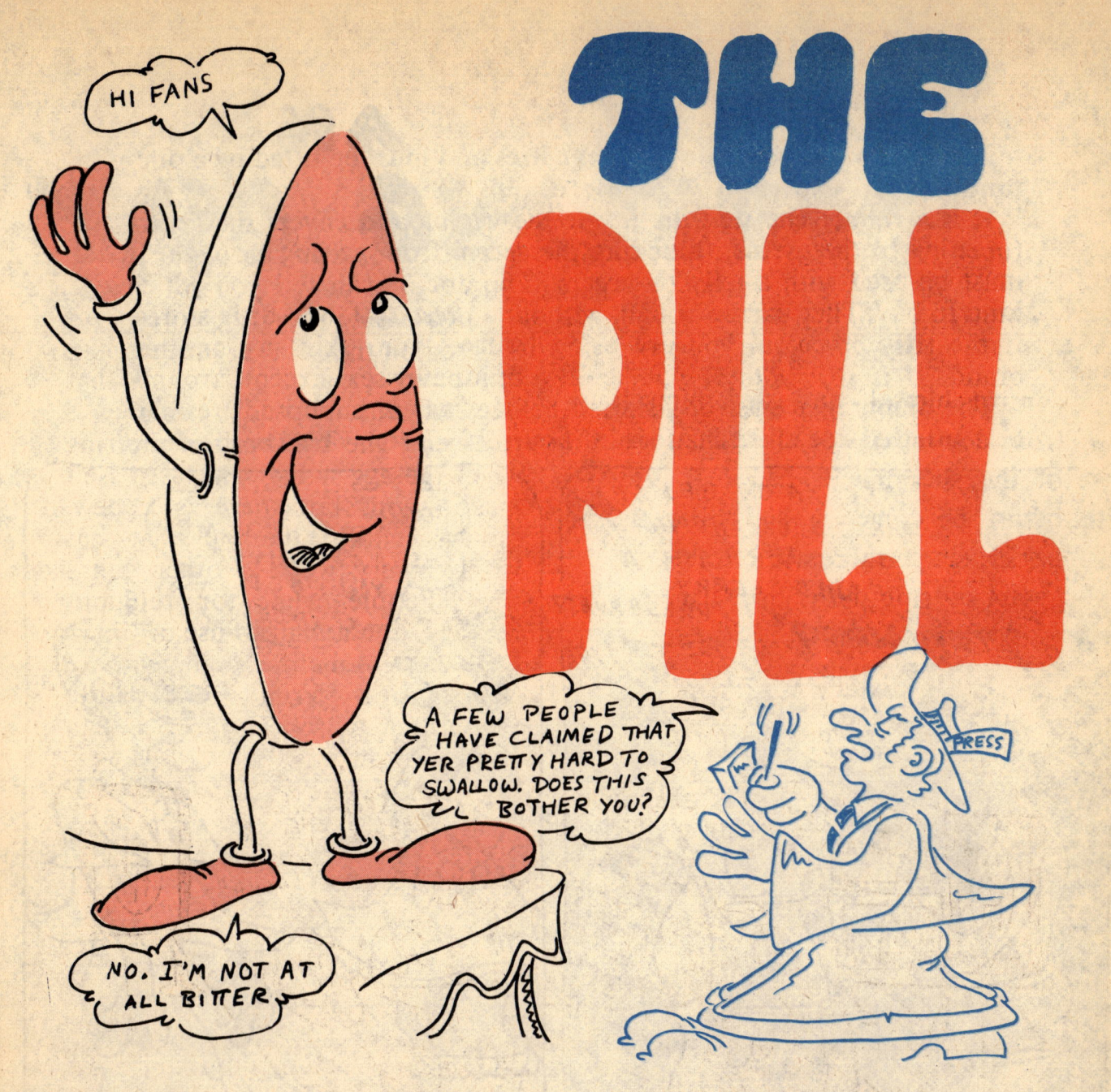

HI FANS

A FEW PEOPLE HAVE CLAIMED THAT YER PRETTY HARD TO SWALLOW. DOES THIS BOTHER YOU?

NO. I'M NOT AT ALL BITTER

In general, if a girl has been menstruating for a year, the Pill is one possible method for her. The doctor will help her decide which type of pregnancy prevention is best. Some girls, for medical reasons, should not use the Pill.

There are different types of contraceptive pills and one kind of pill might affect your body differently than another kind. That's why you should not use someone else's pills. The doctor will know which kind of pill is right for you and will go over the instructions with you.

A girl can get contraceptive pills from her own doctor, a Planned Parenthood Center, or a family planning clinic.

Taking one or two pills a month is no help. You must use your pills as directed. If you forget to take a pill, you should call your doctor.

Remember, despite anything you may have heard about the Pill: more women have medical problems as a result of childbirth than as a result of the Pill.

THE DIAPHRAGM

The diaphragm comes in different sizes and must be fitted by a doctor who will explain how to use it.

It is a rubber cup that fits inside the vagina and covers the cervix (opening to the uterus), blocking the sperm from getting through. It must be used with a jelly or cream. The doctor can tell you which kind to buy. They can be bought without a prescription in drug stores. If the jelly or cream you are using irritates your skin, try another brand. If it still bothers you, call your doctor.

The diaphragm must be inserted before sex. The jelly or cream is best inserted not more than a half hour before sex. This can be done with a special applicator if the diaphragm has already been inserted. Cream and jelly lose their effectiveness about one hour after insertion.

If you do not have sex within a half hour after the cream or jelly has been inserted, or if you have sex again after that time, you must apply it again. The diaphragm must be left inside the vagina for at least six hours after intercourse.

The diaphragm does not hurt. If it is properly inserted, you can't even feel it when it is inside. And neither can your partner. It does not lessen sexual pleasure.

'COIL,' 'LOOP,' 'SHIELD'

MINNIE, I DON'T THINK THIS IS WHAT THE DOCTOR HAD IN MIND WHEN HE SAID YOU MIGHT WANT TO TRY A COIL.

WHEEE...!

BOING

BOING

THE IUD
(INTRA~UTERINE DEVICE)

"Loop," "coil," "shield" are the names of some kinds of IUD. A doctor places this small device (it is usually made of soft plastic) inside the uterus. The doctor can easily remove it any time you like.

Your menstrual periods may be heavier, last longer and be closer together for the first few months (and sometimes longer) after you start using it.

The IUD does not lessen sexual pleasure. You cannot feel it once it is inserted.

GOOD, EASY-TO-GET PROTECTION

A lot of teenagers find it hard to get the Pill, diaphragm or IUD. In this case, the best bet is for the boy to use a rubber and the girl to use foam. When used together, chances of pregnancy are much less than if only one is used.

Rubbers and foam can be bought without a prescription in drug stores. Also, some Planned Parenthood Centers, health departments and street clinics give them out.

If you are embarrassed about asking for contraceptives, go to a drug store where you are not known. You might even want to wait to be served by a clerk of your own sex. Most clerks are used to people who feel uncomfortable about this and will know how to serve you.

When buying rubbers, you might ask for a brand name, such as Trojan, Ramses or Sheik. Ask for a pack of three, six or twelve (lubricated or regular). They cost around $1.00 for three.

DIG, I ER I MEAN, HEH, YOU KNOW MAN, ULP UH, I UH, I'D LIKE A... UH... ...SPONGE?

A FOAM, RUBBER SPONGE?

"HOLD THE FOAM ALREADY!"

FOAM

How to Apply Foam

1. You push the applicator down against the nozzle of the can until the applicator is filled with foam.

2. You put the applicator into the vagina (like you would insert a tampon), and then push the plunger, which squeezes the foam out and into the vagina.

Delfen and Emko are two names of contraceptive foams.

Foam doesn't last long. If you don't have intercourse within a half hour after you've put it into the vagina, you must apply it again. You use one shot of foam before each act of intercourse.

You can get pre-filled applicators, good for one shot, to carry in your purse. One kind is Conceptrol, which costs about $2.50 for a pack of six. Emko Pre-fil has an applicator which may be pre-filled and stored for up to seven days so it is ready for immediate use.

BAGS (RUBBERS)

Rubbers are also known as condoms, bags, safes, Trojans, skins, prophylactics.

Rubbers are not only useful in preventing pregnancy, but they are also very effective in blocking V.D. (venereal disease) germs from passing from one partner to another - although not 100 per cent of the time.

The man protects himself from catching V.D. (such as syphilis and gonorrhea), from his partner and he protects his partner from catching it from him. (You can't always tell if you have V.D. and you can hardly ever tell if someone else has it.) Boys usually know they have V.D., but not girls.

Some guys try to get away without using a rubber, saying that it is too expensive or that they get no feeling when using it. Neither is true. If the girl is not using a contraceptive, she should insist that her partner use a rubber. Even if the girl is using a contraceptive, the boy should use a rubber for protection against V.D. unless they are very sure of each other.

Would you like to come up to my place and see my collection of old bags?

Protect your lover, wear a rubber.

Bag it, Sheik, bag it.

Use a rubber only once.

HOW TO USE A RUBBER

Before Intercourse

Pull the condom over the head of the erect penis (hard on). Leave a 1/2 inch space at the end. (Some condoms already come prepared with this space.)

Slowly unroll the condom until the entire penis has been covered.

After Intercourse

Slowly withdraw the penis, holding the end of the condom with the hand to prevent its sliding off.

PREGNANT?

If you do miss a period and fear that you may be pregnant, go to your doctor for a pregnancy test. If you are pregnant, the pregnancy test will show up positive 14 days after the first expected day of your last missed period or 42 days after the first day of your last actual period.

At any rate, the longer you wait, the more upset you will feel. The longer you wait, the less choice you may have about what to do.

If you find that you're pregnant, you might want the help of trained counselors at places like Planned Parenthood and family planning clinics. If you need financial help, they may be able to send you to a place where you can get it. Once you've decided what to do about your pregnancy, they will be able to tell you where to go. For instance, if you decide that you want to have the baby, they might refer you to an agency or special school program that works with pregnant teenage girls.

If you do find that you've somehow had sex without good protection, go to your doctor or a family planning clinic within 48 hours after intercourse. You may be able to get a "morning after pill" which would prevent pregnancy. (Caution: Many doctors are reluctant to use it because no one is sure how safe it is.) Or, you may be able to arrange for an abortion.

> BUT RANDY, THE CLINIC WON'T GIVE ME A MORNING-AFTER PILL FOR YOUR HANGOVER

> Blaah... ALL NIGHT I ROLLED IN THIS SHEET... I WAS JUST COVERED WITH SHEET..

CHECK YOUR HEALTH

BIG OBS BOOK BIBS BOOB SUD CUK AD!

"THERE'S NOTHIN' WRONG WITH YOUR HEALTH, WOMAN!"

"I JUST LOVE DOCTORS (PANT! PANT!)"

If you are sexually active, you should watch out for V.D. If you think you might have V.D., tell your doctor or go to a local health department clinic. Don't let embarrassment get in the way of your cure. If V.D. is not treated, it can cripple mind and body and sometimes cause sudden deaths. But if the disease is found early, the cure is usually quick, easy and complete. Besides, in almost all states, teenagers can be seen and treated without their parents' knowledge or consent.

It is very important for young women to see a doctor at least once a year for a Pap smear (a test for cancer of the cervix), a breast exam, and a blood pressure count. A girl with high blood pressure, for example, should not use the Pill.

WHERE TO GO FOR INFORMATION AND SERVICES

I DON'T THINK YOU'LL FIND IT UNDER 'KNOCKED UP.'

It is difficult in a lot of places for young people to get the information and services they need. The best place to try first is Planned Parenthood or a hospital or health department family planning clinic. In most cities they have an office you can call. If they can't serve you, they will tell you who can. Other places to contact are a hot line, crisis center, street clinic, free clinic or women's center.

PROTECT YOURSELF

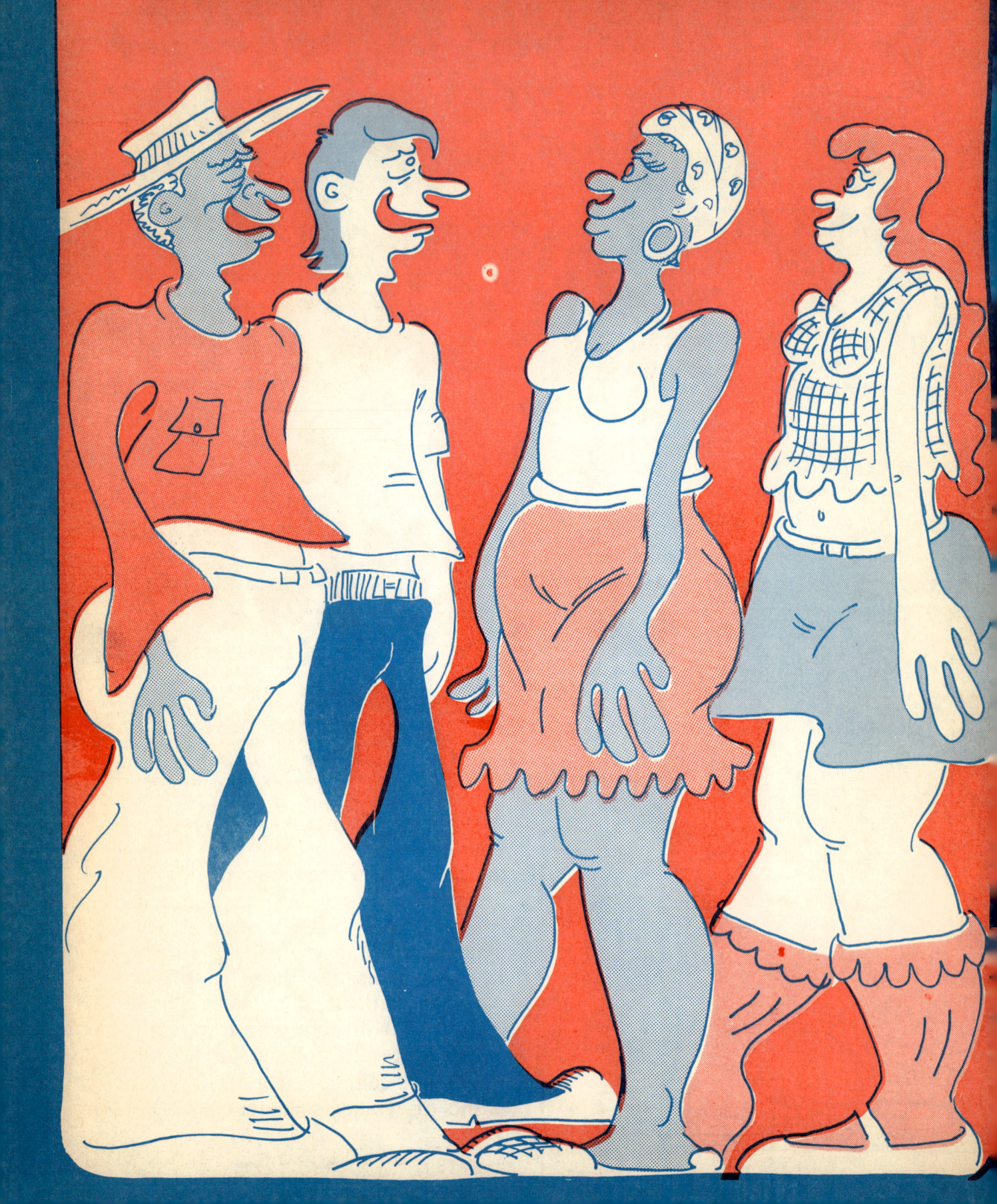

Wing Comix

"DO YOU THINK WE SHOULD JOKE ABOUT SUCH A SICK SUBJECT?"

"WELL, A SICK JOKE BEATS A GROSS DOSE"

"I ONCE KNEW A JOKE SO SICK, IT DIED LAUGHING"

VD CLAPTRAP

New, Improved Edition!
Grosser Than Ever!
The Naked Facts!

When to see a doctor: Page 15

ARE YOU SURE?

There were at least 3 million new cases of VD in 1974. About 95 per cent of these people caught gonorrhea.

Two-thirds of the victims were under 25 years old. The biggest jump in reported cases of VD is among the 11-to 15-year-olds.

Some people don't worry much about VD because they know that a doctor can usually cure it easily. But these are often the same people that don't even know when they have VD.

Untreated, VD can cause all sorts of damage. For example, did you know that gonorrhea is the biggest cause of sterility among men and infertility among women?

Now that you know what you risk by not knowing, can you risk not knowing?

Text: Sol Gordon and Roger Conant
Facilitator: Kathleen G. Everly
Distribution: Del Cusmano
Illustration and design: Roger Conant

Published by Ed-U Press, 760 Ostrom Ave., Syracuse, N.Y. 13210
Ed-U Press is the publishing arm of
Syracuse University's
Institute for Family Research and Education

Other titles in this series of educational comic books include: *Ten Heavy Facts About Sex, Protect Yourself From Becoming an Unwanted Parent, Gut News for Modern Eaters, Juice Use - Special Hangover Edition* and *What Do You Do When You're All Drug Doubt?* Single copies of *VD Claptrap* or any other title are 30 cents each. Bulk rates are available on request.

NEW, COMPLETELY REVISED
Revised January 1975
© 1971, 1975 by Ed-U Press

Has any man ever died from an unsatisfied erection?

HOW YOU CATCH VD

Venereal diseases (VD) spread through sexual contact.

The two most dangerous diseases of this kind are gonorrhea and syphilis. These are two different diseases.

Both gonorrhea and syphilis germs live in warm, moist places -- such as the penis or vagina, the rectum, and the mouth. These germs travel from one person's genitals (or rectum or mouth) after direct contact with someone else's genitals (or rectum or mouth). This could mean a man and woman, two women, or two men.

HOLD STILL YOU LITTLE BUGGERS!

③ You may have heard that you can get VD from toilet seats. However, both syphilis and gonorrhea germs almost always die very soon if they are outside the human body. In other words, people hardly ever catch VD from toilet seats.

If you didn't already know: Whether or not you have pleasurable feelings during the sex act has nothing to do with whether you catch VD.

The gonorrhea germ is very catching. In fact, the common cold is the only disease more catching than the clap.

Gonorrhea usually shows up in men two to six days after sexual contact with the person who has it, although it sometimes doesn't show up for a month or more.

The first sign is usually pus dripping from the penis or a burning feeling while urinating. However, about 10 per cent of the men who get the clap show no signs at all. Just the same, the disease is spreading through their bodies and anyone who has sex with them is likely to catch gonorrhea.

The CLAP

VENUS FLY TRAP

"HOLY COW, THAT WAS HAIRY"

VENUS OR BUST!

"I GUESS THAT'S WHAT HAPPENS WHEN YOU GET TOO CLOSE WITHOUT GOOD SAFETY EQUIPMENT"

"CAN YOU BELIEVE THIS CLAP?"

Signs of gonorrhea disappear after awhile. This DOES NOT mean that the disease has gone away.

4

In women there may be a slight discharge from the vagina with a burning feeling. However, most of the time there are no signs at all. A woman may not realize something is wrong for weeks or months, or even years, after she was infected.

Early in the disease, doctors often can't tell whether a woman is infected.

Tests for gonorrhea have been improved in recent years, but they still aren't 100 per cent reliable. For this reason, many doctors will go ahead and treat a woman if they even suspect that there's a chance she has gonorrhea.

If left untreated, the clap can cause sterility, arthritis, heart trouble and general bad health.

GONORRHEA

HE'S LIABLE TO GET A STRAIN LIKE THAT!

WHAT A JOB -SHEESE!

YE OLE CLAPTRAP

MAYBE HERNIA - NOT GONORRHEA

IT IS A LOT OF CLAP ALL RIGHT

LOOKOUT! A FLYING BOTTLE OF KETCHUP!

You can catch gonorrhea as many times as you have sex with someone who is infected.

SIFF

The first sign of syphilis is usually a sore, which is called a chancre (pronounced shanker). In men it usually appears on the penis; in women it usually occurs inside the vagina.

The chancre, which at first may look like a pimple or wart, soon becomes larger. It doesn't ordinarily hurt or itch. Women usually don't notice it.

If sex contact has been in the mouth or rectum, a sore may develop there.

However, it is possible for the chancre to show up in various parts of the body. It's also possible it won't show up at all.

The chancre will generally appear -- if it's going to -- somewhere between 10 and 90 days after sex contact with a person who has syphilis.

Syphilis left untreated can really ruin your body while you don't even know it.

- The sore goes away in a few weeks. That doesn't mean you are cured.
- You can catch syphilis as many times as you have sex with someone who has it; and you can have syphilis and gonorrhea at the same time.

HERPES VIRUS
(pronounced: her-pees)

Herpes genitalis is a virus that is usually passed during the sex act. In recent years it has become more and more common -- especially among women.

Groups of painful blisters appear on the sex organs or other areas of sexual contact, but they may also show up on the thighs, buttocks and pubic area. They soon break open and ooze yellow-grey pus. These open sores are big targets for more infection.

Between seven and 28 days after showing up, the blisters go away, but the disease may not go away. You can have relapses for years.

Women who have had this disease are strongly advised to get a Pap smear every six months for the rest of their lives, because a woman's chances of getting cancer of the cervix are higher after she's had herpes.

N G U

NGU is an infection of the urinary tract which doctors don't know much about. NGU is short for Non-Gonoccal Urethritis which just means that whatever it is, it isn't gonorrhea.

Doctors are not agreed as to whether this disease (also called non-specific urethritis or NSU) is found only in males. Sometimes NGU seems to be triggered after sexual contact. Other times it shows up after a person has been cured of gonorrhea. (However, it is worse to have gonorrhea than NGU.)

In males, signs of NGU are similar to gonorrhea. Some men have a thin, clear (or cloudy) drip that they never can seem to shake out. Mild to moderate pain may come with urination. Sometimes urination will occur without the man being aware of it.

Men with these signs should waste no time getting to a doctor. For one thing, the infection might spread to the prostate gland, and prostate infections can be very hard to cure. For another thing, it may not be NGU -- it may be gonorrhea.

TRICH...

Trichomonas vaginalis is a disease that inflames the vagina. "Trich" germs may be passed during sexual contact or, occasionally, they may be picked up from toilet seats, towels and the like.

Although trich is considered to be a woman's disease, a man can carry the germs and he may get signs of NGU after intercourse with a woman who has trich.

Signs of trich include redness and itchiness of the vagina, and a smelly, thick discharge which looks like cottage cheese and which may be streaked with blood.

These signs often go away by themselves, but the disease can still be there. Trichomonas is not considered serious if it is treated promptly, but if it isn't cured it could lead to trouble.

Before going to the doctor, don't douche; you may make it difficult for the physician to see what the problem is.

OTHER GENITAL PROBLEMS

Other vaginal disorders

Vaginitis means any noticeable infection of the vagina. Sometimes when doctors don't know what is causing the infection, they call it non-specific vaginitis (NSV). As with NGU in men, NSV in women most often shows up in sexually active females.

Another kind of vaginitis is known as candida albicans, which is a yeast-like fungus. It is not usually transmitted sexually.

You should seek treatment to be sure it isn't gonorrhea and also to stop the infection from traveling up into places like your fallopian tubes.

Crabs

Crab lice are tiny animals that make their home -- by the hundreds -- in the pubic hair (though they travel to other regions). Ordinary soap won't get rid of them. Kwell, available over-the-counter, will do the job. You don't need to shave the infested area. You can pick up crabs many ways, but sexual contact is the most common way.

Venereal warts.

There are various kinds of harmless warts that can appear on the sex organs after sex contact or other close physical contact. Perhaps the most important thing about these warts is that they may not be just warts.

PREVENTION...

Rubbers (bags, condoms, safes, skins, Trojans, prophylactics) are available without a prescription in drugstores. They are very effective in blocking V.D. germs from traveling from one partner to another - although they are not 100 per cent safe. The man protects himself from catching it from his partner and he protects his partner from catching it from him.

You can also buy a pro-kit in a drugstore. A pro-kit contains a rubber, as well as ointment which you must apply immediately after intercourse for it to be of any use. This ointment helps to kill V.D. germs before they start spreading, although it doesn't always work.

It is very helpful to wash with soap and hot water and to urinate immediately after sex - although it is still possible to get infected. Girls may douche (wash out the vagina). However, a girl who is using birth control foam, cream, jelly, or a diaphragm with cream should not douche until six hours after sex, so that the birth control can work.

Of course, the best prevention is not to have sex with someone who might be infected. People who have many sex partners are the ones most likely to catch and spread V.D.

ABOUT RUBBERS

A rubber can cost anywhere from 25 cents to $1.00. Some health clinics and Planned Parenthood Centers give out rubbers free. However, in some states there are laws which do not permit minors to buy rubbers, although this is rarely enforced if you look old enough. Even so, we think that teenagers who are having sex should make every effort to get and use rubbers, not only for protection against V.D., but for pregnancy prevention as well.

Girls should not fall for lines boys use, such as "rubbers are too expensive" or "there is no 'feeling' with it." Today's smart woman won't allow a man in without a rubber, unless she's very sure of him. This goes for women on the pill, too. *The Pill does not prevent V.D.*

How to Use a Rubber

Before Intercourse

Pull the condom over the head of the erect penis (hard on). Leave a 1/2 inch space at the end. (Some condoms already come prepared with this space.)

Slowly unroll until entire penis has been covered.

After Intercourse

Slowly withdraw the penis, holding the end of the condom with the hand to prevent its sliding off.

Use a rubber only once

protect your lover, wear a rubber

PROTECT YOURSELF

Almost all doctors (private or in clinics) want to treat and cure you, but you may run into a doctor or a nurse from the "old school" who treats you as if you should be punished. There are things you can do. If anyone starts giving you a hard time, humor him or her by agreeing with everything said. Be extra polite. Don't let someone else's meanness stand in the way of your cure.

AND OTHERS

Private doctors treat most of the venereal disease cases, but they report only about 20 per cent to public health authorities. This means that many of the V.D. cases are not traced for other possible victims.

If you go to a private doctor and find out that you have V.D., it may be left up to you to tell anyone you've had sex with. If it is left up to you, protect your friends.

> Operation Venus is a toll-free VD hotline. Between 9 a.m. and 9 p.m. call: (800) 523-1885.

we're all outa our minds around here anyway

IT'S BEEN ON MY MIND LATELY

THAT'S WEIRD. IT USUALLY DOESN'T HIT PEOPLE THERE

IF YOU SUSPECT YOU HAVE IT...

If you think you might have V.D., go to your local health center, city venereal disease clinic, or your doctor immediately. The longer you wait, the more damage the disease may be doing. Teenagers in almost all states can be treated without parental knowledge or consent. By law, government health clinics cannot reveal your name when they contact the people you've had sex with.

Venereal disease centers test people for V.D. without charge. If they find that you have V.D., they will provide free treatment (usually penicillin therapy) and contact the people you've had sex with.

Do not try to treat yourself. Treating sores with an ointment containing penicillin only kills the top layers of the germ and leaves the germs underneath alive and spreading.

WHEN TO SEE A DOCTOR

Since the signs of VD often don't appear, women and men who are sexually active should go for VD testing regularly.

If you have any of the following signs, you should go to a doctor immediately.

I REALLY THINK YOU OUGHT TO HAVE SOMETHING DONE ABOUT THAT TRICK KNEE

Men

- Burning during and shortly after urinating.
- Any sores, warts or pimples on the penis or around it or in any other area of sexual contact.
- Any soreness of the penis.
- Any drip from the penis.
- Any unusual coloring of the urine, such as urine which is reddish or very dark.

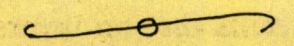

Don't give a dose to the one you love the most.

Women

- Burning while urinating.
- Pain or itchiness in and around the vagina.
- Any soreness or redness in and around the sex organ and anus.
- Any sores, warts or pimples in and near the sex organ or other areas of sexual contact.
- A discharge that is yellow, green, or otherwise discolored. (A normal discharge is usually clear or milky.)
- A thick discharge that looks like cottage cheese.

AFTER THE DOCTOR TREATS YOU

If caught in the early stages, gonorrhea and syphilis can often (but not always) be cured in less than ten days. During this time you should
- Avoid having sex with others until you are cured.
- Avoid masturbating. It can spread the germs to other parts of the body. (Of course, at other times masturbation is both pleasurable and harmless.)
- Not drink any form of alcohol. The alcohol may affect the medicine needed to cure you of VD.
- Tell the people you've had sex with, so they can get treatment.

THANX FER DA SHOT, DOC

MY TREAT

gimme a funky chicken, man

SLIM JIM, MD

Important

The cure for VD is not always automatic. This means that after a doctor has treated you, you should have another test a few months later to make sure you were cured.

SOME FUNNY LINES

Here are some lines kids use. Don't be fooled. Protect yourself.
- I may be poor and screw a lot, but I'm clean.
- Don't worry, you can only get V.D. from a whore.
- Don't worry, I'll pull out before I shoot.
- If you don't want me to shoot, I won't.
- Just for a little while, it takes me a long time before I shoot.

now this joke is what I call an anal extraction

HAHAHA

GIMME A BREAK

REMEMBER
- You can be clean, but you may still catch V.D.
- You can get V.D. from anyone who has it.
- Withdrawal before a guy comes will not prevent V.D. (It's not even a good method for birth control.)
- You can get V.D. from oral sex and intercourse.
- You can get V.D. from a person of the same or opposite sex.

REALIDAD ACERCA DE LA SÍFILIS Y LA GONORREA

- Las enfermedades venéreas son causadas por gérmenes transmitidos por el contacto sexual.
- La sífilis puede atacar cualquier parte del cuerpo, incluyendo el corazón y el cerebro.
- Si no se cuida la sífilis, puede causar esterilidad, enfermedades crónicas, ceguera, locura y aún la muerte.
- Si una mujer encinta tiene sífilis, puede transmitirla al niño que no ha nacido todavía; así éste será enfermizo, desfigurado o morirá prematuramente.
- Si no se cura la gonorrea, puede causar enfermedades generales, esterilidad, artritis, y enfermidades del corazón.
- El condon (capuchón, goma, gorrito) cuando se usa correctamente, es una buena protección.
- Orinar y lavarse con jabón y agua caliente después del acto sexual puede ayudar.
- Si Usted sabe que una persona está infectada, evite el contacto sexual con aquella persona.

- Cuidado con los primeros síntomas, que son: una llaga en el pene o la vagina para la sífilis; una secreción o sensación inflamatoria para la gonorrea. Recuerde que en la mayoría de las mujeres no hay ningún síntoma durante el primer período de la enfermedad.
- Las enfermedades venéreas se pueden curar. El remedio es facil y efectivo si se las trata pronto.
- Las clínicas locales hacen examenes gratis y dan tambien el tratamiento necesario para curarla.
- El tratamiento y la investigación de las victimas es siempre confidencial.
- La mayoría de los estados tiene leyes que permiten que los adolescentes puedan recibir tratamiento sin el permiso o el conocimiento de los padres.

BASIC FACTS ABOUT SYPHILIS and GONORRHEA

- Venereal diseases are caused by germs spread by sexual contact.
- Syphilis can attack any part of the body, including the heart and brain.
- Untreated syphilis can cause general bad health, sterility, blindness, insanity and death.
- If a pregnant woman has syphilis she can give it to her unborn baby causing it to be sick, to be deformed, or to die.
- Gonorrhea left untreated can cause general bad health, sterility, arthritis, heart trouble and other serious health problems.
- The rubber, when used right, is good protection.
- Urinating and washing with soap and hot water right after sex may help.
- If you know someone is infected, avoid sex contact with that person.
- Be aware of the first signs, such as a sore on the penis or vagina for syphilis; discharge (drip) and burning feeling for gonorrhea. Remember, though, that most women show no signs during the early stages of infection.
- V.D. can be cured. Cure is easy and effective if a doctor starts treatment soon after infection.
- Treatment and tracing of V.D. victims is confidential.
- Most states have laws which allow teenagers to be treated without parental consent or knowledge.

A DIRTY BOOK LIKE THIS MIGHT GIVE YOU IDEAS
AT LEAST IT WON'T GIVE ME THE CLAP

third of the nation's breadwinners are women. *Most* of these female-headed families are well below the poverty line.

Therefore, if you want to prevent yourself from being considered "basically passive" by apathetic school authorities, your best bet is to start organizing consciousness-raising groups (among male students too) and to push for women's real needs and views to be expressed in your high school paper.

At this time you have several advantages: Women's liberation is beginning to gain acceptance even among establishment types. There are many women, old and young, on the faculty who strongly sympathize with you, and some liberal male faculty members who might help.

Get with it.

Essential Book: *The Young Woman's Guide to Liberation,* by Karen DeCrow (Pegasus, 1971)

83

A Letter to Brad, My Son –

by Nola Claire*

Last night when you left my house I watched you walk down the porch steps, turn and take hold of the arm of your friend, helping her in the dim light. It was a gesture so "masculine" that later it made me wonder. Where did you learn that? I was watching a man, eighteen years old, protecting a capable woman of the same age who was gladly accepting this gallantry. The reverse could have happened only if you had been on crutches.

At first that combined display of gentleness and strength caused a surge of pride in me. I am still in awe of the tiny infant growing so insistently, in spite of me, because of me, into a kindred human being. That is why it took a few minutes to realize what I had just witnessed. It could have been your father and me at your age.

Even though you and I have been very open with each other, the socialization by the rest of the culture dwarfs my influence. I used to tease you and your sister when you were younger. I would say that you had better not get married, but if you did, not to let me find out. You and your spouse should take off your rings when I was coming to visit and pretend you were just living together. I was half-serious, but you would laugh.

Sometimes I think that I had no right to inflict my values on you, that children have a right to work out their own judgments. But I knew that it was impossible to come on too strong. No amount of proselytizing on my part would begin to balance the constant bombardment of messages which hold up marriage as the ideal state. So complete is this propaganda that in a recent study, emotionally and physically unhealthy married people were often reporting themselves as happy in following societal expectations. Marriage, of course, is something you will decide on for yourself, but I want you to be acutely aware of the factors which are influencing that choice.

From the time you were born, our relatives and friends and even your father and I were treating you in a way that encouraged certain behavior. I dressed you in sturdy overalls, your father tossed you in the air to squeals of laughter, you played with trucks and trains and building blocks. People remarked at what a big strong boy you were and you soon found out that crying was for sissies. Your sister occasionally would wear dresses and people would say how pretty she looked – no one ever said how strong she was.

Gradually you were learning other things. Grown-up men went away in the morning and women stayed home. I held you close and rocked you when you were tired or upset, I fed you, changed your clothes – your father played games with you.

---

*Ms. Claire is a freelance writer and an active worker for NOW.

Even though your immediate role models were traditional, I determined that at least you and your sister would have parallel play experiences as you grew. You both were given similar toys and sporting goods, engaging pretty much in the same activities. But nevertheless, round twelve, you rebuilt an engine and your sister knit herself a dress. Your activities in the neighborhood, with relatives, and in school were giving you different experiences.

The programs you watched on television showed boys and men in traditional roles. When your sister mentioned that she was going to be an astronaut soon after the first rocket to the moon, you quickly informed her that women could not be astronauts. No one had to tell you that in words; you had been seeing that for months on the TV screen. Women only waited on the ground.

We spent hours with Dr. Seuss reading those marvelously creative drawings and verse, learning to imagine, learning to read, but also learning that boys are the heroes, the adventurers. In the grade school readers you used, boys and male animals were overwhelmingly the lead characters, showing curiosity and problem-solving capabilities, while girls needed help and were confused and timid. For math problems, Johnny counted nails, and Susie, clothespins. Adult men were shown engaged in a wide variety of occupations while women were shown as housewives, and occasionally, nurses and teachers.

When you entered junior high you were segregated by sex into industrial arts for boys and home economics for girls. Most of the practical arts could be beneficial, so when you brought home a lamp that you had made, I felt that the satisfaction of making a useful product was positive. You were learning to cook and iron and sew at home as a matter of course. Two years later, your sister attempted to switch from home economics to industrial arts. It was necessary for me to appear at the school with a threatened lawsuit to facilitate this. With that degree of resistance, it became clear that more than a few manual skills were being transmitted. While sawing and planing, you were being carefully taught that the rearing of children and good grooming were appropriate concerns only for females. Your sister found out that her world considered putting a nail straight inappropriate behavior for women. Why shouldn't you and your sister feel equally at ease approaching a table saw and a sewing machine? They are both useful tools.

I want you to be able with these skills to earn a decent living, take care of your own clothes, prepare your meals, understand your car, make simple household repairs, and gain skills in activities that bring you satisfaction. You should be happy with yourself, that is, gain autonomy. Moreover, I want the same things for your sister, your friend and all the men and women in your generation. You could

---

**Meditation is not a way of life.
It is an introduction to old age.**

> **If someone you don't like that much asks you how you are, don't tell him/her the truth.**

approach each other as independent people, able to live on your own. Then, the major decisions in your lives (career choice, if and when to marry or have children) would not be influenced by an arbitrary limitation or a helpless dependence on having others perform services for you.

Besides specific skills you have a right to a full range of human emotions. You should be able to admit ignorance, express grief and joy, show fear without getting ridiculed. In your stride without any self-doubt you should be passive or resourceful, powerful or weak in turn. You are not a super person but neither are you an invalid. The people around you are not, either. If dependence in a woman turns you on, you should examine why. Through magazines and movies, women are being trained to be attracted by half-people – aggressive men (John Wayne), passive women (Playboy foldouts). All people can be assertive and gentle. We must all be aware of what determines the feelings we have. Get in touch with your gentleness, practice tenderness, work and play with little children. "Masculine" and "feminine" are constructs that are determined by the culture. In other words, define yourself.

Brad, I appreciate how difficult it has been at times for you. For many years you have heard me say things that were contrary to what our community believes. Most people will never experience their mothers taking unpopular stands on television and in the papers. But think of what it would be like to be living in a world where all the heads of state were women, where our President and most of the members of Congress were women, where almost all doctors, engineers and lawyers, and all pilots, were women; all cowpokes . . . and even God was a woman. Try to imagine how difficult it would be to aspire to become something. What if your parents, guidance counselors, friends, all said that you will settle down to raise children anyway and if you do not, you will be very sorry someday. Then, in spite of all those odds, you get a job and work very hard, but you never get promoted and you are paid less than your female co-workers. How would you feel when people say that you are not capable even though you know you are?

So you would get married, and because you do not have a good job, you take care of the children for their early years. You do not earn wages even though you know it is vitally important work and you are good at it. When you decide to get some training so you will not have to go back to that unskilled job, your world falls apart. Family, community, strangers, all stand in your way.

I hope you will understand why I cannot make the best of things – why I have to risk everything to spend my life trying to change the world I find so uncomfortable. If you had been born a girl, would you be in the women's liveration movement with your sister and me?

Why We Oppose Votes for Men

by Alice Duer Miller,* 1915

I

Because man's place is in the Army.

II

Because no really manly man wants to settle any question otherwise than by fighting about it.

III

Because if men should adopt peaceable methods women will no longer look up to them.

IV

Because men will lose their charm if they step out of their natural sphere and interest themselves in other matters than feats of arms, uniforms and drums.

V

Because men are too emotional to vote. Their conduct at baseball games and political conventions shows this, while their innate tendency to appeal to force renders them particularly unfit for the task of government.

---

*Alice Duer Miller, novelist and poet, lived from 1874 to 1942

ZION'S HERALD.

PUBLISHED BY SOLOMON SIAS, FOR THE NEW-ENGLAND AND MAINE CONFERENCES OF THE METHODIST EPISCOPAL CHURCH.....B. BADGER, EDITOR

Vol. III.   BOSTON: WEDNESDAY, OCTOBER 5, 1825.   No. 40

LADIES' DEPARTMENT.

FEMALE VIRTUES.
Extracted from the Ladies' Literary Gazette.

Society, which requires of men, each according to what he has received, the various gifts which nature has distributed, seems to demand of *woman* a tribute nearly uniform. It is hers to be the comfort and ornament of the domestic habitation, to render herself beloved and useful, and scatter here and there the flowers of life under the feet of those who surround her. It is hers to cheer, to bless, and to console; to brighten the hours of joy, sweeten the draught of pleasure, and aid in drinking the cup of pain.—To her, the avenues of power and grandeur are shut; but she can establish an empire of affection and confidence, of which she may be herself the centre; and enthroned in the hearts of those to whom her virtues have endeared her, it is hers to dispense those inestimable gifts, which increase the happiness and diminish the pains of life.

Cast often by this duty into a tempest of cares and business, man is assailed by the passions of his nature, which find, unhappily, a thousand ways to deprave him. Trained, from his infancy, to the bustle and activity of his business, he is drawn into a whirlpool of schemes, projects, and speculations; of hopes which are destroyed and renewed without cessation; and he precipitates himself, rather than advances, towards the termination of his career, and attains, without perceiving it, the passage to a more permanent state. He consumes his life in anxiety, he calculates its years with sorrow; and demands with bitterness, "*What then, is the space which should separate childhood from dotage?*"

Devoted to occupations more peaceful, more sweet, more uniform, WOMAN can tranquilly number her days, and signalize them by a thousand acts of virtue. In truth, her virtues must be exercised in the shade, and in silence. Fame will not speak of them, nor will posterity regard them; but *hope* cherishes their remembrance, for the great day of reward. Does she not resemble those flowers, whose hues are brighter by the aid of a favorable obscurity, than when they are exposed to the rays of a burning sun? The hope of finding a diamond, may induce a man often to grovel in the dirt; but a *woman* can preserve unsullied, the border of her garment.

Finally, to love all that is worthy, useful, good, and virtuous, and to fly all that is opposed to it—*is what society demands of woman.*

LOVE OF THE BIBLE.

Susan G. a poor but respectable widow, applied some time since to one of the committee for instruction in

88

BEING REASONABLE
WITH YOURSELF

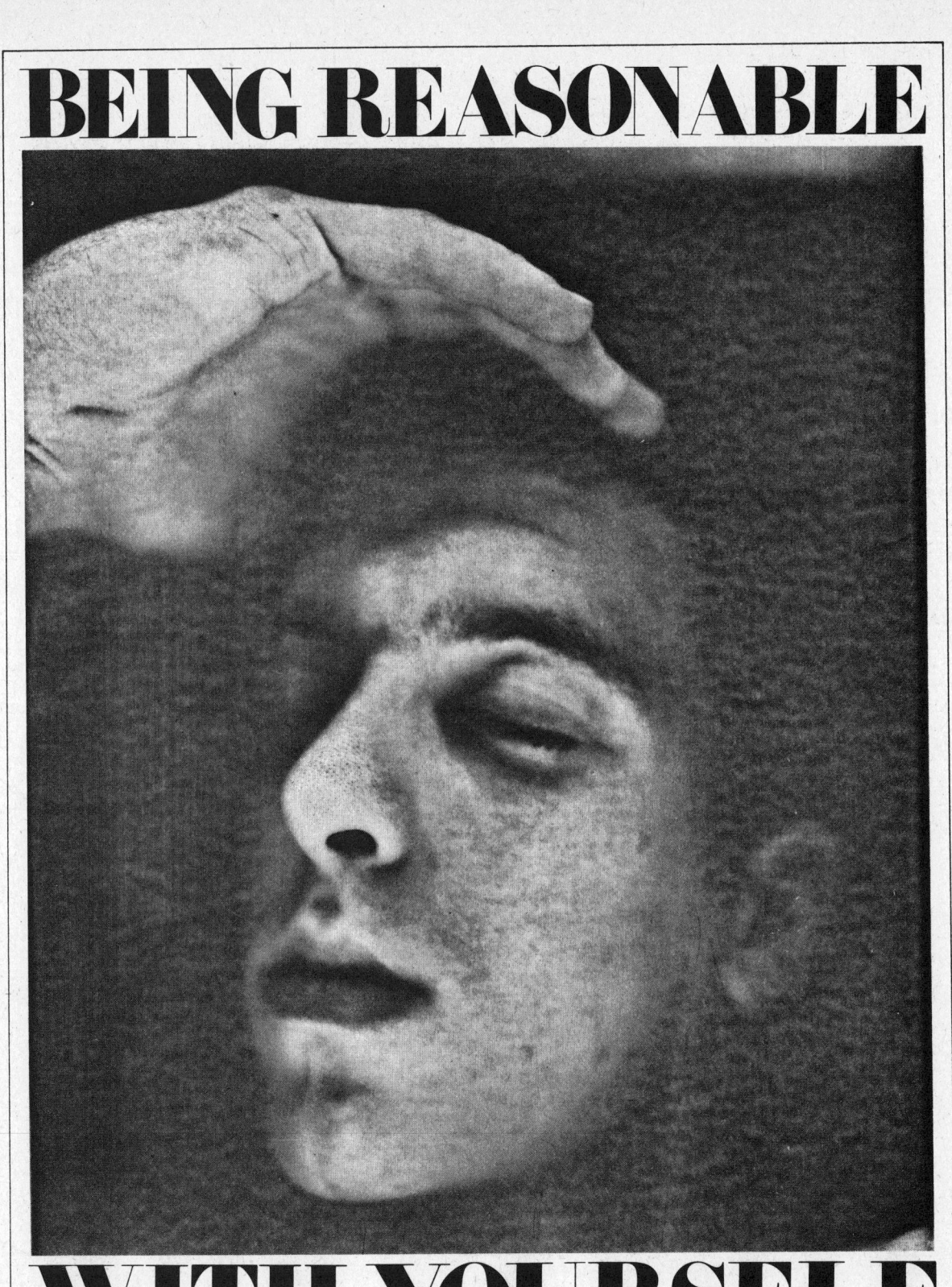

by Tom Miller

Note: I admire the work of Albert Ellis — but not everything he writes, as I do not agree with his views about religion or his rejection of the unconscious. But I believe that his rational, emotive therapy is one of the most important contributions to societal self-acceptance in our time. So I asked one of my students who admires my work (and not everything I do, either) to interpret what he feels Albert Ellis is all about. Given a few pages, it is clear that Tom can swim in Ellis' sea extremely well. If you are intrigued, follow it by reading *Guide to Rational Living*, by Ellis and Harper. (S.G.)

A very common belief is that other people can make you feel a certain way — like angry, upset, hurt or happy. But if you think about it, *you* make yourself feel almost every emotion you experience (the only exception is physical pain).

Let's say you've been anticipating the great date you have on for tonight, and your parents just said, "No dice. You're not leaving the house." You then get angry at them for not allowing you to go out. Why? Because you probably have the idea or belief, *I should get what I want, and when I don't it's terrible and awful*. This particular attitude is the reason for your low tolerance of frustration. By holding this idea, you almost guarantee that you will make yourself angry at your parents, because when something terrible and awful happens to you, you have to get very upset about it. Your self-talk goes something like this:

> **(1)** "It's awful that I can't go out tonight, I should be able to."
> **(2)** "They have no right to do this to me. They should not have said that."
> **(3)** "They are being so unfair I can't stand it."
> (I'm sure you can think of other things you would say to yourself.)

While you are angry at your parents, it is quite likely that you will say or do things which will make it harder for you to get what you want. At the very least, you will use up time and energy feeling angry and hostile.

Let's look at a different attitude: *It is not awful or terrible when I don't get what I want. It's just unfortunate. It is unrealistic for me to expect to get what I want all the time.* Starting with this idea, you will be able to rationally figure out a few more things to keep you from blowing your stack:

> **(1)** "This is one of those times I am not getting what I want."
> **(2)** "It is not terrible or awful that I can't go out tonight. It's just unfortunate. I can take it."
> **(3)** "I would prefer they had said I could go out; however they did not, and that is how it should be because that is what happened. If I want something to happen, then I had best work at fulfilling the requirements for its happening."*
> **(4)** "I can accept this, because it did happen, although I definitely do not approve of it."

*For example, if you want to go skiing, you have to have boots, bindings, skis and some snow on the ground.

If this is what you had told yourself, you would have been, at most, somewhat frustrated, irritated, annoyed, disappointed—but not raging "out of control." You could then ask yourself the question, "Is there anything I can do to approximate getting what I want?" You might be able to think of some acceptable options, such as having your date come over to your house, talking with her/him on the phone, finishing up some work so you have more time to date in the near future, or having a reasonably enjoyable evening, given the circumstances, rather than feeling miserable all night. There's no law that says you have to get jerked out of shape whenever someone else says or does something you don't like.

The beauty of realizing that your way of thinking (rather than the event itself) causes your emotions, lies in the fact that your thinking comes from inside you and that therefore you control it. If you believe "it" (the event) causes you to feel and/or behave in a certain way, then you are permitting yourself to be controlled by forces outside yourself.

Some other common faulty assumptions are:

> **(1)** "I need to be loved or approved of by almost all the important people I know, in order to feel worthwhile."
>
> **(2)** "In order to be worthwhile, I have to be thoroughly competent, adequate, and achieving in all possible respects."
>
> **(3)** "Some people are bad and they should be severely blamed and punished for their misdeeds."

Understanding the Saying

PUTTING YOURSELF DOWN

How worthwhile do you believe your "self" to be? Your rating depends on the decisions you have made about how much love and approval you ought to get, and how competent or adequate you think you are. For example, you accidentally overhear your parents talking with your teacher. All three of them are raving about how wonderful you are, and what a great job you are doing at home and school. You feel great and you think you are more worthwhile. But the opposite also works. If you overheard them saying how poorly you were doing, you might feel not only disappointed, but also less worthwhile. *You* are then putting yourself down! By *relying* on what others think of you, you *need* to do whatever it takes to please them. If I happen to know how much you need my positive affection and how terrible it is for you when you get my negative attention, then I can jerk you around like a yo-yo. You believe I can make you feel miserable or ecstatic. If I am really this powerful you had better take good care of me.

Luckily, you don't have to operate on the concept of worthiness. You can choose self-acceptance. Self-acceptance, unlike self-worth, has nothing to do with what other people think of you, or even with how you rate yourself. Under self-acceptance, you define you "self" as existing. You can't rate, measure, or evaluate it. *You just are.* Your behavior or what other people think of you does not affect this view of "self." You say, "I am", but not "I am OK" or "I am not OK" (this is self-worth talk).

You are not the same as your behavior. A distinction can be made between your behavior and your "self." For example, notice the subtle but important difference between the following statements: "Jane is a great swimmer." "Jane can swim extremely well." The first is self-worth talk, and implies Jane is the same as her behavior; the second statement places no label on her, it only describes her behavior and your rating of it. This is self-acceptance talk.

If one of your goals is to increase pleasure and decrease pain, then just accept *yourself*, and *criticize your behavior* as worthy/unworthy. These evaluations of your performance, while helpful, have nothing to do with the value of your "self," because "self" can have no value. All they mean is you behaved well or poorly. If you can follow these suggestions and if you will stop worrying so much about what other people think of you, you will be released to try to do more of what you want to do. This is the "opportunity" Sol Gordon talks about so much. Life is only a search for "meaning" when you operate on the worthwhileness continuum. Life can be a pursuit of opportunity — a process of trying — one of working at fulfilling the prerequisites for approximating your goals.

Probably the most important message I want to get across is that each of us is a *fallible human being.* YOU ARE A MISTAKE MAKER. That is, "I have a right to be human, and to be human is to make mistakes." If you are able to apply this idea not only to yourself, but to everyone, then you will not need to engage in self-blame (guilt or anxiety) or other-blame (hostility). For how could you blame anyone for behaving poorly when you already have granted them the fact that by being human they are imperfect and will make mistakes?

There do not *have to* be good people or bad people; there *can* be just people, who sometimes behave well and sometimes poorly. The next time someone asks you the question, "Who are you?" consider my answer: "I am a person, and my name is Tom. I do many things, some of them I do well and some not so well. If you want to hear some of the things I do, I'd be happy to tell you."

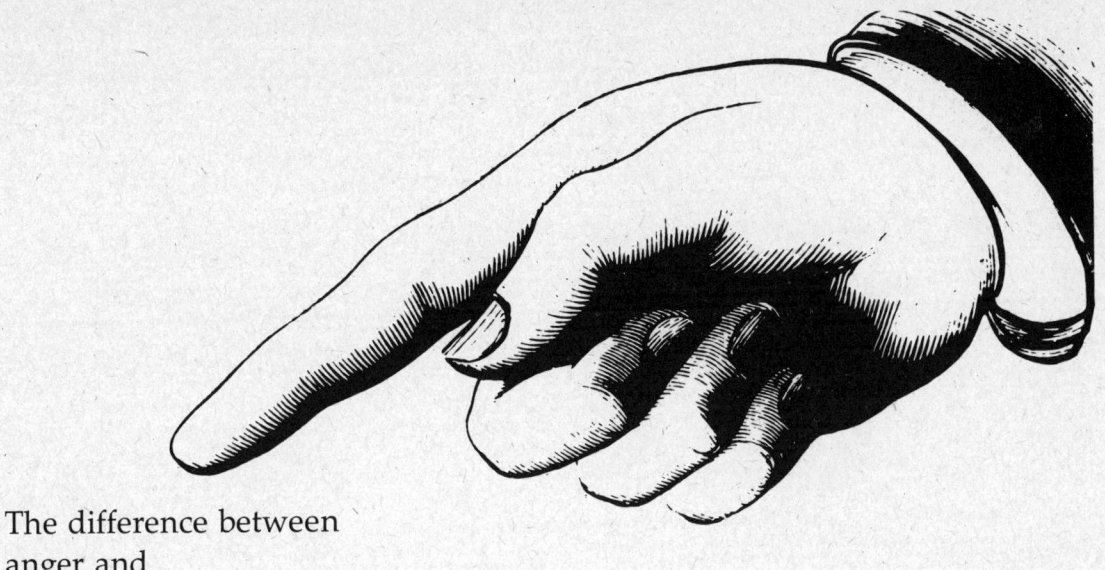

The difference between
anger and
hostility
        toward a person
you care about

   Anger is usually a mature response; not long lasting and energizing. It propels you toward the person you care about in your effort to confront or resolve the problem.

   Hostility is usually an immature response; long-lasting and exhausting. It keeps you away from the person you cared about because of your preoccupation with revenge.

   Most mature people feel angry about something every once in a while.
   They express their anger to the people involved. They try not to express it to innocent bystanders.

   Most mature people feel hostility about something every once in a while. They try to control the hostility and convert it into anger. A not very simple task when confronted by someone who *is* hostile.
   People who are generally hostile are not liked.

   It seems like a good idea to sort out whether you want the people you care about to experience your anger or your hostility.

Who was it who said:
   The most peaceful can not live in peace if it does not please an evil neighbor?

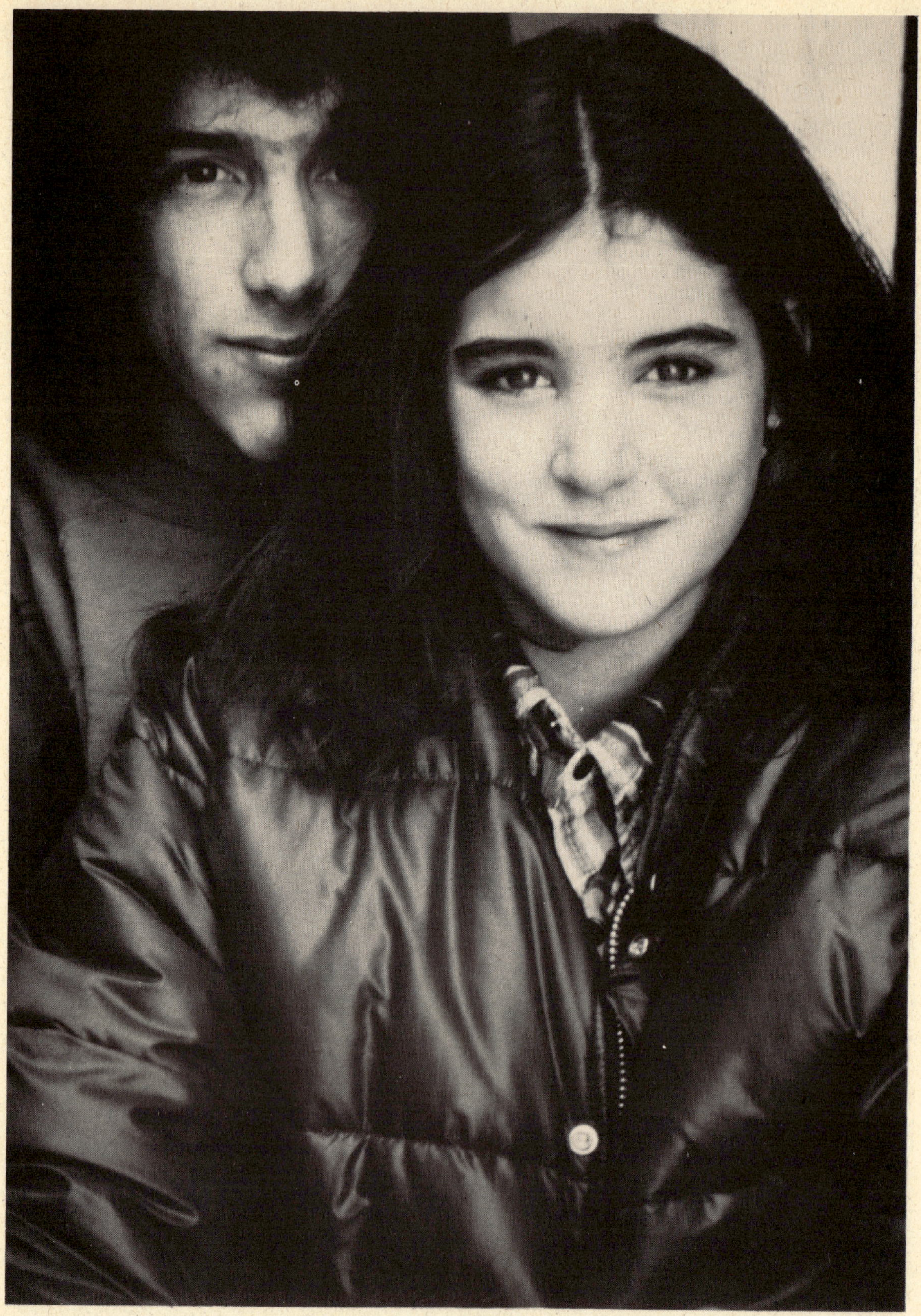

COPING WITH YOUR PARENTS

There are some kids living at home who get along with their parents; some have been able all along and some have struggled to reach this point. That's fine!

This part is for those of you who are not doing too well because you feel your parents are either:

☐ too strict ☐ too old fashioned ☐ too opinionated

☐ too prying ☐ too smart ☐ not smart enough ☐ too busy ☐ not busy enough

☐ too sarcastic ☐ smothering ☐ not understanding enough

☐ too observant (they think they know or notice everything you do)

Let's face it, all parents are old fashioned — especially those who claim that they are modern. Starting with the premise of having old fashioned parents will help you develop strategies of getting along. This is essential at some time, because kids who don't come to an understanding with their parents are haunted by them, often through their entire lives. Even though they are determined never to be like their parents, as adults they imitate their parents' worst traits. The exception to this general rule is the kid who is genuinely more mature than his/her parents. These particular kids need to free themselves from parental influence as soon as possible and eventually to learn to understand and love — if not respect — their parents.

In the final analysis everyone needs to become reasonably independent. Thus you are in a strong position to cope with parents only if you are working toward independence for yourself.

This means
    You have strong interests of your own and
    You are working toward a goal.
It could be:

- Going to college (even if you have no idea of what your major is going to be).
- Earning your own living (in a career of *your* choice, not of your parents').
- Wanting to live on a commune (even if your parents ridicule the idea).
- Planning to become an artist (even if you're expected to join the family business).

You cannot have any "claims" on your parents if your response to them is avoidance of responsibilities or if your relationship to them is hostile-dependent (meaning you can't get along with them or without them).

Here is a formula for successful coping with your parents. The odds are that what we're going to suggest *won't* work for you. (You didn't expect that, did you?) The gimmick here is that working in the right direction will eventually offer you the independence you will want *even if* your current family situation does not improve much. If you can hack our advice, your situation will improve. The problem is, of course, that you can't expect your parents to change much — but your attitudes toward them can change drastically.

Here goes . . .

The one-month politeness campaign — which can be especially effective when you want something badly (a car, a trip, more money, almost anything except permission for pre-marital sex or a motorcycle).

Make it a point to be very polite without being sarcastic.

It takes a bit of faking it.

You must be able to say at appropriate times:

- Good morning.
- Thank you.
- I appreciate your doing "it" for me.
- I'm sorry, I didn't mean to upset you.

(and, if possible, at least once a week without being asked):

" I'll be glad to take out the garbage.

I'll be glad to help clean up.

Can I get anything for you? or, Is there anything I can do for you? I have half an hour to spare.

I'll be glad to stay home with so-and-so (a younger sibling). "

Chances are your parents will flip.

You might even overhear them ask each other if they should send you to a psychiatrist.

The main thing is not to fall into any traps they set. Their response might be:

(1) You want something from us. (Your polite response: "Of course. You always said I should work for something I wanted.")

(2) Some snide remark like: "What's gotten into you?" or "Now you want to be helpful . . . where have you been all my life?" (Your response: "I haven't been very considerate before. I'm trying to change to see if being considerate will get me anywhere.")

After a month ask for what you want in this way:
"I'd like to talk to you about something, but I would appreciate it if your first response is not 'No.' "

Chances are fifty-fifty you won't get what you want — you may have to extend the campaign.

You may discover in the process that politeness makes things much easier for you, even if you didn't get what you wanted. In any case it is extremely important to know that politeness is not a method for getting closer to your parents; it is a way of establishing a distance which permits you to discover your own way. You may want to use the distance as an opportunity to get closer, but that's up to you.

☞ These are courtesies appreciated by most parents: ☜

- Make it a point (or a sacrifice) to spend a couple of hours a week with your parents. Talk to them about anything, or just watch TV with them, but be sure to talk to them during the commercials.
- Every once in a while ask a parent who works outside the home: "How are things going?" (and if s/he says "Fine" say: "I mean, I'd like to hear about your job/business.")
- Not too often — perhaps a couple of times a month — ask one or both parents for their advice about something not too crucial so you can occasionally follow their suggestions.
- Experiment with telling the truth every once in a while — but start by saying: "I worry that if I tell you the truth you'll be very upset" or "When I tell the truth, the whole thing gets blown up out of proportion."
- Clean up your room at unexpected times.
- Praise them for things they do well.

THINGS NOT TO DO:

- Don't ever announce your good intentions, such as: "I'm going to study all weekend." Instead, say, after the fact: "I was surprised at how much I accomplished."
- Don't say, "You don't understand me." No parent can handle it. Say instead: "I guess it's been difficult for me to explain myself to you" or "I feel badly that I have not been able to help you understand me."
- Don't send cards or cheap presents to your parents on birthdays, holidays,

98

etc. Instead, try to do something original like preparing a meal and cleaning up afterward; write a poem; or make something on your own.
- Don't tell your parents you're in love with someone unless you want to risk being made fun of or humiliated. If anything, understate your interest in another person.

With rare exceptions, parents don't expect much from their kids these days, so they are really quite easy to please.

    The best way to think of your parents is
(First and Foremost):
    They mean well
(Last but not Least):
    Their good intentions will not always lead you where you want to go.

ONE OF THE MOST DIFFICULT PROBLEMS
FOR SOME PEOPLE TO FACE IS THE FACT THAT
THEIR PARENTS ARE REALLY NICE PEOPLE.

For teenagers Whose Parents Are About to Be or Who Have Recently Become DIVORCED or SEPARATED

☆

Obviously, you can't — and shouldn't — eliminate all your grief and guilt, but know this:

Children are almost never responsible for the break-up of a marriage!

So stay off the heavy guilt, self-punishment trip (which is always harmful).

Stifling your feelings to please a parent usually does more harm than good. In general, the best policy is one of enlightened self-interest.

As a teenager, you have a right to make some decisions, including having some say about which parent you live with. It shouldn't be a matter of custody, but of choice. Talking these things over isn't easy, but it's important for you to struggle to have a voice in the decision-making process. Your decision should be based on your needs rather than on feeling sorry for a parent. If you are able to do this, you won't fall into the trap of "taking sides" and assigning blame (which is a bummer). In this respect, you may want to say, "I'd like to live with *you* for awhile, *but* I'd like to have the right to change my mind if, after a year or so, it doesn't work out."

If necessary, you may have to start out by saying, "I know this upsets you, but my intent is to protect myself, rather than try to please somebody..."

This idea of enlightened self-interest can also be carried over to your brothers and sisters. It might be a good idea for all of you to discuss it among yourselves and then for each of you to decide whom you would like to live with. The idea that all of you should stay together *at any cost* is foolish. Maybe yes, maybe no.

If one of your parents has died,
read the section on Death - especially
the part about guilt.

If you've spent most of your life with one parent, you should know that one in three adult Americans is currently not married to anyone. Single adults number around 43 million in this country.

100

Of course, you may have to accept certain defeats and some unpleasant limitations (such as visitation hassles). Some decisions will be beyond your control. Sometimes there is no fair and just way to settle these matters.

There are many reasons why it seems better to have a mother and a father living in the same home as you do — at least until you are eighteen. But it's better only if both parents usually get along with each other.

Remembering that it's too much of a strain not to ventilate your feelings and talk things out, you may be able to help your parent not feel sorry or deprived by suggesting something like:

> *"It's bad enough not having two parents around, why make it harder by feeling sorry for yourself – let's see how we can help each other."*

or

> *"I can't take the place of the missing parent and I don't want to.
> I want to remain your child, even if it does mean added responsibilities."*

or

Reassure your parent that you like it better without the tension that may have been an overbearing part of his/her married state.

So even if you accept that the whole thing is tragic, *the worst thing that you can do is to feel sorry for yourself.* If you go around feeling ashamed of your family's status, you'll find the pressure of covering up that shame to be enormous. For example, when someone asks you about your parents, you try to avoid discussion. It would be much better to simply say, "They're divorced (or separated)." The first few times, you may find it difficult to admit it, but what a relief it is to be able to speak freely. Don't compare your situation unfavorably with anyone else's. It's surprising how often the intact, wonderful family across the street, that you've admired and felt jealous about, falls apart without warning.

Be aware that everyone has troubles. One family has a retarded child, another has children and doesn't want them, other families can't make ends meet, while many families are not satisfied despite great affluence.

In spite of everything, most kids like their families — even though there are times when they don't. The fact that your family is not a currently conventional one should not make much difference in the long run, especially if you don't use your "orphan" status as a cop-out.

All really meaningful experiences are of brief duration (which can be repeated).

THIS PAGE IS FOR PARENTS (AND OTHER ADULTS)

Expressions guaranteed to turn off young people:

1. I want to have a serious talk with you.
2. We trust you.
3. When I was your age . . .
4. Because we say so.
5. As long as I don't know about it.
6. Act your age.
7. It's about time you (got good grades, straightened your room . . .)
8. Just a minute.
9. Ask your father/mother.
10. Are you telling me the truth?
11. That's not your idea, is it?
12. Don't you dare talk to me that way.
13. Get off your high horse.
14. Wipe that smile off your face.
15. What will the neighbors say . . . ?
16. After all we've done for you . . .

And in response to a love affair:

17. You'll get over it.
18. When you get older, you'll laugh about it yourself.
19. It's puppy love.
20. Of course you can't take out the garbage, you're in love.
21. Don't do anything I wouldn't do.
22. Where did we go wrong?

IF YOU EVER Become A Parent

Do It Right Your Time Around

Despite rumors, "scientific" research and popular "Y we R like we R" books, some psychologists like myself readily admit that we don't really know why people turn out the way they do. Too many of us have seen rotten, self-destructive kids come from what seem to us to be reasonably, if not perfectly, mature families. (Of course, the more fancy among us can always come up with some kind of unconscious or latent hostility to explain everything.) And we have seen really terrific kids emerge from rotten, self-destructive families. The plain fact is that some kids are more adequate than the families that nurtured them.

Life is complex. We don't really know how much influence parents have in contrast with brothers and sisters; nor whether stable mothers working outside the home are more effective than nervous mothers at home all the time; nor how much input comes from TV, peers, living in a materialistic society and what have you. There are a few things we seem to know, however. Children exposed to extremes, such as rejection or smother love, don't turn out very well. Children brought up in a poverty-stricken, crime-ridden neighborhood get into more trouble with the law and tend not to earn as much money when they grow up as do children brought up in the affluent suburbs.

Self-confidence and feelings of adequacy are transmitted by adults who are confident and comfortable with their impulses. But, too often, our society and culture operate in opposition to the impulse life of the child. Many mothers seem to have developed child-rearing practices based on notions inspired by popular women's magazines. Fifteen years ago we were supposed to be strict with children; ten years ago we were supposed to be permissive. Today, we don't love them enough, but are allowed to beat them occasionally. Ten years ago a schedule was all the rage; three years later we were supposed to feed permissively. Recently, it was discovered that fathers are important.

I have seen homes where the parents were strict, homes where the parents were permissive, and other homes where both parents were neurotic. In all these cases the children have been perfectly normal. But children do grow up confused, unhappy and neurotic when the mother is insecure about her role as a mother, or when there is conflict between the mother and father about the child. Parents have become confused by an overabundance of advice from magazines, from their own mothers and fathers, and from neighbors. As a result, many parents cannot respond in a spontaneous way to their own children.

One of the most dynamic results of spontaneity is the courage to accept the impulse life of the child. Let me illustrate some of the ways we might respond to children's impulses.

A child has a nightmare. S/he wakes up in terrible fear and screams for mother. The mother might say, "Oh, there's nothing to be afraid of." But the child is frightened. What we need to say to the child is, "Yes, it is very frightening to have a nightmare." Then, we must reassure him/her that s/he is loved and not alone.

Another example: Jimmy is six, his brother Johnny is four, and Jimmy doesn't like his brother. Mother says, "But you're supposed to like your brother, he *is* your brother," as though this has any meaning to the child. This mother could be saying "You don't have to like your brother, but I still don't want you to hit him."

Sandra is seven and comes home from her first day in school and says, "I don't like my teacher, she is a nut." Too often, Mother replies, "Oh, you mustn't say that!" As a matter of fact, Sandra may be right.

DEW DROPS

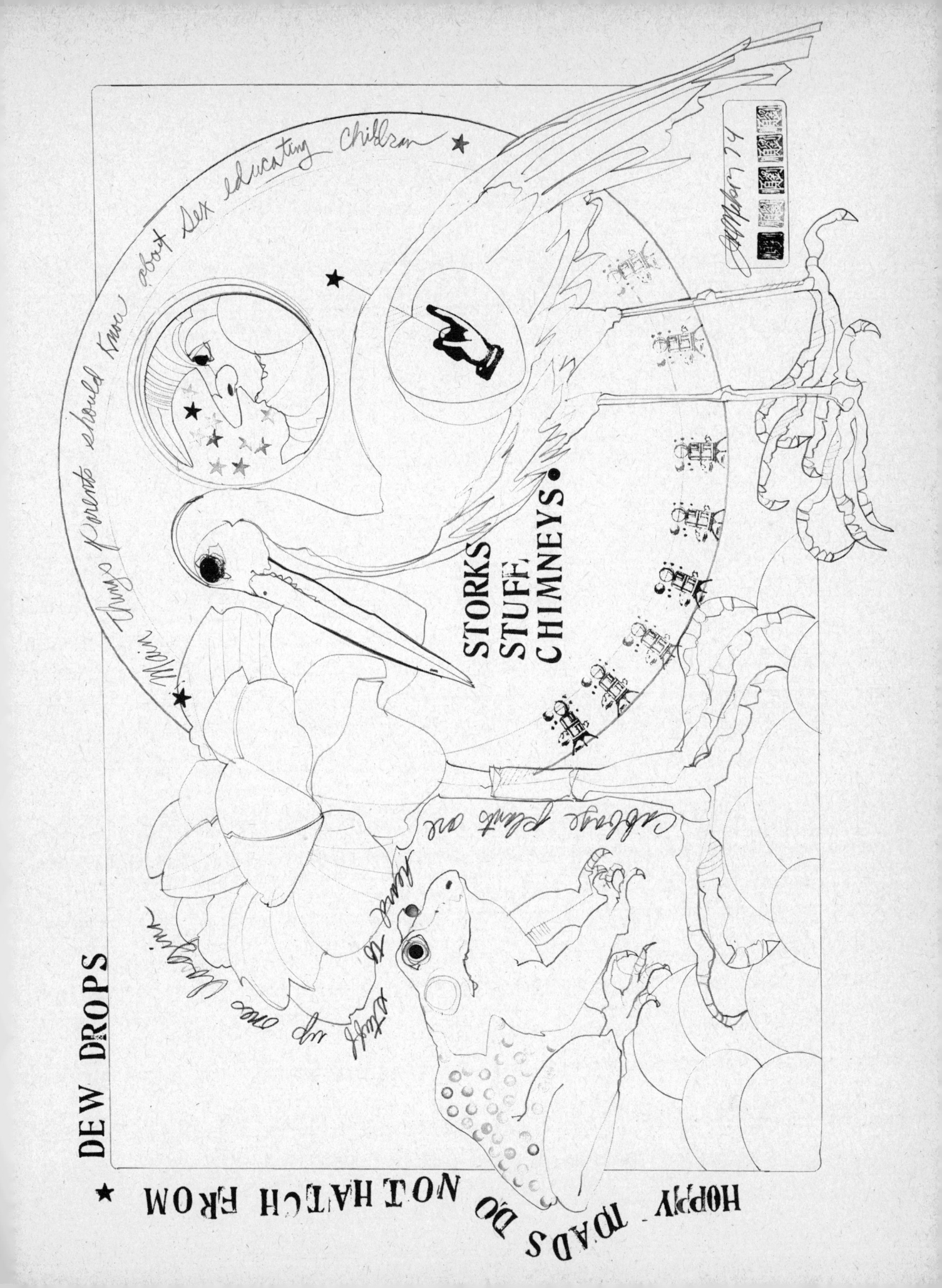

HOPPY-TOADS DO NOT HATCH FROM ★

STORKS
STUFF,
CHIMNEYS.

Many things Parents should know about Sex educating Children

Cabbage Plants are stuff up one way or...

Why are we unable to accept the free, spontaneous statements of children? They are often correct. Spontaneity is mental health in action. Acceptance provides the child with a sense of security. Children who are secure will learn in school with a good teacher or a poor one. Characteristic of a secure child is his inner striving to become a more complete person. Characteristic of the maladjusted child is his struggle against his mother, his father and other authority figures.

Of course, not only should parents be able to talk freely with each other, but they must also be able to respond to their children's questions as they are asked and not work on the assumption that the less a child knows the better off s/he is. The opposite is true.

It is also not possible to tell a child too much. Children simply ignore or are bored by knowledge they cannot understand — they'll turn you off. Contrary to what some people think, information doesn't stimulate socially inappropriate behavior. Ignorance does.

Besides, what neighbor has ever worried that *his/her* kid will tell *your* kid the cock and bull story about the cabbage leaf or Mr. Stork? It's time that the kids whose parents have given the correct facts become the sex educators in their own neighborhoods.

SPECIAL ALERT

Don't have children mainly to satisfy your parents' "grandparent" complex or to bolster a deflated ego (no child can blow it up for you).

Have children for the sheer joy of it, knowing full well that it can also be a drag. And once they are grown, know that you will never have the control over them you think you should have or deserve to have.

Consider Tommy, a nine-year-old, who is caught drawing a "dirty" picture. His mother gets very excited. She snatches the picture from the boy's hands. (In this country, you need evidence.) Apart from disturbing Tommy, she has revealed to her son that she has a sex problem. She calls in her husband, who also gets very excited, indicating that he, too, is threatened by the question of sex.

Consider the parent who is terribly orderly and preoccupied with cleanliness. Anyone preoccupied with cleanliness worries about dirt most of the time. Why project your concern with dirt upon children? If children feel that their thoughts are dirty, their ideas dirty, and their behavior dirty, they end up feeling guilty and insecure.

Having said all that, we must say that most parents mean well and want to bring up their children so they can be happy, creative, self-supporting members of society.

Since most of you reading this will marry (despite your best intentions) and will bring into this world at least one, probably two children (despite the fact that you may be happier without children), we would like to offer some advice about doing it right your time around (which as you know will be difficult to do even if you want to).

1. First, talk to your spouse about advantages and disadvantages of having children and decide about the timing. Plan and agree about sharing responsibilities in advance. (While it's not always a disaster to have an unplanned child, it often is.)

2. Both you and your spouse should read Dr. Spock — and Lee Salk's parenting book — if you want to get into it heavy, or my parenting book if you want to get into it light.

3. Decide that you don't have to do everything right to be a good parent, and be willing to admit to your children that you are not always right even if you think you are not often wrong.

4. Realize that open, genuine affection for each is probably the most important gift you can offer your children.

5. Appreciate that bringing up a creative child has little to do with prescribed or pre-determined standards of performance. Creativity usually means that parents will have to allow for some lapses in discipline.

6. One good way to test your readiness for parenthood is to consider your attitudes toward sex.

Here are the main things
we think you should know
(in a nutshell, of course)
about sex-educating children.

Masturbation: Playing with one's genitals is a common and normal activity for children and should not be a source for scolding, punishment or milder forms of disapproval, such as substituting a toy. The child needs to explore her/his body and should not be discouraged. As the child gets older (say three or four) s/he can be taught to masturbate only in private.

Nudity: Nudity in the bath and bedroom is a healthy introduction to sexual differences and sexuality. The child will let his parents know when his/her modesty dictates privacy by closing the door, or asking to bathe alone, etc. Parental privacy needs to be protected too, sometimes.

Proper Terminology: Giving correct names for parts of the body is important. It's just as easy to teach a little boy "penis" as it is "ding-a-ling," or "bowel movement" or "b.m." rather than "poo-poo" or some other term. Similarly, a child should know the correct words for sexual intercourse and sexual behavior.

Obscenity: If a child repeats a word that s/he heard in the street or from adults, use the word, and explain what it means. This approach has several advantages. First, your child will know s/he can't use it as a weapon against you. Second, the child will realize that such questions won't make you uptight. Third, by explaining it with proper terminology you are treating the subject of sex with respect, instead of relegating it to the street.

Touching: Children often grow up with the feeling that touching and expressing affection are inappropriate. This attitude develops primarily because they rarely see adults *touch*. Consequently, they grow up not knowing how to express themselves physically. As teenagers, they will believe that touching another person is only a prelude to sexual intercourse. Parents should not cut off physical affection from their children after infancy, since a child still needs this physical reassurance of his/her parent's love.

★

LOVE IS...

Mature Love* is . . .

. . . when your caring about the other person is *just a little* more important to you than having the other person care for you. The relationship is mutually enhancing and energizing.

Immature Love is . . .

. . . when the other person's caring for you is a *lot more important* than your caring for the other person. Your love is a burden on the other person and the state of being in love is exhausting.

It's too bad that many people think that when they find true love "everything will be perfect." They think that there must not be any disagreements and that each partner will always want to be with the other. When a problem comes up they are likely to end the relationship thinking that "love has died." Then they go off looking for someone else with whom they can experience "the real thing." As a result, they find every relationship a disappointment, and they may wonder why no one seems to be as sensitive as they are.

Sometimes people say and believe that they are in love, but they act in a way that is sure to sabotage the relationship. They neglect their studies or their work; or they're careless about their appearance; or they're jealous, irritable and petty when they are with the other person; or they fail to keep promises or assume the obligations that are natural when two people really love each other.

People who are in love will be so intent on making themselves the best possible partner for the loved one that they are inspired to improve their work, to enhance their appearances and to show the best side of their

---

*In this context we are referring to responsive love: being aware and concerned about the impact your love has on others. Love can start out as mature and degenerate into a nightmare by becoming possessive, stifling or controlling.

personalities. The true lover tries in every way possible to make him/herself a better person, so that s/he will be worthy of the love that is desired.

Real love is best when it's a shared experience. It sometimes happens that a man falls in love with a woman who does not return his feeling (or vice versa). When this happens to a mature person, s/he makes every reasonable effort to evoke affection from the other person. If this fails, s/he will be disappointed, but after awhile will admit that s/he can't have what s/he wants, and will seek out another relationship.

It is not true that "really" being in love is something that can happen only once in a liftime. It is possible to be in love many times. Even an intense love affair, when it comes to an end, may be followed by another relationship that is even more deeply rooted and more satisfying.

DO YOU WANT TO BE A LOVER?

If you were loved and taken care of as a child you will be in the best position to love and care for others. If that part of your life was not exactly the way you wanted it to be, try (in this order):

1. To care for and love yourself.
2. To care for and love, or be close to, people of your own sex. These are the best preparations for learning to:
3. Love and care for people of the opposite sex.

Once you are able to develop all three, they remain part of your life forever, and you are ready to:

4. Love and care for your children.

It's no accident that people who reject relationships with members of their own sex or who go out of their way to be with members of the opposite sex (like the woman who says: "I don't care to relate to women; they bore me" or the man who says "Man, I love women; I need to be with a woman all the time") are rarely able to establish a meaningful, mature and lasting relationship with a member of the opposite sex.

"Let no one who loves
be called altogether unhappy.
Even love unreturned
has its rainbow."

James M. Barrie

ON BEING INTIMATE WITH A CHESTNUT

Sometimes we talk about intimacy. We quickly agree that people can be sexual without being intimate. But, ah, can anyone be intimate without sex? Perhaps, but what about intimacy without touching?

We decide that there are many different levels and intensities, like in love or enchantment. The intimacy we care about seems to be being at one with, at any one moment, in harmony with:

another person
  an imaginary friend
    God
      nature
        a stuffed animal
          a real dog
            your family
              a doll
                Jesus
                  your horse
                    your genitals
                      your motorcycle
                        a blanket
                          grass
                              yourself
                                even a chestnut

It's not easy, this intimacy business. One thing we know for sure is that the path to its fulfillment can be treacherous. First you must reveal yourself. But when you do, you risk humiliation or betrayal. But you also have a chance of a response that you want. Intimacy means being responsive, not reactive.

A person falls in love with you.
God is revealed.
The motorcycle sends out vibrations.
Your doll, dog or horse listens to you as no one else has before.
Or your music captures the soul.

Most people are afraid of being intimate.

Some people don't even know how to be.
    What a pity!
How can you tell about intimacy?

> It is joyous
> and sad
>
> It is sharing and giving,
> and open-ended and
> taking your mind off yourself
> momentarily

Have you ever touched anyone with your body or mind?
And then someone talked about being intimate with a chestnut. For an entire summer he fondled, confided in, and loved her. The response of the chestnut was simply marvelous to behold.

If someone asks you, "Can I trust you?" say, "No."

Whom Not to Marry (if You Do Marry)

Everybody gives advice on *whom* to marry. Few listen. So we'll advise you on *whom not* to marry. Maybe you'll consider it.

Don't marry if one or more of the following conditions exist:

[1] If one of you relentlessly asks questions like, "Do you love me?" or "Do you really care about me?"

[2] If when you are together you spend most of your time disagreeing and quarreling (even if you miss each other when you are not together).

[3] If you don't really know each other as persons, even though you have spent a great deal of time together.

[4] If you are both still very young (roughly under 20). Most young marriages end in divorce or separation.

[5] You are marrying mainly to get away from your own home and family or to have someone "mother" you.

[6] If you find that your decision to get married has been largely influenced by your prospective father-in-law or mother-in-law. Don't laugh! Not a few young people are led into matrimony by the warm acceptance, the flattery, the wealth or even the cooking of a potential in-law.

[7] If you keep having thoughts like, "Maybe things will be better after we're married," or your prospective mate insists on a particular behavior you don't like before marriage and promises "to change" after marriage. It rarely happens.

[8] If your fiance has behavior traits that you can't stand (such as non-stop talking) and you avoid the issue for fear of giving offense.

[9] If your partner insists that you drop all your old friends and start afresh.

[10] If, after you've given it some thought, you discover you are marrying a sex object, not a person. A "showpiece" marriage becomes unbelievably boring after awhile.

[11] Whatever you do, don't marry to "cover" an untimely pregnancy, especially if your main motive is to "do the right thing."

MENTAL ILLNESS

IF YOU THINK
YOU MIGHT
BE GOING CRAZY

For one thing, nobody is in perfect mental health. But the important thing is that there is a difference between an emotional problem and mental illness. You can hardly hope to get through life without suffering from some emotional hassles, just as you can't think that your body will never catch a virus.

When you are going through an emotional disorder, part of your

Zing Comix

What Do You Do When You're All DRUG DOUBT?

If you're having a rough trip, turn directly to page 19.

First aid for overdose: page 18

It is common for people to try to fake their way through life, but it is much more interesting to

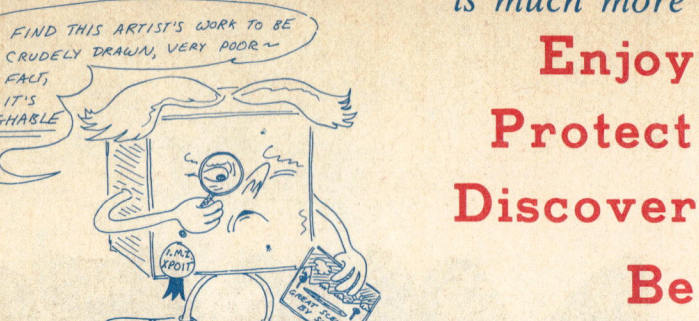

Enjoy
Protect   Your Self
Discover
Be

Written, illustrated and designed by Roger Conant
Psychology consultant: Sol Gordon
Humor consultant: Tibor G. Csicsatka
Facilitator: Kathleen G. Everly
Distribution: Del Cusmano

Published by Ed-U Press, 760 Ostrom Ave., Syracuse, N.Y. 13210
Ed-U Press is the publishing arm of Syracuse University's
Institute for Family Research and Education

Other titles in this series of educational comic books include *Juice Use -- Special Hangover Edition, Ten Heavy Facts About Sex, V.D. Claptrap, Protect Yourself From Becoming an Unwanted Parent,* and *Gut News for Modern Eaters.* Single copies of *Drug Doubt?* or any other title are 30 cents each. Bulk rates are available on request.

NEW, UPDATED EDITION
Revised July 1973, January 1975.
© 1972, 1973, 1975 by Roger Conant

WHAT ARE YOU WAITING FOR?

Are you waiting for tomorrow
or the end of time?

Are you waiting for the Martians
or the end of crime?

Are you waiting for The Answer
and some peace of mind?

Are you waiting for somebody
whom you can't seem to find?

Panel 1: ABSOLUTELY FREE! "HEY, THEY'RE GIVIN' OUT FREEBEES"

Panel 2: ABS FREE! "HERE YA GO (HEH, HEH)" "WE'VE BEEN IN LINE AN HOUR" "Gee thanx"

Panel 3: "OUCH! THAT SONOFABEE!" BZZZ "FOR THIS WE WAITED?"

WHAT ARE YOU LOOKING FOR?

If you have a low self-image, you can start to feel better inside by finding yourself:

1. something new to do and learn
2. someone to BE with

If you are turned off to learning anything much, then you are turned off to life. Who was it who said: "Real knowledge is self-taught?"

If you are afraid to let at least one person know what you're really like, then you won't have anyone to talk to about your deepest needs and feelings. But revealing yourself is a risk. The other person might reject you or humiliate you. Or, s/he might accept you and like you.

If you can't risk failure, you won't be successful.

so they want to get stoned

ouch!

YOU HAD TO ASK ABOUT THAT...

Life is Not a Meaning; It is an Opportunity

CAN YOU TRUST US?

Why should you trust us? We could be full of it.

You're the one who must figure out what's for real and what isn't. After all, even people with good intentions can throw you a curve. Nobody knows all the truth about everything.

Besides, you can't tell who is a right-on person and who isn't by whether s/he is old, young, freak, straight and like that. And, most important, you can't really judge people by what they say. Their actions tell the real story.

But look over what we have to say in this comic. Does it make any sense?

Mature love
is when meeting the other person's needs are just a little more important than satisfying your own wants. Mature love is energizing and helps you feel good about yourself.

Immature love
is when your own needs are a lot more important than meeting the other person's needs. Immature love is exhausting. You feel angry, depressed and jealous a lot.

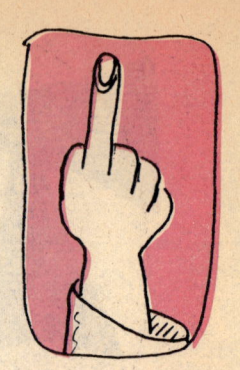

LOVE

HEY! YER BREAKIN' MY HEART

here ya go chump

ZUG A GUT WORT

BILL OF GOODS

$3

GUILT

text ©1975 by Sol Gordon

Mature guilt
is when you feel bad about something you really did wrong. Mature guilt doesn't last too long and helps you organize yourself, so you won't do "it" again. Mature guilt is a good thing, as long as you don't sink into

Immature guilt
disorganizes and overwhelms you. You feel rotten about something you didn't do wrong (such as having an ugly thought). Or: even if you really did something wrong, you use your guilt feelings as "payment" which allows you to go out and do the same thing again.

P.S.: Feeling guilty about "evil" thoughts that suddenly spring up on you will cause you to have those thoughts again and again.

SEX ANYONE?

"HERE COMES OLD GOOFBALL"

"SPEAKING OF A GOOF BALL, HE HUNG LOOSE ALL NIGHT LAST NIGHT"

"BEAT IT... THIS IS JUST TOO MUCH COCK 'N' BULL"

snort

- If you need a drug to get horny, you are really uptight about yourself.

- Heavy drug users quickly lose interest in meaningful sex.

- Pregnant women should avoid all drugs and medicines unless very strongly recommended by a doctor.

- If you want to heighten sensuality, the best way is to really turn on to the other person. Some drugs may seem to increase sexual pleasure, but they also turn you in on yourself, cutting off the other person. Thus, the drug tends to rob the experience of meaning.

Bad habits (such as boasting, overeating, goofing off. . . .) are ways of dealing with life's tensions. When you start to fight the habit, you will probably be socked with enormous rushes of anxiety.

If you have the guts to withstand these attacks of tension, you'll be able to change your behavior for the better. When the temptation is great, go find something interesting to do. But even if you fail to hold out sometimes, don't give up the ship.

If you keep working at a behavior long enough and hard enough, you will eventually conquer. It may take just a few days, or it may take years.

(This hard-to-follow advice also goes for people addicted to alcohol, tobacco or other drugs.)

HUNG UP?

THERE'S GOTTA BE A **!!¿*! CIGARETTE HERE SOMEWHERE

One of the worst things about heavy drug use is the way it doesn't solve problems.

People who feel that they don't have much control over their lives often look for an answer in the pleasures of drugs. This is strange, because the more you do drugs, the less control you have in your life.

Drugs cannot achieve anything.

Ever noticed that people who drink a lot never seem to get much done? Likewise, if you spend most of your time grass-eyed, you won't accomplish much more than lying around listening to music.

If you put off things that you know need doing, then all your pleasurable experiences are reduced to copouts. Besides, the process of not doing something that needs doing is much more tiring than just going ahead and doing it.

People use and overuse a mind drug because it gets them high -- and they like it.

We all know that alcohol loosens "inhibitions." Likewise, the other mind drugs in some way or other reduce *some* inhibitions.

What many people forget is that these same drugs reduce *judgment* -- that inner you that says, "This is important, this isn't;" "This is real, this is fantasy;" "This is O.K., this is not."

Mind drugs tend to put your thoughts in charge of you, rather than having you in charge of your thoughts. LSD is the most extreme example.

TRASH

Panel 1: "HERE, TRY THIS" / "HEY, OUTA STATE"
Panel 2: doo de doo / glug
Panel 3: OOPS / POW!
Panel 4: "SORRY PAL, I JUST WANTED TO GET A HEAD" / "WHAT A RIPOFF" / PLUNK

Some people will swallow anything and everything -- all at once. That's why they are called trash-heads.

Too much of any *one* drug may be harmful. And since "too much" depends on things like age, sex, weight and health, how do you know how much is too much (even if you know how many micrograms are in a particular dose)?

When it comes to mixing drugs, not even druggists can always predict what will happen. Sometimes drugs combine with each other in the body, causing freaky changes -- such as death. For example, mixing alcohol and barbiturates has caused thousands of deaths.

One trio to avoid: Speed, booze and barbiturates. The three of those together can bring on temporary insanity so fearful that you might do a lot of damage to yourself or somebody else before you get straight again.

ALCOHOL

Alcohol is by far the world's worst drug problem. About one in ten people who drink at all cannot control his or her drinking (how often and/or how much).

People who are becoming alcoholics usually don't know it or can't admit it to themselves. Chances are fairly high that if you drink heavily for several years, you will wind up addicted.

Teenagers can be alcoholic.

You don't have to be alcoholic in order to be one of the drunks who cause thousands of fatal accidents every year.

TOBACCO

Are you aware that people who smoke *and* drink regularly are 15 times more likely to get cancer than people who do neither?

Ever noticed that cigarette ads are aimed at immature teenagers? The kids who take up smoking are trying to *look* cool. Dumb, isn't it?

Panel 1: ♪ a hunnerd bottles a beer on da wall... ♪

Panel 2: FIRE! FIRE!

Panel 3: YOUR HOUSE IS ON FIRE! PLEASE COME TO THE WINDOW. / unnh...?

Panel 4: CAN YA HOLD IT A MINUTE? I CAN'T FIND MY CIGARETTES

11

- **BARBITURATES.** Here are some names: Nembutal, Tuinal, Seconal, Veronal, Luminal, Amytal Sodium, Phenobarbital. Slang: goof balls, sleeping pills, sleepers, yellow jackets, purple hearts, blues, blue dragons, blue heavens, rainbows, reds, red birds, red devils, tooies, nemmies. Regular use of too much barbiturate quickly leads to very bad addiction. Withdrawal illness is very dangerous. An overdose can kill. Mental illness is not uncommon.

- **TRANQUILIZERS.** There are two kinds: "major" and "minor." Thorazine is a "major tranq." "Majors" are not addicting, but death from overdose and other unpleasant side effects are possible. Minor tranqs are overused more. Some brands: Equanil, Librium, Librax, Miltown, Phobex, Suavatil, Valium. It is harder to get addicted to minor tranqs than to barbiturates, but continued overuse for several months can lead to addiction that is just as bad as barbiturate addiction.

- **HYPNOTICS.** The most popular of the hypnotics are called Sopors (also known as methaqualone). Overuse may lead to addiction.

DOWNERS:
barbiturates, tranquilizers, hypnotics

SPEED AND COKE

Nowadays "speed" usually means just about any strong stimulant other than cocaine. But cocaine is also a powerful stimulant. In general, stimulants make you feel super-alert and full of phony energy. Users frequently get hung up in silly details.

One big branch of the stimulant family is the amphetamines, which are also known as Methedrine, meth, crystal, Benzedrine, bennies, Dexedrine, Dexamyl and others. Other stimulants include Plegine, Ritalin and effedrine. Many diet pills are strong stimulants (a side effect of most stimulants is a lack of hunger).

WHATCHA DOIN', HARE?

WRITIN' A NOTE TO THE MILKMAN

SCRIBBLE SCRIBBLE

Though not truly addictive, stimulants are sometimes mixed with addictive drugs like barbiturates (as with Dexamyl, Tedral) and, when injected, with heroin. Very high doses of stimulant may result in temporary mental illness and once in a while a user may get violent toward him/herself or others.

Sometimes people who are high on big doses of stimulant black out without any warning.

A cocaine overdose can bring on convulsions (a fit) and death.

SMACK AND OPIATES

HEY HORSE, LEMME BORROW SOME OF THE STUFF YOU GOT IN THE BAG – I GOT THE SHIVERIN' SHAKES

YOU GOT WINGS – FLY

YOU DON'T UNDERSTAND – I'M A SITTIN' DUCK

The people who take heroin to knock out the pain of life also knock out its meaning.

Where opiates (like heroin) enter, three driving forces of life leave: sex, action and hunger. Users "fly low and die slow" (and sometimes not so slow).

Only 10 to 15 per cent of junkies get complete cures.

Opiates are derived from the opium poppy (a flower). Druggists also call them narcotics. Besides heroin, the opiates include morphine, opium and codeine.

The most powerful is heroin, alias: smack, scag, stuff, H, horse, him, harry, jones, junk, duji. Morphine, a medication, is sometimes called M or Miss Emma. Codeine is found in some cough syrups and other medicines.

Man-made opiates include methadone, demerol, Mepergan, Percodan, Percobarb.

All these drugs are highly addictive. O.D. deaths from bags bought in the street are not uncommon.

Withdrawal sickness is painful. Smackheads have high rates of liver disease (from dirty needles) and lung diseases -- among other problems.

ACID and others

Though LSD is not addictive, you can never be sure how your mind will be affected. No matter how many good trips you've had, you cannot predict when the next one will be a bummer.

LSD and other hallucinogenic drugs tend to "control" the user more than s/he controls them.

Mental illness triggered by such drugs may last hours, days or years. Hallucinations and false beliefs brought on with this type of mind drug have led to a number of deaths.

Many users claim that these drugs help them understand life better. It *is* true that one or more doses may wake a person up to the unpleasant discovery that much of his/her behavior is unthinking, immature and selfish. Other "insights" are more often than not serious distortions of reality. If you want to know what reality is, just beware that drugs lead you further into illusion.

Other hallucinogens: peyote, mescaline, psilocybin, "magic mushrooms," morning glory seeds, jimson weed, DMT, DOM, MMDA, STP, and even poisons such as strychnine (from the deadly nightshade plant).

IT IS NOT TRUE THAT 'MENTALLY STABLE' PEOPLE ARE SAFE FROM BUM TRIPS

Marijuana and its sister drug, hashish, are both derived from the marijuana plant.

• These drugs are not physically addictive. But people whose *main bag* is grass (or any drug) are trying to avoid something in their life that makes them unhappy. The trouble is, you get a lift at first, but later you feel much worse because the problem is still there.

• These drugs hardly ever move people to violence or a life of crime. However, it is not well known that grass *can*, at times, bring on terrifying episodes of paranoia, even among long-experienced users. One guy we know went stoned to see *The Exorcist*. Guess what? He came within an ace of losing his marbles.

grass and hash

• Occasional use rarely does much harm to mind or body, but if it makes you feel guilty, don't do it. Since the drug relaxes your inner controls, it is possible for the guilt to get out of hand and bring on a bum trip.

• Long-term use may have serious mental and physical effects, but that doesn't mean it is worth it to outlaw it. In some cases, drug laws are used as a political weapon against people with unpopular views or life styles.

• Be on your guard. There are more people around than you think who would get a kick out of screwing up your mind while you're helplessly stoned or otherwise drugged out.

Looking for a rush or a jag, people have sniffed not only model airplane glue, but fumes from things like benzine, cleaning fluid, lighter fluid, nail polish remover, paint, varnish thinner, and hair spray. Users soon need more than a couple whiffs to get the feeling -- which is similar to barbiturate drunkenness.

People have been found dead of suffocation with their heads in bags of fumes. Others choked to death after filling their lungs with hair spray.

Inhaling these fumes may result in damage to the blood, heart, liver, kidneys and brain. Brain damage is permanent. Though most of these fumes are not addictive, the death rate among users is very high.

FUMES

First Aid For Overdose

Get Medical Help as Fast as Possible

PASSED OUT, cause unknown. Check breathing first. If poor or stopped, give mouth-to-mouth breathing (if O.K., do not give artificial respiration). Drug O.D.s are often hard to get started breathing properly, so keep at it. Once the victim is breathing satisfactorily, turn his head to one side and very gently roll him onto his stomach. Keep all parts of the body still.

PASSED OUT from too much heroin, morphine, or other narcotics; cocaine; barbiturates or tranquilizers; glue fumes or other fumes. Follow the directions above about breathing, but keep changing the position of the victim's body.

CONVULSIONS. Some drug overdoses bring on convulsions (a fit).

Don't try to hold the victim down as he jerks, but do push nearby objects out of the way and gently push him clear of dangerous places like stairwells. If possible, keep him from biting his tongue. Put something that won't break between the teeth at the side of his mouth. The edge of a hard book cover will work. Or: a spoon handle wrapped in a handkerchief, a rolled up magazine or belt, even a shoe. Do *not*, however, force his mouth open if it is clamped shut. Once the seizure is over, loosen collar and have him lie flat, turning his head to one side. If his breathing is shallow, give him mouth-to-mouth breathing.

AWAKE, but CONFUSED and SLOW (possibly staggering), as a result of overdosing on one or more of these drugs: cocaine, heroin, morphine, barbiturates, tranquilizers, fumes. DON'T LET THE VICTIM GO TO SLEEP. Keep him walking and moving until you get him medical help.

If you know he *swallowed* the drug a short time ago, try making him vomit. (Do *not* make him vomit if he inhaled fumes.) Ways to induce vomiting: Lots of water. Better yet -- several teaspoons of baking soda or milk of magnesia mixed with water or milk. Another way -- he can put his finger in his throat. Have him get it all out. If your first tries don't work, try again several times.

SPEED O.D. People rarely fall down and pass out from too much amphetamine (though they sometimes black out momentarily). When they do faint, the drug was likely mixed with a barbiturate or narcotic. In that case, follow the directions above for a person passed out from overdose. If the user is awake he may show signs of (temporary) mental illness -- especially if the dose was very high. He may be violent or suicidal. Stay with him to make sure he does nothing too rash. Death from a speed O.D. is rare (though it has happened), but it is hard to tell what other drugs were mixed with the amphetamine. It is best to call for medical help, or, at the very least, to get in touch with a drug crisis center in your area.

More Aid

Aside from drug crisis centers, which handle immediate emergencies and related (and unrelated) hassles, there are other programs for drug users who need and want help.

Mostly, these are for heroin users, though some accept other drug problems. Under the care of doctors, addicts and ex-addicts help each other through withdrawal sickness, talk out emotional problems, and in general, support each other.

Some names: Daytop in New York City; Synanon in San Francisco; Argosy House and Odyssey House in New York and other cities.

Many states encourage methadone maintenance programs. Methadone is at least as addictive as heroin, but it is legal and cheap, and it prevents heroin withdrawal sickness.

What to Do About a
ROUGH TRIP

If you are having a hard time, you should know that:

You cannot be hurt by
thoughts
images
fantasies
sounds
Actions are much more important

You are not your thoughts
You are yourself

Try not to fight these thoughts so much. Let them go. Right now they are mostly automatic anyway.

You are a live human being,
which, by itself, is *good*.

It is not likely that you will be able to figure out what's bothering you while you are tripping. Leave that for later and relax a little now.

YOU ARE FOR REAL.

It is your thoughts, stimulated by the drug, which are confused. But you will come around.

TRY:
- Soothing music.
- A warm bath or shower.
- A change of clothes (clean and loose, if you have).
- If you are religious, pray.

Sometimes doctors use valium to help trippers slow down. But don't give yourself any other drug, because this may make your trip even worse.

There may be a drug crisis center in your community. If you're feeling really bad, go there or call there. Or go to a hospital emergency room if really necessary.

If your friend is bumming, read the above. **IMPORTANT:** Stick with him/her or have someone else stay with him/her.

No one can make you feel inferior without your consent.

Rx: LIVE A LITTLE

THE LAST WHOLE EARTH CATA- LOGUE

There is nothing more harmful than trying to live up to someone else's idea of what you should be like.

constructive energies is knocked out, but you still manage to hang in there somehow.

People who are mentally ill are so disoriented that they are almost completely unable to care for themselves, or, if they do get by, they find it almost impossible to take care of anyone else for long.

Although most people don't talk about it, just about everyone you know has a relative who is or has been in a mental hospital. (Just as almost everyone has a relative who is alcoholic and/or who has committed suicide.)

Just because Uncle Joe is mentally ill doesn't mean you will become psychotic, even if you have some of his mannerisms. Sometimes members of your family may make remarks such as: "Now you're acting just like Uncle Joe." So what? Don't let such remarks mean anything.

IF YOU THINK SOMEBODY ELSE IS CRAZY

Some people who are called "mentally ill" are not. Sometimes people are committed to institutions just because they are going through a temporary period of confusion, or are an emotional burden on their families, or are threatening to relatives and neighbors because of "odd" or "out of character" behavior.

People with unpopular or disturbing ideas may be shut out by being branded "mentally ill."

Sometimes mentally retarded individuals are accused of being crazy. Only a very ignorant or a very insecure person would make such a judgment.

MOST IMPORTANT FACTS ABOUT MENTAL ILLNESS

- Mentally ill people can and do recover.
- The more a mentally ill person is mistreated or ignored, the less chance s/he has.
- The mentally ill person, whether s/he or others know it or not, is suffering from enormous mental anguish. The mentally ill person has an extraordinarily difficult time accepting intimacy with anyone. Many mentally ill people have abandoned hope — and this keeps them sick.

SUICIDE

Almost everyone at times has thoughts of suicide. Having such thoughts now and then does not mean you are suicidal or mentally ill.

Suicide may be "the decision to end all decisions," a response to overwhelming pain (sometimes physical, but usually mental), a result of overdosing on alcohol or drugs (frequently in combinations), or it may have been an accident.

Remember:

1. If life is so overwhelming that you are seriously thinking about murdering yourself, first do something constructive, such as summoning up all your strength to say a prayer (it can't hurt). Then call up a friend. If you can't do that, call up a hotline. If you can't do that, write a letter to a newspaper. Do something constructive. Think about this: If you are alive, that — all by itself — is good.
2. Overdoses of drugs and/or alcohol can weaken your inner strength to the point that you are at the mercy of your unconscious. Many people have gone berserk and destroyed themselves after downing speed, barbiturates and alcohol.
3. Sometimes people will threaten to commit suicide as a desperate way of crying for help. What they want is attention, not death. But it may happen that while they are teetering on the bridge they lose their balance, or they turn on the gas and close the windows but the expected relative doesn't show up at the usual time.

WHEN SOMEONE THREATENS SUICIDE

Obviously, anyone who makes an attempt at suicide needs immediate professional attention.

However, people who *talk* about suicide (even if casually or jokingly) — often have been going through some very unpleasant experiences. If no one takes them seriously and instead says things like "That's silly" or "I'll join you" or other self-conscious remarks, these people become convinced that no one really cares enough to ask what's wrong. It is most helpful to take an active concern in the person by communicating: "Listen, you've been threatening to kill yourself lately and I'm very concerned — can we talk about it?" If the person is not responsive, you might call up your local suicide prevention center. Most cities have an emergency service (often it is listed as Contact).

DEATH

Almost everybody seems to be into death these days. The whole idea bores me. Sure, we need to appreciate it as a part of life. But to study it, prepare for it, even praise the sick parts of other cultures that glory in it, seems deadly to me.

Dead should certainly not be considered a four-letter word. It's more like sad, a three-letter word.

We feel it powerfully when someone close to us dies. And the grief and the mourning is part of caring for ourselves and sharpens our own respect for life.

From a psychological standpoint, the most important fact to know about the death of a member of your immediate family is: Your first impulse is to feel guilty about it.

It's all right to have regrets that perhaps you didn't do enough for or be kind enough to this person. But don't let such a feeling hang you up for too long. Look at it this way: if you feel bad that your relationship with this person wasn't as good as you would like, the only thing that makes sense is to improve your relationships with those around you who are living.

Many people carry around a burden of *irrational* guilt after the death of a loved one. For example, the daughter who was away at college when her mother died becomes obsessed with the idea that maybe it would have turned out differently if only she had stayed home.

Don't freeze on that first impulse to feel guilty. People are always dying at unexpected and inopportune times. That's part of life. Again: Your obligation is to the living.

The part of death that horrifies me is the wanton, fierce human murder of millions of people — a holocaust. That is worth studying. In the forgetting, we become accomplices.

Sure, there is a lot more to it, because a response to a death is so deeply personal. And that's the way I'd like to leave it.

Is Religion Dead?

"Here I am."

— Abraham

What's At The Bottom of Your Beliefs?

Is religion too phony, too incredible or too heavy for you? If you don't have a religion you enjoy or if you've rejected the religion of your parents, why not figure out your own religion? It's really good to believe in something. But that doesn't mean you shouldn't be cautious when it comes to religious ideas. After all, if your religion gives you nothing to think about, it doesn't offer much.

And if you don't think about the basis of your moral beliefs, you make way for the self-righteous hypocrites to set themselves up as the guardians of *your* (and everybody else's) morality. It's no accident that certain unscrupulous leaders make a big show of their religion. They'll tell you what to think and what to believe — if you let them.

Part of living in a democracy is having respect for the values of other people. To take an extra-sensitive example: Abortion. While we don't favor abortion as a method of birth control, we believe that *compelling* someone to give birth is evil. As it happens, most Americans agree with the Supreme Court's ruling that lawmakers may not interfere with a woman's right to have an abortion in the first twelve weeks of her pregnancy. Some people are flatly opposed to abortion. They have a right to express their feeling. But that does not give them the right to make abortion illegal.

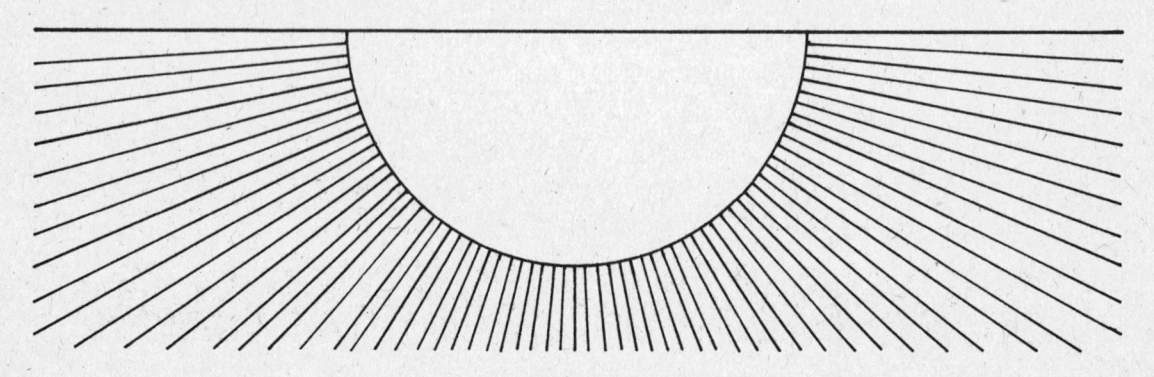

The real test of your religion is the effect it has in your personal life. Does it make you a better person?

Being a better person means:

1. You feel good about yourself, but still want to grow.
2. You can say: "I am." Being alive requires no justification.

This permits you to care for and love others.

A better person doesn't manipulate and exploit people, and balances selfish interests with the needs of others.

A better person strives for good relationships, intimacy (with one or more people), and to contribute as a citizen of the community and the world.

We will still be mean, selfish and inconsiderate at times, but most often won't feel the need to hold a grudge, carry feuds to the extreme or antagonize people we don't get along with or don't know.

Test your own religion, or the basis for your moral beliefs, in the above terms. If it doesn't jibe, maybe you have not understood the message that no religion is motionless (even if God be changeless). New and different understandings take place through inspired/inspiring leaders.

AN APOTHEOSIS TO MY LORD*

If God is dead He must have Been
If He was, He is
If He is, He could not have Been

God		YOU
Is		ARE
Not Free		Free
To Tell	You	To
YOU	Must	Respond
What To		To
Do	Find	Him
	Your	
	Own	
	Way	

*A poem by Sol Gordon with hidden connections, meanings and vibrations

One of our favorite books is "The Catcher in the Rye." One popular book we can't stand is "Jonathan Livingston Seagull." If you are wondering why, read the next two reviews.

THE CATCHER IN THE RYE

A Generation After: Irrelevant?

by E. Marion Fagan

From the well-deserved resurrection of seminal rock-n-roller Chuck Berry to television's "Teen Angel" of 7-Up commercial fame, America is now enjoying (or, if you prefer, enduring) a nostalgic frenzy over the period labeled "The Fabulous Fifties." The Fifties has been fabulous indeed for its merchandizers, including films, books, a Broadway show, and innumerable recordings among its more profitable manifestations.

Conspicuously absent from this revival has been any re-examination of that period's most acclaimed novel of adolescence, J. D. Salinger's, *The Catcher In The Rye*. *Catcher* was very nearly required reading for the literary-minded high school and college student of the fifties and early sixties, and was considered a minor masterpiece by many critics and reviewers of that era. Today, the book is not much discussed.

One possible reason for *Catcher's* current neglect is that young people don't read as much as those of the book's generation. Nurtured by television rather than the story book, they receive most of their information and entertainment from the electronic media.

Another reason is that *Catcher* is highly unsuitable material for the purpose of nostalgic celebration. A deceptively gentle and brutally honest story, it tells the truth about an era that people wallowing in said era's mythology don't wish to review. Nostalgia is a pain-killer, a narcotic to aid in withdrawal from a threatening and unbearable present. *Catcher*, on the other hand, is a sensitizer, a delicate painting in pain of a massive communications breakdown.

How has *Catcher* stood up over the quarter-century since its creation? Are Holden Caulfield and friends hopelessly dated, quaint and irrelevant to their present-day counterparts? *Catcher* is rife with authoritarianism, hypocrisy and sexism, all anathema to today's young readers. But these elements are not the root ingredients of the novel.

Both *Catcher* and its main protagonist are dated now as to cultural climate and life styles. At that time, "The Bomb" was in its infancy, Indochina was a French problem, and the issues of ecology and women's rights were the underpublicized dreams of a pioneering few. But this is not what *Catcher* is about. *Catcher's* primary concerns are alienation, loneliness, thwarted sexuality, the inability to communicate intimacy — all of the life-killing blocks that stand in the way of happiness, self-actualization, and love. If these problems ever become irrelevant, we will have reached the millenium.

Holden Caulfield, the novel's narrator-protagonist, is in an almost permanent state of confusion, torn between "reality" as it is presented to him, chiseled in stone and handed down by unimpeachable "authority" (home, school, society) and the deeply felt reality of his own perceptions. The stiffly worded motto of his prep school sums up his dilemma: "Since 1888 we have been *molding* [emphasis mine] boys into splendid, clear-thinking young men." The rigid, codified, lock-step-to-success atmosphere of prep school is strangling him. He'd rather watch the ducks in Central Park, or spend as much time as possible in his rich fantasy world. He has no faith in reality as it is packaged and sold to him, and very little in the validity of his own inner experiences.

The role models offered for success in his world both bore and frighten Holden, torn as he is between hating that role and his fear that he'll never be able to fulfill it. The part he is asked to play is personified in his school acquaintance, Harry Stradlater. Stradlater is fully decked out with all the desired equipment — good looks, athletic ability, popularity, and a great "snowing" technique for obtaining sexual favors. His most outstanding asset is his ability to manipulate those around him, as the borrowed-coat sequence early in the novel demonstrates. His capacity for warmth and intimacy are practically nil. He is a good user of people.

Harry's female counterpart is Sally Hayes, another successful adjuster and manipulator. She is busily conforming herself into a desirable choice for the "right" kind of man. She dresses correctly, behaves properly and expresses the most fashionable attitudes in the approved tribal language (upper-class version). Her only apparent goal is that of status — the status gained by acquiring a high-status male, and hanging his scalp on the wall of a split-level tepee.

Holden Caulfield is ill at ease in this predatory world. He can't stand Stradlater, but allows Harry to use him. After all, Harry's a winner and he's a loser. Sally Hayes is sexually attractive to Holden and helps him to pass some lonely hours, but he is bored with her as a person. With either party there is little possibility for the satisfaction of his greatest need — the longing for intimacy, the desire to get next to and into another human being, the drive to share his own unique reality with others, and to receive the same in return. While he can't understand or even accept his feelings, he can express them in bursts of insight, but is too beaten down by the effort of living up to the demands made upon him to recognize these insights for the experiential truth they represent.

Unsurprisingly, sex and love are Holden's most troublesome concerns. "Women kill me . . . they really do . . . I just like them, I mean," he remarks in bewilderment. His despairing comment about male-female relationships, "You never know where the *hell* [author's emphasis] you are!" points up his difficulties in dealing with the labyrinth of false roles and expectations involved. Sex and sexual relationships are something one is expected to perform and be good at: "A woman's body is like a violin and all."

Holden can't reconcile his sexuality with his need for intimacy. He can't fathom why he can feel "in love" with a girl for a brief time, and then almost in the same moment realize that he doesn't even like her. His failure to perform adequately with a prostitute in a seedy Manhattan hotel room leaves him dazed and miserable — "I know you're *supposed to feel* [emphasis mine] pretty sexy when somebody gets up and pulls their dress over their head . . . I felt much more depressed than sexy."

Aside from the demand to perform in the approved manner, sexual expression is strictly defined and limited. In that same hotel, Holden observes a neighboring transvestite through the window and says to himself, "In my mind, I'm probably the biggest sex maniac you ever saw . . . sometimes I can think of *very* [author's emphasis] crummy stuff I wouldn't mind doing . . . I can even see how it might be quite a lot of fun . . . the thing is though, I don't like the idea."

Holden's real needs are expressed with lyrical tenderness as he holds fantasy dialogues with his much beloved and long-dead younger brother, Allie, and enjoys his closeness with his "nice skinny-roller skate skinny" little sister Phoebe. His beautiful fantasy of being *The Catcher In The Rye* — just looking after children at their play — compellingly illuminates his need to give love and caring to others.

The most exquisite and sensually significant of Holden's experiences is a brief moment in a movie theatre. He is with his only real girl *friend*, Jane, someone with whom he has been able to share himself, and the gentle touch of her hand on the back of his neck is a profoundly moving sensation, a pure crystal fragment of shared sensuality.

Many of the societal problems described in *The Catcher In The Rye* are now painfully making their exit. People are trying to deal with one another in terms of human needs rather than artificial demands. We have many new or newly recognized problems: drug abuse, alcoholism, and venereal disease are the most prominent among today's adolescents. But these are only new symptoms of the same basic dissatisfactions expressed so poignantly in *Catcher*. As long as these dissatisfactions are relevant to the human condition, so will be *The Catcher In The Rye*.

BE THE FIRST KID ON YOUR BLOCK TO READ THESE 10 RECENTLY FORGOTTEN NOVELS

1 **One Flew Over the Cuckoo's Nest** *by* Ken Kesey ● Who's crazy - the patient or the staff? ●

2 **The Razor's Edge** *by* Somerset Maugham ● An old fashioned search for meaning. ●

3 **I Never Promised You a Rose Garden** *by* Hannah Green
● A moving account of one girl's breakdown and her struggle for a breakthrough. ●

4 **The Sun Also Rises** *by* Ernest Hemingway ● "Bulls have no balls!" the hero shouts. ●

5 **The Chosen** *by* Chaim Potok ● A Jewish thing in a popular setting for goyim. ●

6 **Siddhartha** *by* Hermann Hesse ● A modern Buddha dilemma. ●

7 **God Bless You, Mr. Rosewater or Pearls Before Swine** *by* Kurt Vonnegut, Jr.
● Just plain hysterical. ●

8 **When She Was Good** *by* Philip Roth ● Great expectations, a baby, insanity. Sad. Sad. ●

9 **The End of the Road** *by* John Barth ● Savage satire, leisurely told. ●

10 **"The Circus of Dr. Lao"** *by* Charles G. Finney
● "See the werewolf turn into a real flesh-and-blood woman - right before your very eyes" - "Step right up . . . if you dare!" ●

★

JONATHAN LIVINGSTON SEAGULL

Hard Core Corn

by Roger Conant

Pornography is derived from the Greek *porne*, meaning "prostitute," and *graphein*, meaning "to write." One definition of *prostitute* is "to apply talent, sex, etc. to unworthy purposes."

A book which reduces humanity's most profound insights and speculations to inane cliches and then pretends to be inspirational is hard-core porn/corn.

One of the most extraordinarily successful and clever fakes to come down the pike during the last few years has got to be *Jonathan Livingston Seagull*, by Richard Bach.

There are few things more annoying than sentimentalism which suckers the heart but which means nothing. Soap operas are painful enough, but at least they don't pretend to be something they aren't.

I don't want to take much time damning such a flea of a book, but it is important to ask how such a book, in which nearly every sentence is a super-slick cliche, finds so many enthusiastic readers (even though it is, I hope, already passé).

But first, let's consider a couple of quotes:

The subject was speed, and in a week's practice he learned more about speed than any gull alive.

Pretty good, huh?
Check this out:

"Chiang . . ." he said, a little nervously.

The old seagull looked at him kindly. "Yes my son?"

"Chiang, this world isn't heaven at all, is it?"

The elder smiled in the moonlight. "You are learning again, Jonathan Seagull."

Heavy, heavy.

What really troubles me is the number of presumably intelligent young people who fell for such a feather-brained book. I suppose it just goes to show that a great many people are philosophically infantile.

Of course, the tendency to buy simplistic nonsense illustrates the well-known fact that a great many young people, unwilling to accept Pharisaic religion, want something more. But, alas, most people (no matter what their generation) are, when you get down to nitty-grittys, rather uncritical.

After all, ours is a culture of con-persons: "Everything will be all right"; "We'll take care of everything"; "Don't trouble yourself." If you're willing to have life fed to you on a silver spoon, there are plenty of opportunists ready to make it easy for you; "Just sign here." (And, if you're confused, all you have to remember is that the good guys still wear the white hats.)

We're so accustomed to being spoon-fed that when someone reduces religion to mindless mush, we hardly give it a thought.

The massive swallowing of

Special for people into reading - see our next page for 142 modern writers we think you'll like. How many have you heard of? How many names would you add to the list?

S. J. Agnon
Kingsley Amis
Sherwood Anderson
Sholem Asch
W. H. Auden
Jane Austen
Isaac Babel
James Baldwin
Honore de Balzac
John Barth
Simone de Beauvoir
Samuel Beckett
Max Beerbohm
Saul Bellow
Bertold Brecht
Martin Buber
Pearl Buck
Albert Camus
Lewis Carroll
Willa Cather
Anton Chekhov
Leonard Cohen
Colette
Joseph Conrad
Frank Conroy
Thomas B. Costain
Hart Crane
e. e. cummings
Charles Dickens
Emily Dickinson
Isak Dinesen
Owen Dodson
John Dos Passos
Fyodor Dostoyevsky
Theodore Dreiser
Lawrence Durrell
Jonathan Edwards
George Eliot
T. S. Eliot
William Faulkner
Lawrence Ferlinghetti
F. Scott Fitzgerald
E. M. Forster
Robert Frost

John Galsworthy
Jean Genet
Andre Gide
Ellen Glasgow
Johann Goethe
Maxim Gorky
Robert Graves
Graham Greene
Edith Hamilton
Thomas Hardy
Heinrich Heine
Robert A. Heinlein
Joseph Heller
Ernest Hemingway
Hermann Hesse
A. E. Housman
Aldous Huxley
Henrik Ibsen
Christopher Isherwood
James Joyce
Franz Kafka
Knut Kamsen
James Kavanaugh
Nikos Kazantzakis
Ken Kesey
Arthur Koestler
Selma Lagerloef
D. H. Lawrence
Doris Lessing
Ludwig Lewisohn
Jack London
Federico Garcia Lorca
Malcolm Lowry
Norman Mailer
Bernard Malamud
Andre Malraux
Thomas Mann
Somerset Maugham
Guy de Maupassant
Herman Melville
James A. Michener
Arthur Miller
Henry Miller
Alberto Moravia

Iris Murdock
Carson McCullers
Vladimir Nabokov
Pablo Neruda
Sean O'Casey
Eugene O'Neill
George Orwell
Kenneth Patchen
Sylvia Plath
Chaim Potok
Marcel Proust
Thomas Pynchon
John Reed
Rainer Maria Rilke
Edwin Arlington Robinson
Romain Rolland
Philip Roth
J. D. Salinger
William Saroyan
Jean Paul Sartre
George Bernard Shaw
Isaac Bashevis Singer
I. J. Singer
C. P. Snow
Alexander Solzhenitsyn
Gertrude Stein
John Steinbeck
Stendahl
Lawrence Sterne
Wallace Stevens
August Strindberg
John M. Synge
Rabindranath Tagore
Dylan Thomas
Henry Thoreau
J. E. E. Tolkein
Leo Tolstoy
Ivan Turgenev
Mark Twain
Sigrid Undset
Paul Valery
Kurt Vonnegut Jr.
Jacob Wasserman
Evelyn Waugh

Franz Werfel
Elie Wiesel
Oscar Wilde
Tennessee Williams
Thomas Wolfe
Virginia Woolf
Herman Wouk
Richard Wright
William Butler Yeats
Emile Zola

_____
_____
_____
_____
_____
_____
_____
_____
_____
_____
_____
_____
_____
_____
_____
_____
_____
_____
_____
_____

Bach's bait underscores the desire of so many people to have everything pre-packaged and watered down. They yearn for the realm of the spirit — but not *really*.

People don't like to be uncertain (afraid), so they respond by not thinking much at all or by toying with "questions" that aren't too threatening (as in *Seagull*) or by seeking salvation within some totality that does not permit questions (such as communism, fascism, cultism). Consider the current spectacle of hordes of young people flocking to all sorts of false prophets who hint that they are the only one with the key to the millennium, or that they are the Messiah, or even God Himself.

But, of course, Jon Seagull, who — after three or four seconds of troubled deliberation pops back to earth to teach other gulls to Fly — does not believe in messiahs. As he eloquently pleads with one of his devotees: "Don't let them spread silly rumors about me, or make me a god. O.K., Fletch?"

May The Great Gull Deliver Us

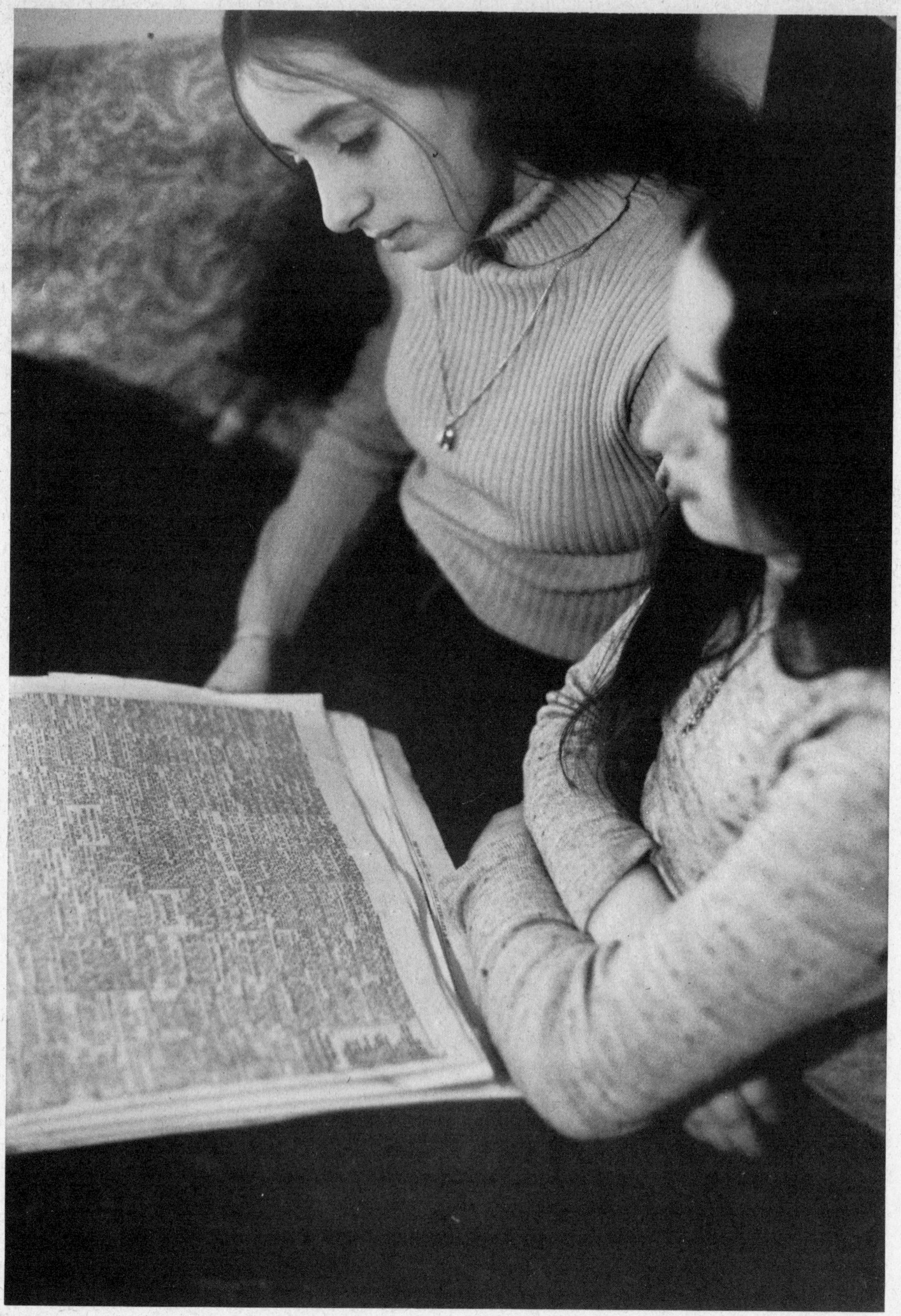

CLASSIFIED

★★★★★★★★★★★★★

1 ALCOHOLIC PARENT?

If one or both of your parnts cant hndle drnkng, write to:
Al-Teen Family Group Headquarters, Inc., Bx 182, Madison Sq. Sta., N.Y., N.Y. 10010.

2 BOOKS & MAGAZINES

Anthropology, Anyone?

Start by readng *The Frontiers of Anthropology*, ed. by Ashley Montagu.

If you dont thnk you are much

I Ain't Much, Baby—But I'm All I've Got, says Jess Lair, who wnts you to free yrslf w/his proven progrm of slf-acceptance, slf-enrichmnt & love.

Awareness

POLITICAL:
Being Free—The Possibilities of Freedom in an Overorganized World, by Gibson Winter.

SELF:

Discovering who we are:
Awaken Your Awareness, by M. Beckington; *Awareness: Exploring, Experimenting, Experiencing*, by J. P. Stevens; *Awareness Through Movement*, by M. Feldenkreis; *Behold the Spirit*, by Alan Watts; *Highest State of Consciousness*, ed. by John White; *Meditation: The Inward Art*, by B. Smith; *Mind Games: The Guide to Inner Space*, by R. Masters and J. Houston; *Mystics of Our Time*, by H. Graef: *Practicing the Presence*, by Joel Goldsmith; *Prayer and Meditation*, by F. C. Happold; *Religious Values and Peak Experiences*, by A. H. Maslow; *Ways of Growth: Approaches to Expanding Awareness*, by John Mann and Herbert Otto; *Between Man and Man*, by Martin Buber; *Test Pattern for Living*, by Nicholas Johnson; *Concentration and Meditation*, by Christmas Humphreys.

Deservng of spcl mention:
- *The Transparent Self*, by Sidney M. Jourard.
- *Toward a Psychology of Being*, by Abraham H. Maslow.
- *The Pursuit of Loneliness*, by Philip Slater.
- *Feel Free*, by David Viscott.

Be a winner—or at least be yrslf
- If you waste the precious & lmtd time of your life impossibly tryng to make up fr disappointng past events, then *The Winners Notebook*, by Theodore Isaac Rubin, is fr you.
- "Now I think any person is a poem," says *The Revolution Is to Be Human*, by Walter Lowenfels.
- Krishna Murti wonders why we cannt find clarity fr ourslvs in our own minds & hearts—without any distortion; why need we be burdened w/books? he asks in *Flight of the Eagle*.
- *Why Am I Afraid to Tell You Who I Am?* is the best of the religiously oriented popular prsnl-growth books. By John Powell, S. J.
- *On Becoming a Person* is really nt a bd idea, says Carl R. Rogers, one of the leadng exponents of group therapy.
- "Today I don't want to live for, I want to live."

I-am-what-I-am excitemnts frm *Notes to Myself*, by Hugh Prather. Frm Real People Press, which also pblshd *Embrace Tiger & Return to Mountains* (the essence of T'ai Chi).
- *In and Out of the Garbage Pail* (Junk & Chaos, Come to Halt!) The autobiogrphy of Frederick S. Perls.
- *On the Taboo Against Knowing Who You Are*, by Alan Watts.

Biography Freaks: Look!

The Autobiography of Alice B. Toklas, by Gertrude Stein.
O'Neill, by Barbara & Arthur Gelb.
Ladies and Gentlemen—Lenny Bruce, by Albert Goldman.

Books Without Reading

If yre not into reading but still wnt to be stimulated by bks, there are ways to do it.

Heard any gd bks lately?
Try listening to an intrstng bk. Caedmon & Spoken Arts put bks into cassettes. Try *The Great Gatsby*, by F. Scott Fitzgerald, read by Alexander Scourby. Send fr catalogs frm R. M. Karen, 200 Park Av. S., N.Y., N.Y. 10013 & Listening Library, 1 Park Av., Old Greenwich, Conn. 06870.

Looked at any gd wordless novels lately?
See Lynd Ward's *Storyteller Without Words*, novels in woodcuts. Stunning beyond belief.

Death

If death fascinates you, theres a wealth of new bks to choose frm, because death hs jst rcntly become fashionble. For starters, try *On Death and Dying*, by Elisabeth Kubler Ross, & *Facing Death*, by Robert E. Kavanaugh.

Fantasy Specials

Lord of the Rings, by J. R. R. Tolkien. If you arnt crazy about the Rings trilogy your frnds will think theres smthng wrong w/you. There isnt.

The Sword in the Stone, by T. H. White. In the days of Arthur & Merlin magic ws a way of life.

Alice's Adventures in Wonderland & Through the Looking Glass, by Lewis Carroll. Alice is rarely read these days, fr no gd reason. Do you suppose its because Tweedledum said to Alice, "You know very well you're not real"?

Free Things

The bk *1001 Valuable Things You Can Get Free*, by Mort Weisinger, tells where to get goodies wo/paying.

Gay?

If you think you are gay, read:
The Gay Liberation Book (ed. by Richmond & Noguera).
Out of the Closets: Voices of Gay Liberation (Links). Includes resrces & people to contact.

Other bks on gays and the gay situation:
Homosexual: Oppression and Liberation, by Dennis Altman.
On Being Different, by Merle Miller.

How-To

Do It Yourself Environmental Handbook (Dayton Museum of Natural History).
How to care fr someone else is careflly elucidated by Milton Mayeroff in his short, care-full bk, *On Caring*.
How to fnd out how Thoreau did it: *Walden & Civil Disobedience*.
How to do smthing abt wrld population: *Ark II*, by Pirages & Ehrlich.
How to weave, mk pottery, do macrame, work w/leather, silkscreen & a lot of fine stuff in *Woodstock Craftsman's Manual*, provoked by Jean Young.
How to Make Psychology Work for You, by Abraham P. Sperling.

Legal Rights

Want to knw mr about your legal rights if yre under 21? Read the paperbck bk *Up Against the Law*, by Jean Strouse.

Loneliness

The basic message of *Loneliness*, by Clark E. Moustakas, is that loneliness is a condition of human life which enables you to sustain, extend & deepen your humanity.

Love &/Or Marriage

"To live in love is life's greatest challenge. It requires more subtlety, sensitivity, understanding, acceptance, tolerance, knowledge and strength than any other human endeavor or emotion . . ."
From *Love*, by Leo Buscaglia.

Other bks to read:
Massage for Lovers—How the Body Feels, by Byron Scott.
It's Me and I'm Here, by Harold C. Lyon Jr., is about *real*izing your potential.
Only Two Can Play This Game, by James Keys (the penname fr G. Spencer Brown, who wrote the *Laws of Form*).
The Risk of Loving, by Simon & Reidy.
The Magic Book of Love Exercises, by Ann-Elizabeth.

Media

Many of our attitudes are subtly shaped by the mass media, whthr we like it or nt. As A. J. Liebling once said: "Freedom of the press is guaranteed only to those who own one."
Check into *Oh What a Blow That Phantom Gave Me*, an anthropological excursion into the media by Edward Carpenter.
Power to Persuade, by Robert Cirino, documents one case aftr anothr of news distortion. Did you know that during the Vietnam War no major news agency in the U.S. referred to Asian troops hired by the CIA as "mercenaries"? Instead, they were usually called "allies."

W. A. Swanberg's biographies, *Pulitzer*, *Citizen Hearst*, & *Luce and His Empire*, give intimate portraits of the 3 greatest press lords spawned in America.

Mental Retardation

Best all-around bk is Burton Blatt's *Souls in Extremis*.

Mountains

Befre you climb a big one, write fr a free nwslttr frm Mountain Safety Research, Inc., 625 S. 96th St., Seattle, Wash. 98108. Theyve tstd & dsgnd equipmnt your life dpnds on.

And two gd prntd rsrces:
*The Book of Survival, by Anthony Greenback
*Wilderness Camping magazine, Bx 1186, Scotia, N.Y. 12302

Myths, Faking It & Nonsense

(Are you aware that a myth is almost always based on a little bit of truth?)

The B.S. Factor, by Arthur Herzog, is a skeptics-wherever-you-are-unite bk.
Myths to Live By, by Joseph Campbell, & *The Ignorance of Certainty*, by Ashley Montagu & Edw. Darling (who also wrote The *Prevalence of Nonsense*).
Into Greek myths? Read *The Greek Myths*, by Robert Graves, & *Mythology*, by Edith Hamilton.

Neglected Books

e. e. cummings' *The Enormous Room*.
Romain Rolland's *Jean Cristophe*.
Franz Kafka's *Amerika*.
Thomas Wolfe's *Look Homeward Angel*.
Irving Stone's *Lust for Life*.

Novels That Cld Change Yr Life (but probably wont)

● All the novels of Nikos Kazantzakis frm *Zorba the Greek* to *The Last Temptation of Christ* are mind busters. If you read one, youll want to read the rest.
● *Billy Budd*, by Herman Melville, hs been called "the greatest short novel ever written."

- *Herzog,* by Saul Bellow, is a Jewish answer to James Joyce's *Ulysses.*
- *The Plague,* by Albert Camus, who also wrote *The Stranger* and *The Fall.*
- Imagine turning into a television set and *Being There* with Jerzy Korsinski.
- Fr a real head trip, look into Iris Murdoch's *A Severed Head,* or any of her other bks.
- *Joseph and His Brothers* and the *Buddenbrooks,* by Thomas Mann, will dazzle and razzle you.
- *Steppenwolf* and, really, any of Hermann Hesse's bks.
- *The Possessed,* by Fyodor Dostoyevsky.
- *One Day in the Life of Ivan Denisovitch,* by Alexander Solzhenitsen.
- *The Jungle,* by Upton Sinclair.
- *Babbit,* by Sinclair Lewis.
- *Darkness at Noon,* by Arthur Koestler.
- *The Naked and the Dead,* by Norman Mailer.
- *Catch 22,* by Joseph Heller.

Poetry

For people who are into it:

"The Love Song of J. Alfred Prufrock" is one of T. S. Eliot's greatest. Albert Cullum hs written a marvelous poetry bk w/a poem as its title:

> the
> Geranium
> on the
> Window
> Sill
> Just died
> But
> Teacher
> You
> Went
> Right On

For people who arnt into it:

Sample the *Collected Poems* of Kenneth Patchen. Includes "the origin of baseball."

Propaganda

Tired of all that "Good Old Days" propaganda? Get *The Good Old Days—They Were Terrible,* by Otto L. Bettman, and show it to anyone who's feeding you that nostalgia stuff.

Radical Road

Two gd radical mgzines:
*WIN, Bx 547, Rifton, N.Y. 12471
The Realist, 595 Bwy., N.Y., N.Y. 10012

Religion

(Is religion dead? Is God dead—or hibernating?)

IN GENERAL:

- Dscvr what Thomas Merton thnks abt *Mystics and Zen Masters.*
- Check out the *Year One Catalog—A Spiritual Guide for the New Age* (ed. Ira Friedlander).
- *Tales of the Dervishes*—The Teaching Stones of the Sufi Masters (compiled by Idries Shah).
- *The Psychology of Consciousness,* by Robert Ornstein, is an excllnt companion to *On the Psychology of Meditation,* which he wrote w/Claudio Narenjo.
- "A sorcerer has no notion that he is in two places at once. To be aware of that would be the equivalent of his facing his double and the sorcerer that finds himself face to face with himself is a dead sorcerer." From *Tales of Power,* by Carlos Castaneda, who also wrote *A Separate Reality—Further Conversations with Don Juan.*
- Harvey Cox says in the *Seduction of the Spirit:* "Make-believe involves setting aside for a brief period the role, self-image, identity and world view within which one operates most of the time and trying out another way of being."
- Sam Keen's marvlous *Apology for Wonder* ends w/a quotation frm Dag Hammarskjold: "God does not die on the day when we cease to believe in a personal deity but we die on the day when our lives cease to be illuminated by the steady radiance, renewed daily, of a wonder, the source of which is beyond all reason."
- How cn you consider yrslf an educated Westerner if youve nvr actually read much of the Bible? If you appreciate clear, direct language, try out the *Living Bible* (Tyndale Press). This version is easy, fascinating readng—unlike most super-literal trnsltions, which are oftn confusing and murky.

For those of you intrstd in an exceptionlly accurate trnsltion, try David Lamsa's. For xmple, one line in the Lord's Prayer is traditionally rendered: "Lead us not into temptation . . ." Lamsa, an xprt in Aramaic, translates: "Do not let us enter into temptation . . ." If you want to know a little bit abt religions, read *The Religions of Man,* by Huston Smith.

For Jews

- *9-1/2 Mystics*—the Kabbala Today, by Herbert Weiner. A stunning intrdction to Jewish mysticism & tradition conveyed in a cntmprary settng.
- Buy the Modern Jewish Family Calendar—*A Time For Living*—beautflly illstrated w/wise sayings. For xmple: "A people's memory is history: and as a man without a memory, so a people without a history cannot grow wiser, better." —Isaac Leib Peretz.
- Devour evrythng Elie Wiesel hs wrttn. Start w/*The Oath*. (Doesnt rlly mttr where you strt.) Read *Souls on Fire* fr history or, if you like short bks, *Dawn, The Accident, The Town Beyond the Wall.* Wiesel is the heart & conscience of the mdrn Jew who hs survivd the holocaust.
- Dont listen to what anybdy says, read *Exodus* by Leon Uris. Evryone shld hv his/her own exprnce of this mdrn drama.
- *Joys of Yiddish,* by Leo Rosten. Vry imprtnt to know the meaning of such words as farshtinkener, fartootst, faygelch, fress and feh.
- *The Wisdom of Israel* (an anthology compiled by Louis Browne) frm the Old Testament to the Gemara. Xmple: "A rabbi saw a man give a penny to a begger publicly. He said to him: 'Better had you given him nothing, than put him to shame.'" Another: "If one man says to thee: 'Thou art a donkey,' do not mind. If two speak thus, purchase a saddle for thyself."
- *In the Days of Simon Stern,* a novel by Arthur A. Cohen.
- When you start gtting serious,
The Story of Judaism, Bernard J. Bamberger.
Basic Judaism, Milton Steinberg.
Guide to the Jewish Holidays, Hayyim Schauss.
What Is a Jew?, Morris Kurtzer.

Encourage your school or univ. to hlp you remembr the Holocaust. Write to United Federation of Teachers, 260 Park Av. S., N.Y., N.Y. 10010 & ask fr the 12-pg teachrs rsrce unit called "The Holocaust, The Jewish Ordeal in Nazi-Occupied Europe 1933–45."

(Visit Israel. The least you cld do is eat bagel, lox and crm cheese for brunch on Sunday.)

FOR CATHOLICS

If you wnt to gt bck into religion a new way, try:

- Andrew Greeley's *The Touch of Spirit & The Jesus Myth.*
- Anthony Padavano's *Dawn Without Darkness.* Expansve, poetic, universal, graphic . . . highly spiritual.

- Henry Nouveu's *Intimacy*. Interpersonal, humanistic.
- Eugene Kennedy's *The Pain of Being Human*. He also wrote . . .
- *What a Modern Catholic Believes About Sex*.

FOR PROTESTANTS

- Coordinator of Family Ministries, 475 Riverside Dr., Rm. 711, N.Y., N.Y. 10027 has all sorts of intrstng literature.
- Subscribe to *Faith at Work*, Bx 1790, Waco, Tex. 76703. $7 fr one yr. "Seeking God in a face to face encounter . . . determining what you are afraid of and heading in that direction. All growth begins with new awareness."
- Look ovr an issue of the *Christian Century* if you are the intellectual sort.
- Try *Preludes to Prayer* (365 Daily Meditations). Get into C. S. Lewis's *Mere Christianity* or dscvr the "hidden" meaning of his science fiction trilogy.
- What do you knw abt people like Rosemary Radford Ruether or James Gustafson, or the German theologians Jurgen Moltmann or Karl Barth?
- Two exceptional bks: *Situation Ethics*, by Joseph Fletcher, and *The Dynamics of Faith*, by Paul Tillich.

Sayings & Aphorisms

The best collection of short thoughts by famous people is *Collected Thoughts for Living*, by William Sentman Taylor & Phoebe L. S. Taylor.

Science Fiction

A Canticle for Liebowitz, by Walker M. Miller Jr. In a hellish, barren desert in the 32d century, a humble monk unearths a fragile link to the 20th century. Its a handwrittn documnt from the blessed saint Liebowitz w/the holy words: "Pound pastrami, can kraut, six bagels—bring home for Emma."

Rendezvous With Rama, by Arthur C. Clark. By the yr 2130 the Mars-based radars were dscvrng new asteroids at the rate of a dozen a day.

Cat's Cradle, by Kurt Vonnegut.

Sex

Sex and Birth Control, by E. Jane Lieberman & Ellen Peck.

Sexual Myths and Fallacies, by James L. McCary.

The Sensuous Person, by Albert Ellis.

The New Intimacy: Open Ended Marriage and Alternate Lifestyles, by Ronald Mazur.

Commonsense Sex, by Ronald Mazur.

The Sex Book, by Goldstein & others.

The Joy of Sex, by Alex Comfort.

Masters and Johnson Explained, by Nat Lehrman.

Facts About Sex for Today's Youth, by Sol Gordon.

The Sexual Adolescent, by Sol Gordon.

Sex in a Plain Brown Wrapper, by the Student Committee on Sexuality at Syracuse Univ. (send $1 to Ed-U Press, 760 Ostrum Av., Syracuse, N.Y. 13210).

Startling Theories

Worlds in Collision & Ages in Chaos, by Immanuel Velikovsky. When Velikovsky's bks apprd, the scientific estblshmnt ws outraged.

The Late Great Planet Earth, by Hal Lindsey. Do the Scriptures forecst the End in Our Time?

Teaching

If tchng's your goal, read *Teacher*, by Sylvia Ashton Warner.

John Holt is one of the mst imprtant figures in educ. today. Check out *How Children Learn*.

Trips

Zen and the Art of Motorcycle Maintenance, by Robert M. Pirsig. Another Moby Dick? Some say so.

I See By My Outfit, by Peter S. Beagle, N.Y. to Calif. on a motorscooter by the author of the immensely absorbng *The Last Unicorn*.

Travels With Charlie, by John Steinbeck.

A Moveable Feast, by Ernest Hemingway.

Weird (but attractive)

Trout Fishing in America, by Richard Brautigan. Hardly abt trout only, but it seems to be abt America.

What's Normal?

People who are nt different usually dont hv much to offer. Here are 3 essential bks by different writers.

*The Politics of Experience, by R. D. Laing.

*Where the Wasteland Ends, by Theodore Roszak.

*The Second Sin, by Thomas Szaz.

If you cn handle it, *Civilization and Its Discontents*, by Sigmund Freud, is short & easy to read.

3 CATALOGS & PAMPHLETS

Black?

Fr a catalog of 600 bks on the Black experience, write to Robin's Distributing Co., 6 N. 13th St., Philadelphia, Pa. 19107.

Books About Almost Anything

Dover Publications, 180 Varick St., N.Y., N.Y. 10014, has a wide, wild assrtmnt of bks, lots of them gd & cheap. Write & ask to be put on their mailing list; yll get a flood of flyers & catalogs.

Or write to Publishers Central Bureau, Dept. 379, 1 Champion Av., Avenel, N.J. 07131 for reglr listngs of discount bks, prints & records.

Cheap

PAMPHLETS & BOOKLETS (& EVEN BOOKS):

Really gd, cheap pmphlts abt practically evrythng. Write to:
   Public Affairs Pamphlets, 381 Park Av. S., N.Y., N.Y. 10016
And all srts of infrmation on almst anythng you cn think of, plus trnscrpts of happenings like the House Judiciary Committee impchmnt

hrngs. Gd & cheap. Write for catalogs to Sup't. of Documents, Govt. Printing Office, Wash., D.C. 20402

PROPERTY:

Your own U.S. govt. sells a lot of surplus property cheap. Write to the Supt. of Documents & ask for *How to Buy Surplus Personal Property*. Costs 25c.

Sources & Resources

- *The Great Escape*—A srcebk of delights & pleasures fr the mind & body. For xmple: Aikido, Arica, Ascid, ashrams and astrology.
- *Real Time I*
- *Toward Social Change*—A handbk fr those who will.
- *PsychoSources*—A real psycho mish-mash. Vry stimulatng.
- *Source*—An organizng tool fr exploitng communcations rsrces.
- *Peoples Yellow Pages of America*—A directry of non-rip-off type srvces, like where to meet people, alternatve education, growth prgrms, & how to raise money & travel cheap.
- *Public Works*—Everythng.

4 EMOTIONS

Crisis?

If yre really in a bad way, try Recovery, Inc. Evry mjr city hs a chapter of this really sensible self-help group. Learn more abt it by writng to them at 116 S. Michigan Av., Chicago, Ill. 60603.

Call Contact or your local hotline or crisis cntr. If you dont know where to reach a crisis cntr or hotline, try the nearst college campus student cntr.

For a directory of hotlines, switchboards and related services, write to:
The Communication Co., 1826 Fell St., San Francisco, Calif. 94117.

Call your local mental health assoc.

Write to the National Institute of Mental Health, HEW, Public Health Service, 5600 Fishers Lane, Rockville, Md. 20852, & ask them to snd you their pamphlet *Pressure* (DHEW Publication No. ADM 74-21). Ask them also to snd a list of other pblications that cld be helpful.

Try talkng thngs over w/someone you like.

Hung Up?

- Try helpng yrslf first.
Or send $5.50 to the Assn. fr Rational Thinking, 117 W. Main St., Madison, Wisc., & ask fr Maxine C. Maultsby's *Handbook of Rational Self-Counseling*.
- Or find out how to live rationally by gettng into *Guide for Rational Living*, by Ellis and Harper.
- Or maybe you can find security in a rapidly changng wrld by *Shifting Gears* à la Nena & George O'Neill.
- Or dscvr how to be an *Authentic Person* (in a wrld in crisis) Sydney J. Harris's way.

5 ENVIRONMENT

Ecology

It's your planet & theres no way to ignore it (it wont go away & you cant get off). Do smthing, now. Gd rsrces:
Read *The Organizers Manual*, from Bantam Books, & *The Environmental Handbook*, from Ballantine. Then act.
Join the Sierra Club, Mill Tower, San Francisco, Calif., 94104 (there are regional chpters all arnd the cntry) and get the *Sierra Club Bulletin;* or the National Audubon Society (local chptrs all ovr) & get the fantastically beautiful *Audubon* magzine.
Write to the National Wildlife Federation, 1412 16th St. N.W., Wash., D.C. 20236 fr a copy of their *Conservation Directory*, which lists every conservation grp in the cntry. Pick one nr you & wrk for it.

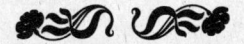

Natural Healing

Want to be nturlly healthy, vibrantly alive & in tune w/the whole earth? Greg Brodsky tells all in *From Eden to Aquarius*.

Nature

Dont get so wrapped up in the urban, suburban or schl life that you forget (or nvr discvr) the joys of open cntry, frsh air & whats left of the Good Planet Earth. Why nt:
    camp on a mountaintop
    watch the moon rise
    go on a bike trip or picnic
    backpack alng the Appalachian Trail or Rocky Mountain Trail
And if you jst cant get away, stay in touch by reading the bks of Rachel Carson (*The Sea Around Us, The Edge of the Sea, Under the Sea Wind*) — informative, factual & incredibly poetic & moving.

Plants as Pets

Theres mr to raisng plnts than jst watrng them when theyre thirsty & gvng them sunlight. Plnts grw bttr if you play music & sing fr them & stroke their leaves & love them.

Buy your first plnts at a greenhse & gt their advice on waterng, fertlizng & light. Once you understnd the basics, tke cuttings frm friends' plnts & mke a terrarium, bonsai or a vivarium (a terrarium w/small animals to kp the plnts cmpany).

Strnge, how plnts nvr stp growing, while adult people shrink.

Rural & Wild

Publications

Two of the best pblications on the country existence that pick up where the Whole Earth Catalog (now revised and called the Whole Earth Epilog) leaves off:
    Natural Lifestyles, Bx 1101, Felton, Calif. 95108
    Mother Earth News, Bx 70, Hendersonville, N.C. 28739

The mst intrstng magazine fr people who wnt to find out abt & do the Appalachian folk art scene. Sbscrbe to *Foxfire* (about $6), write to The Foxfire Fund, Inc., Rabun Gap, Ga. 30568.

Read:
   The Mother Earth Hassle-Free Indoor Plant Book, by Lynn & Joel Rapp
   Free Food & Medicine (provided by nature, no charge)

Read:
   Ginseng and Other Medicinal Plants, by H. D. Harrington. (What did people do befre there wr pills? The folk-lore of healing has its roots in wild herbs & plants.)
   Western Edible Wild Plants, by H. D. Harrington. (What to eat & what nt to eat on the trail. If yre going to pick your own, be careful! Sm harmfl varieties are nearly identical to the gd ones.)
   *The bks of Euell Gibbons: *Stalking the Wild Asparagus, Stalking the Blue-Eyed Scallop, Stalking the Healthful Herbs, Stalking the Good Life, Beachcomber's Handbook.*

Wild About Wilderness?

Survival With Style, by Bradford Angier, is for picknickers, hunters, fishermen & campers.

Look into the Wilderness Society, 729 15th St. N.W., Wash., D.C. 20005, & National Parks & Conservation Assoc., 1701 18th St. N.W., Wash., D.C. 20009. Lots of wilderness trips, bks, articles.

6
FILMS

(Some) of the best (oldies) of all time:

*King of Hearts
*Rashomon
*The Bicycle Thief
*Children of Paradise
*Citizen Kane
*Open City
*La Strada
*City Lights
*Modern Times
*The Great Dictator
*Potemkin
*Alexander Nevsky
*The Blue Angel
*The Informer
*Casablanca
*The Seventh Seal
*A Night at the Opera
*A Day at the Races

7
FOOD AND COOKING

Grow Your Own
You don't even need a garden w/earth. Try hydroponics; all you need is air and water. Send 25c for *Hydroponics as a Hobby* to: U. of Illinois, College of Agricltre, Extension Srvce in Agricltre & Home Econ., Urbana, Ill. 61801.

Spice of Life:
Grow your own herbs to go along w/the food yre going to grow (or maybe just w/the food yre going to cook, if you dont want to tackle the food-growing part jst yet). Write to Nichols Garden Nursery, 1190 Pacific Hwy., Albany, Ore. 97321, or Meadowbrook Herb Garden, Wyoming, R.I. 02898.

Brew Your Own
Or Your Very Own Brew (tea, that is, not beer). Lots of dffrnt knds of teas. Try sm. But first read *The Book of Tea*, by Kakuzo Okakura, or *About Tea, Coffee and Spices*, by John A. Murchie.
   Free catalogs of fruit, vegtble and flwr seeds. Send to Clyde Robin, Bx 2091, Castro Valley, Calif. 94546, or W. Atlee Burpee Co., Riverside, Calif. 92502.

Cook It Yrself
Whethr you grow it or buy it, do your own cookng, even if you live at home. Start w/a paprbck cookbk and then improvise once you understnd basic fryng, bakng, etc. *The Joy of Cooking*, by Rombauer & Becker, & *The Natural Foods Cookbook*, by Hunter, are gd places to start. Also *Let's Cook It Right*, by Adele Davis, & *The Impoverished Students Book of Cookery, Drinkery and Housekeepery*, by Jay F. Rosenberg. Or just ask mom.

Food Nut?
"Food Is More Than Just Something to Eat" is free frm Nutrition USA, Pueblo, Colo. 81009.

8
GETTING INVOLVED

Action
If yre over 21 & looking fr smthing exciting to do fr the nxt 2 yrs, cnsdr joining either the Peace Corps (srvce abroad) or Vista (in this cntry). Write to Action, Wash., D.C., for infrmtion on how to qualify.

Lend A Hand
Want to hlp poor people? Send 25c fr a catalog of stuff (clthes, jwlry, etc) handmade by poor people in the South. Write to Liberty House, Bx 3468, Jackson, Miss.

Work w/older citizens. Get details frm Future Homemakers of America, 2010 Mass. Ave. N.W., Wash., D.C. 20036.

Summers
(See Also Working and Volunteering)

If yve got an entire summer free & wnt an entire education (sort of), read *Civilization,* by Kenneth Clark. Simply the whole wrks, slightly condnsed, bt profusely illustrated.

Dscvr America (or redscvr it). Find out abt Amer. Youth Hostels, Inc., Natl Campus, Delaplane, Va. 22025.

Know where you wnt to go? Write to McDonald's Maps, Bx 11189. Chicago, Ill. 60611, & ask fr a Heritage road map of the areas you wnt to visit.
   Want to work in parks & forests? Apply, starting each December, to SCA Olypic View Dr., Rte 1, Bx 573A, Vashon, Wash. 98070, or write to Youth Conservation Corps, Bx 2975, Wash., D.C. 20013.

Volunteering
(Volunteerng is a gd way to prepare fr the work wrld. Besides, its jst a gd thng to do.)

Read *A Public Citizen's Action Manual,* by Donald K. Ross (w/intro by Ralph Nader).

Write (or tlk) to:
Commission on Voluntary Srvce. & Action, 475 Riverside Dr., Rm. 665, N.Y., N.Y. 10027 (Phone 212 870-2707).
International Secretariat for Voluntary Service, Geneva, Switzerland.
National Center for Voluntary Action, Dir. of Communications, Wash., D.C. 20006

If you feel you waste a lt of time, do smthing obviously worthwhile; its really nice to be hlpful to another human being, even if yre nt a Boy or Girl Scout.
Contact:
Assoc. of Volunteer Bureaus of America, Bx 7253, Kansas City, Mo. 64113, or National Cntr for Volunteer Action, 1735 I St., N.W., Wash., D.C. 20006.

Working

What to Read
Working, by Studs Turkel, will hlp you know wht to expect.
If you arnt worried abt hazards at wrk, you shld be. Read *Work Is Dangerous to Your Health,* by J. M. Stellman & Susan M. Daum, a handbk of health hazards on the job & wht you cn do about them.
Working Loose, availble frm the Amer. Friends Servce Committee, 2160 Luke St., San Francisco, Calif., 94120, will tell you how to find work you wnt to do.

Work Abroad
Club de Vieux Manoir, 10 rue de la Cossonerie, Paris 75011 France.
Experiment in Intl Living, Putney, Vt. 05346.
Information, Council on Intl Educational Exchange, 777 UN Plaza, N.Y., N.Y. 10017.
International Personnel Pool, 53055 Monteriggioni, Italy.
Kibbutz Aliya Desk, 575 Av. of the Americas, N.Y., N.Y. 10011 (for work on a kibbutz in Israel).
Strichting Internationale Werkkampen (Intl Wrk Camp Foundtion), Breestraat 53, Lerden, Netherlands.
Read *How to Get a Job Overseas,* by Curtis Casewit.

Work in the U.S.
Amer. Friends Srvce Committee, 2160 Luke St., San Francisco, Calif. 94120.
Outward Bound, 165 W. Putnam Av., Greenwich, Conn. 06830.
Sierra Club, 1050 Mills Tower, San Francisco, Calif. 94104.
Work Force, Vocations for Social Change, American Univ., Wash., D.C.

9 HANDICAPPED

If you are handicapped or concernd about someone who is, pose sm questions to Closer Look, Bx 1492, Wash., D.C. 20013. Ask to be placed on their mailng list. Its a srvce of the National Special Education Information Center (Health, Education & Welfare Dept.). Their purpose is to help people w/handicaps find educationl, social & career rsrces within the community.

Or write to: Committee for the Handicapped, The People-to-People Program 1218 New Hampshire Av. N.W., Wash., D.C. 20036.

10 INTELLECTUAL?

Subscribe to:
*The New York Times (229 W. 43 St., N.Y., N.Y. 10036).
*Partisan Review (Rutgers Univ., 1 Richardson St., New Brunswick, N.J. 08903).
*Society (Rutgers again).
*Saturday Review/World (450 Pacific Av., San Francisco, Calif. 94133).
*Commentary (165 E. 56 St., N.Y., N.Y. 10022).

11 I.Q. OUT OF SIGHT?

Find out if your I.Q. is high enough to join the exclusive MENSA. Bx 86, Bklyn., N.Y. 11223.

12 MONEY

How to handle the hassle
Read: *How to Travel Without Being Rich,* by Norman D. Ford.

How to Make It
Good ways (nt the usual stuff like shvlng snow, mwing lawns, etc.).
*Buy, or design, your own nmbr stencils (at least 3″ high) & paint people's house nmbrs on their curb or mailbx. Chrge 2 bits, do 10 an hr.
*Write and mimeogrph sheets of paper tllng of all the odd jobs yd be wllng to do (gt acrss the idea that the wrk is gd & the prices cheap). Distrbte the sheets arnd yr neighbrhd, tck them up in the sprmrkt, etc.
*Orgnize a Strday or Sndy play progrm fr little kids so the parents cn go shpping. Gd w/a friend.
*House-sit while people are on vcation. Feed & wlk pets, water plants, etc.
*Snd jokes to Playboy or Reader's Digest (& mk up true stories fr confession mgzines).
*Hv a water fight &, whle yre at it, wash a few cars.
*Cllect your neighbors' junk & hv a yrd sale.

13
NEW EXPERIENCES & GOOD THINGS TO DO

Acting, Theater, etc.

Many people are actors without really knowing it. They imitate movie or stage stars, sing along w/the radio or TV, mk up their own funny voices. There are opportunities evrywhre to join theater & drama grps. If music is your thng, try out fr a chorus or orchstra, or tk your instrmnt a little mr seriously & strt yr own grp.
Gd rscrcs:
Stage Makeup, by Herman Buchman
Filmmakers Newsletter, Bx 115, Ward Hill, Mass. 01830
The Puppet Theater Handbook, by Batchelder.

Assorted Ideas

How to make thngs like slotted animals, Kiko's seagull bed friend, windowshade maps & murals, tissue fish, questions & solutions. All in *Making Things—The Handbook of Creative Discovery*, by Ann Wiseman.
How to Find Out About Biofeedback by Turning On the Power of Your Mind, by Marvin Karlrus & Lewis M. Andrews.
A Catalog of the Ways People Grow, by Severen Peterson, Brief dscriptions of patanjalis yoga, aikado, Gestalt therapy, Alexander technique, Hadidism, hatha yoga, har, etc., etc. . . .
How to make it as a vegetable (eater). *Victory Through Vegetables*, by Joan Wiener.

Or why not try:
*Yoga
*Yogurt (?)
*TM (Transcendental Meditation ws intrdced into this cntry by Maharishi Mahesh Yogi early in the 60s)
*Massage (there are lots of gd bks)
*Kung Fu
*Memorizng *Kung Fu Meditations* (& Chinese Proverbial Wisdom) selectd by Ellen Kei Hun.
*Rememberng dreams, First read Erich Fromm's *The Forgotten Language*.
*Get hold of this yr's *World Almanac* and dscvr a wrld you didnt know much about.
*Plan to get to Europe somehow.
*Enroll in a Red Cross first aid course, jst in case.
*For house plant freaks: *The N.Y. Times Book of House Plants*.
*For organic garden freaks: *The Organic Gardener*, by Catherine Osgood Foster.
The Secret Life of Plants

Be An Activist

Write a lttr on imprtnt issues to local or natl newspapers or magazines. See how many you can gt printd in one yr. If none are placed, follw up w/mr lettrs askng why the originls wrnt used.

If you spot a hazardous toy or product call (toll-free) 800-638-2666 (Consumer Product Safety Commission).

Join Common Cause, 2030 M St. N.W., Wash., D.C. 20036.

Clean It Up

If your neighbrhd is dirty, littrd & smthing to walk thru wo/seeing, get yr frnds & whoevr else will hlp to spnd a Saturday cleaning it up. See if a local deli will spnsr sm free food. Ask the local DPW to lend a truck to haul away junk & tools to pick it up with. Gd projct fr clubs, community organiztions, etc.

Come To Your Senses

(& then theyll come to you)

Dont talk all one day.
Dont eat all one day.
Wr a blindfld all one day & hv someone lead you arnd. The point is to bcme mr sensitive to your own senses & to appreciate the situation of people who cant enjoy them all.

Explore Your Mind

Theres mr there than you may know. Try sm (or all) of these xprmnts to find out where yre at.

*Give away smthng you are really attachd to, fr no special reason.
*Gv up your worst habit fr a wk, or do it til' yre sick of it.
*Mk up a cultural value all your own.
*Lrn to do smthing (like play the guitar) so you dont have to spnd the rest of your life saying "Gee I wish I could play the guitar."

Future

Freakng out on the future? Get in touch w/the World Future Society, 4916 St. Elmo Av. (Bethesda), Wash., D.C., 20014.

Leonard Cohen

If you arnt into his songs, begin w/Suzanne (for you've touched her perfect body with your mind).

Mind Games

Psychics hv alwys claimed they cn do outrageous thngs & the latest crop is no exception. Besides the usual seances & tble levitating, the mst unusual is Michael Manning, who rprtdly bends forks & spoons w/his mind. People concntrtng together on one prticlr thought are said to accmplsh other phenomena.

In one of those odd moments when yve got nthing to do, you & sm frnds wld probably get a chrge frm exprmntng w/the unknwn. (You cld start w/ouija brd & wrk your way up to—bending spoons?)

Nostalgia

Hv you noticd that a lt of "getting back to the good old days" is media hype to entice you to buy thngs you wldnt ordinarily want? One of the thngs we cld really get bck to is pride in ones own craftsmnship. (People didnt used to bld thngs dsgnd to fall aprt in a few yrs.) Its fantastic to mke smthing yrslf. Bake bread. Mke your own clothes. Assmble a collage that rprsnts an idea, or yrslf. Start w/makng thngs fr yrslf, then give them away (gd vibes).

Nothing to do on Sunday?

Read the N.Y. Times
Or watch educationl TV or sm of the public-srvce programs such as news docmntaries or intrvw shows à la Meet the Press or Face the Nation. (By the way, public TV is usually boring on wkdays—but rarely on Sundays.)

Throw Your Voice

A new twist to the pen-pal idea is to xchnge tapes of your voice w/people thru the mail. Fr complte details write The Voicespondence Club, Bx 207, Shillington, Pa. 19607.

Travel

Fr sm intrstng variations on trvlng, write to American River Touring Assoc., 1016 Jackson St., Oakland, Calif. 94607., or International Bicycle Touring Society, 846 Prospect St., La Jolla Calif. 92037.

14
OTHER CLASSIFIEDS

Watch the ads in these publications. There are lts of srprises.
- The National Observer
- The Village Voice
- Saturday Review/World
- Sunday N.Y. Times (the back of the sports sction)
- Mother Earth News

15
RUNAWAYS

If you knw someone who has run away frm home, ask him/her to at least call Operation Peace of Mind, 1-800-231-6946, a confidential, toll-free number, which cn reassure parents of aliveness.

16
SCHOOLS & WHAT TO DO ABOUT THEM

Alternatives

COLLEGE

(Thinkng of going to college but afraid the traditional scene wll trn you off? Invstgte these non-traditional colleges w/their innovations in free-spirited learning.)

Franconia College, Franconia, N.H. 03580
Goddard College, Plainfield, Vt. 05667
Hampshire College, Amherst, Mass. 01002
Simon's Rock College, Gt. Barrington, Mass. 01230

HIGH SCHOOL

(If yre planning to drop out, there are bks available to gv you sm idea of your state's h.s. equivalency prgrm. It may nt be as diffclt as you thnk.)

Keep posted on the alternative h.s. scene thru New School Exchange, Pettigrew, Ark. 72752. Sbscription to this magazine costs $10.
Or write to:
*National Alternative Schools, School of Educ., U. of Mass., Amherst, Mass. 01002.
*National Consortium for Options in Public Education, School of Educ., Indiana U., Bloomington, Ind. 47401.
*Alternatives, 1526 Gravenstein Hwy, No. Sebastopol, Calif. 97452 (ask for their directory of Free Schools; Personal Growth; Social Change).

If yre trying to chnge schools, contact The High School Project, 3130 M St. N.W., Wash., D.C. 20007. Phone (202) 965-4880 or, in the Eastern states, call toll-free (800) 424-9216.

FREE SCHOOLS, NEW RULES

Fr infrmation on free schools fr yrself or your own children, write to:

*Do It Now Foundation, 6136 Carlos Av., Hollywood, Calif. 90028
*Teacher Drop Out Center, Bx 521, Amherst, Mass. 01002
*Observations From the Treadmill, 357 Hidden River Rd., Narberth, Pa. 19702

SCHOOLS BY MAIL

Test out your interest & motivation in a subject by taking a correspondence course. For a listing of extension & correspondence courses availble frm regionally accredited colleges & universities, write to National University Extension Assoc., 1 Dupont Circle, Suite 360, Wash., D.C. 20036. Fr a list of private companies offering correspondence courses, write to National Home Study Council, 1601 18th St. N.W., Wash., D.C. 20009.

SCHOLARSHIPS, ETC.

Find out abt schlrships, fllwshps, loans, part-time jbs, etc. Send 50c for "Need A Lift?" to: Amer. Legion, Dept. S, Bx 1055, Indianapolis, Ind. 46206.

Campaign

Try a subtle campaign to intrdce *Psychology for You* into your school. This txtbk by Sol Gordon contains vibrations appreciated mainly by yng people.

Re-Examination

If your school is re-examining itslf, fnd out abt other schools that are too. Write to: Jeff Hanson, Wentworth College, Spokane, Wash. 99251.

Deschooling

Are you tired, rundown, bored, disappointd, crazy, ugly? Hv you come a long way for nothing? Are you spnding more time on English 101 and enjyng it less? Wld you rather do it yrslf? If you answrd yes to any of the above, yre ripe for deschooling. Get a copy of *School You*, by Margaret R. Johnston, available only by snding $2 to School You, Bx 1082, Binghamton, N.Y. 13902.

135

17
UNKNOWN ARTIST

Find out abt—& dscvr—Egon Schiele (b. 1890 in Austria, d. 1918).

18
V.D.

Worried about it?
Every major city has a V.D. hot line, or call toll-free "Operation Venus" at 1-800-523-1885
Protect your lover, wear a rubber.

19
WOMEN'S LIBERATION

Advice For Men

"The most unsatisfactory men are those who pride themselves on their virility and regard sex as if it were some sort of athletics at which you win cups. It is a woman's spirit and mood a man has to stimulate in order to make sex interesting. The real lover is the man who can thrill you by just touching your head and smiling into your eyes."
  Frm *My Story*, by Marilyn Monroe
  Read *The Liberated Man* (subtitle: Beyond Masculinity: Freeing Men and Their Relationships With Women), by Warren Farrel.

Advice For Women

Join NOW now, or a women's consciousness-raising grp. Write NOW, 5 S. Wabash, Suite 1615, Chicago, Ill. 60603.
Subscribe to *Ms* magazine, 123 Garden St., Marion, Ohio 43302.
Find out abt pblications, pmphlts, etc., frm KNOW, Inc., Bx 86031, Pittsburgh, Pa. 15211.
Materials abt sexism are availble frm N.E.A., The Academic Bldg., Saw Mill Rd., West Haven, Conn. 06516.
Today's changing roles: An Approach to Non-Sexist Teaching, dvlpd by Educational Challenges, Inc. The National Foundation for the Improvement of Education, Suite 91B, 1156 15th St. N.W., Wash., D.C. 20005.

Read:
And Jill Came Tumbling Down—Sexism in American Education.
Fear of Flying, by Erica Jong, Vry sexual, vivid & female (whatever that means).
The Female Eunuch, by Germaine Greer.
Getting Closer—Body Work for Women, by Anne Kent Rush.
Our Bodies, Our Selves, by the Boston Women's Health Book Collective.
Rebirth of Feminism, by Judith Hole & Ellen Levine.
Everything a Woman Needs to Know to Get Paid What She's Worth, by Caroline Bird.

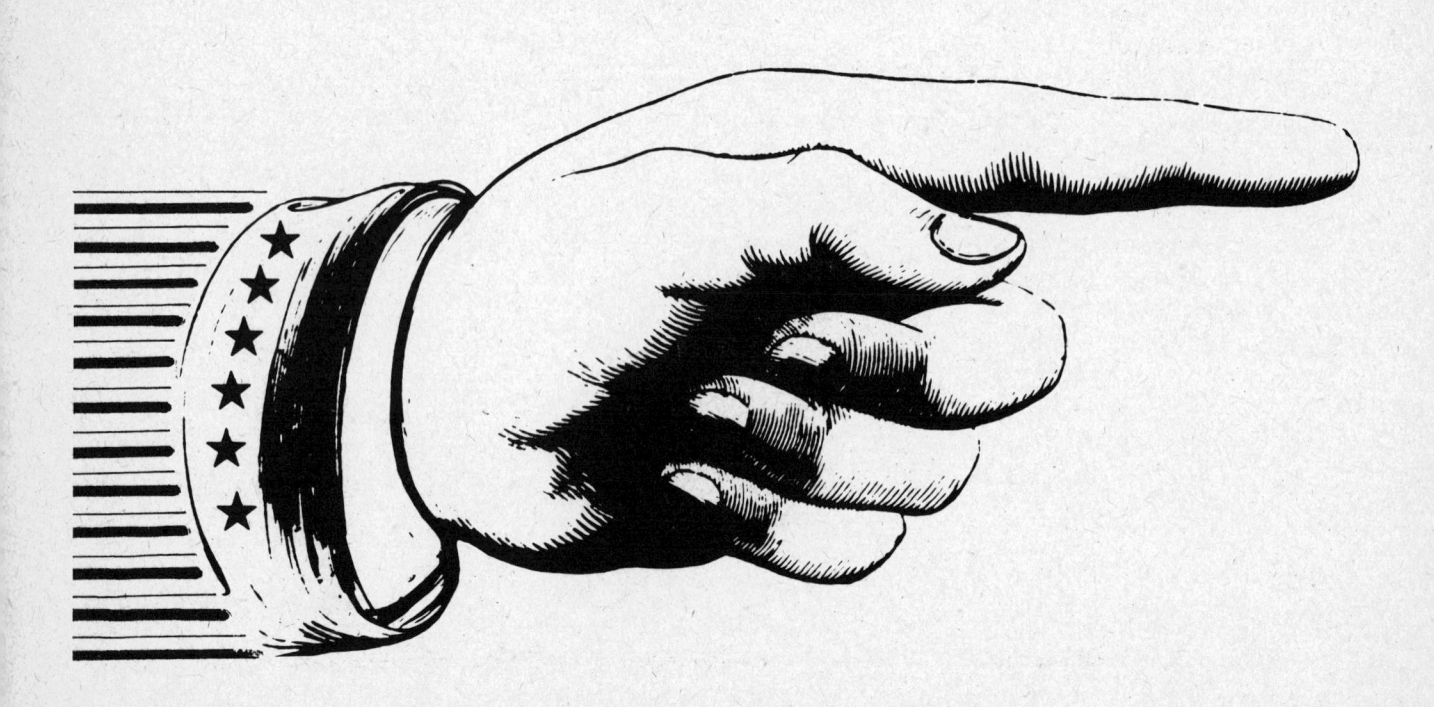

ABOUT THE AUTHORS

SOL GORDON, Ph.D. is a professor of Child and Family Studies at Syracuse University's College for Human Development. As a psychologist, his specialties include: teenagers, education that works, sexuality, turning people on to life, and writing controversial stuff.

ROGER CONANT is a professional writer and cartoonist. He co-authored the text of four of the comic books contained herein — as well as designing and illustrating them. He also contributed many survival ideas to the overall book and was instrumental in the preparation of the manuscript.

HERE IS WHAT THEY HAVE TO SAY ABOUT THEMSELVES:

WHO AM I?
by Roger Conant

"Know them by their fruits."

Look at my cartoons. I think that, despite a few inevitable restrictions, they show the real me — for better or worse. Could you tell from them that I am a Jesus freak?

Creative Infidelity
On Being Happy In An Unhappy World

by Sol Gordon*

How can I be happy if I have public memories like

> The Spanish Civil War
> The Second World War
> The Soviet carnage
> The American Black experience

and for me the special disasters

> The Holocaust
> Vietnam
> The assassination of heroic possibilities
> The Yom Kippur War

---

*The author wishes to use the occasion of this publication to come out of his closet and declare that he is polymorphous perverse. He dedicates this piece to all the women in his life, to all the men in his life, and especially to the wife in his life.

This statement appeared originally in *The Humanist*, January 1975.

and private tragedies

    Bill, is it true that only the good die young?
    J., will you ever love me?
    Mom and Dad, you would have been so proud
     had you lived nine more years!
    And Bobby, not even 30 years old - why
     did you blow your brains out?

And yet

  I'm mainly happy

because

  I believe

life is not a meaning but an opportunity.

  life is not
   harmonious
   congruent
   rational
   or heroic (for me)

All really pleasurable experiences are

  of brief duration
  repeatable from time to time
  but brief
      love
      orgasm
      sunsets

I love many people

  in love with only one I can
  count on always

I love to do many things

  (and I have the money for everything
  I want that costs money)

I'm clever

  enough to play with clever notions

like

  cheap is expensive
  relevance is boring
  if God is dead, She must have been alive once
  if you are bored, you are boring to be with
  all thoughts are normal (guilt is the energy
   for obsessive unacceptable thoughts)

I know what to do when I'm depressed

  I learn something new

I'm a big proponent of the "Sug a gut wort" theory. I'm nice to most people, even people I don't know or like.

I have little patience for people who claim they are objective, fair or non-directive.

Sometimes

>I'm sad for this world
>and for my lack of heroic possibilities

But

>I do the best I can
>I give humorous talks and write books

Yet,

>I sacrifice little
>I eat all my meals enjoyably
> without thinking about India
>I make bigger than most people's charitable
> contributions
>I'm politically left, socially right
>I select and don't settle

And these are the fifty-one* "things" I enjoy the most:

1. Daydream the destruction of the forces of evil

2. Nightdream the current love of my life

3. A New York City weekend with my wife

    (a) gourmet meal
    (b) ballet
    (c) topped off by the Sunday New York Times in the bathtub of a luxurious hotel. (Ever since I can remember I've always thought that if it didn't appear in the New York Times, it didn't happen - little of me has appeared in the Times so I feel compelled to read it religiously)

4. Marc Chagall

5. Bittersweet stories and chocolate

6. Mozart

7. Lots of cities

    Jerusalem
    Copenhagen
    Florence
    Bruges
    to say nothing of San Francisco and Rome

---

*If we want to grow up and not old we should be able to intensely enjoy at least the number of things equal to our age.

8. Lots of museums

    The Met, Hermitage, MOMA, Frick,
    Prado, Uffizi, Tate, Gardiner
    and would you believe the one in Philadelphia?

9. Lynd Ward and Kathe Kollwitz

10. Starting a new Iris Murdock novel on my way to California and finishing it on my way back

11. Having a marvelously funny, reminiscent day with one of my friends, taking in a walk, a scenic meal and sometimes a deeply agonizing but liberating philosophic dialogue

12. The joy of Owen Dodson, one of America's finest Black poets

13. Harold and Maude, all of Charles Chaplin's and about 31 films in my life with "Les Enfants du Paradis" as the supreme triumph

14. When someone says to me, "Oh, so you are Sol Gordon"

15. Saying "no" when someone asks, "Can I trust you?"

16. Sad, serious plays like "A Long Day's Journey Into Night"

17. The boredom of Andy Warhol

18. The agony and music of my Judaism

19. Public television: Upstairs and Downstairs

20. Elie Wiesel, because he reminds me of who I am

21. Making fun of people who are "so busy" but accomplish little

22. Uninterrupted classical music

23. Sending out vibrations to perfect strangers and then asking if they got them. Some do and we become friends

24. Virgil Thompson and Gertrude Stein's Four Saints in Three Acts—even though I seem to be the only one left who adores it (Pigeons on the Grass, Alas)

25. Risking intimacy quickly

26. Presently alive people whose "work" I admire, but I suspect we wouldn't hit it off if we met: Leonard Cohen, Sidney Lumet, Ralph Nader, Marlon Brando, Gloria Steinem, Bella Abzug, Ingmar Bergman, Hugh Prather and Maude

27. Feeling younger now than I felt 27 years ago

28. Being alone sometimes

29. Nature, but not too much of it at a time

30. Walks

31. Reading slowly the good novelists, like Mann, Camus, Thomas Wolfe, Dostoyevsky, Herman Melville, Romain Rolland, Virginia Woolf, I. J. Singer and would you believe Sholem Asch and the fellow who wrote The French Lieutenant's Woman

32. The big, beautiful house we live in although everyone says it's too big for the two of us

33. The excitement of the opera at the Met

34. The paintings of the now-known Fasanella and the still-unknown Howard Siskowitz and Rita Dominguez

35. Imagining the surprise of everybody when they discover who I really am

36. Fantasizing the number one or two spot for my still unpublished "Sex Is" book on the New York Times best sellers list

37. Realizing as an ultra busy person I have the time for everything I want to do

38. Convincing people I read minds

39. Playing with remedial educators with my slogan, "Don't try to unblock a block with a block"

40. The Tchaikovsky Trio in A Minor, op. 50 with Arthur, Jascha and Gregor

41. Britten's Serenade for Tenor (Peter Pears) Horn and Strings

42. T.S. Eliot's, "Let us go you and I"

43. Being warm and intimate with people I care about

44. Remembering my mother's expressions like, "How can good food be bad for you?"

45. The furniture of George Nakashima

46. Sex

47. I love teaching, influencing, intellectualizing (especially with people who appreciate my sense of humor)

48. I love being influenced by and learning from people who are really smart and who don't take themselves too seriously

49. I enjoy introducing to new friends my ideas and experiences such as the ballet and things Jewish

50. When asked to do something I don't want to do with the incentive "You'll make a lot of money"—I revel in responding, "I'm not interested. I'm independently wealthy"

51. Not wasting my Time by reading it in the john.

   I stay happy, partly by being unfaithful to my humanistic aspirations. With a little imagination, anyone can

   Why travel heavy
   When you can travel light?

ABOUT YOU

1.

**LET'S START A NEW TREND!
ACKNOWLEDGE, ENCOURAGE
PEOPLE WHO ARE DOING GOOD WORK
PROTEST INEQUITIES & INDIGNITIES
CONSERVE ENERGY BY DECIDING
   WHAT CAUSES ARE IMPORTANT...**

...TO YOU